22-44

# The COMPARATIVE POLICY PROCESS

# The COMPARATIVE POLICY PROCESS

T. Alexander Smith

STUDIES IN COMPARATIVE POLITICS
Series Editor
Peter H. Merkl

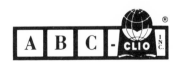

SANTA BARBARA, CALIFORNIA
OXFORD, ENGLAND

**Library of Congress Cataloging in Publication Data**

Smith, T Alexander, 1936—

The comparative policy process.

Includes bibliographical references and index.
1. Comparative government. 2. Policy sciences.

I. Title.
JF51.s545      320.3      75-2373
ISBN 0-87436-210-5
ISBN 0-87436-211-3 pbk.      *JF*
                            *51*
                          *,S545*

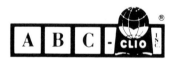

CLIO BOOKS
American Bibliographical Center—Clio Press, Inc.
2040 Alameda Padre Serra
Santa Barbara, Calif. 93103

European Bibliographical Center
Woodside House, Hinksey Hill
Oxford OX1  5BE, England

Designed by Jack Swartz
Composed by Datagraphics Press, Inc., Phoenix, Ariz.
Offset and bound by R. R. Donnelley & Sons Co.,
Crawfordsville, Ind.

# PREFACE

THIS book was written with the conviction that students of comparative politics devote insufficient attention to theorizing about the policy process. As a result there has been much unsystematic talk about policy, or policies, but little in the way of theoretical conceptualization. In developing my own perspective I should say at the outset that I owe a profound intellectual debt to Professor Theodore J. Lowi of Cornell University. His work in the American policy field provided inspiration for many of the positions adopted in this book. By agreeing to contribute the two cases on West German politics, Professor Margot Nyitray made this a more broadly-based study than was otherwise possible. Professor Dan Nimmo of the University of Tennessee was especially helpful with problems of organization. Professor Peter Merkl, a constant source of encouragement, read the entire manuscript and offered many useful suggestions relating to accuracy, style, and content. Portions of the manuscript were also commented upon by Professor Alan Wyner of the University of California, Santa Barbara as well as by three of my colleagues at the University of Tennessee, Professors Thomas Ungs, Paul Schulman, and Thomas Hood. Candice Burger, Dorman Francisco, and Nancy Runion, students at the University of Tennessee, read the manuscript either completely or in part. Invaluable editorial assistance was given by Miss Kathy Grover of the English Department of the University of Tennessee. I would also like to express my appreciation to Mrs. Nancy Davidson for editorial aid and to Mrs. Mary Williford for typing the manuscript. Finally, I would like to express my gratitude to Mr. Lloyd W. Garrison, editor and publisher of Clio Books, who has given me much advice and encouragement during these past several months.

T. Alexander Smith

v

# CONTENTS

# INTRODUCTION

## A PAUCITY OF LITERATURE

Comparative government occupies an old and honored niche in the discipline of political science, but the comparative study of the policy process largely has been ignored by political scientists. Books and articles about other areas of the discipline appear more often than those devoted to comparative analyses of policies in various nations.[1] This absence of interest in comparative policy making is perplexing since one of the features that distinguishes political science from other disciplines—e.g., sociology, history, and psychology—is a unique focus upon policy, i.e., the substance of policies and the processes by which they are made. Sociology, for example, has long been concerned with the socialization of citizens, voter preferences, and community stratification, but its interest in national policy-making processes has been marginal at best. Hence, political scientists have drawn upon sociology to develop theories of behavior, but they have found sociology of little help in understanding the policy process.

There are various definitions of the term public policy, but in this book it is useful to think of policies as bundles of government decisions based on issues. This definition includes more than mere decision making by political elites, interest group struggles, or even, in the language of systems analysis, "inputs" and "outputs." Such concepts or approaches reflect only a segment of the present definition. The study of the policy process requires the analyst first to understand and then to impose order on the numerous and varied decisions made by governments, or on what is referred to metaphorically as the "black box" or the "conversion process" of political activity. The study of the policy process therefore concentrates upon the patterned flow of issues which ultimately become government decisions. However, to grasp intellectually the process as a whole, one

1

must also look upon the policy process somewhat independently of particular political groups, decision makers, and political institutions and instead think of it as encompassing all of these.

From this standpoint the investigation of the policy process is a central concern of political science.[2] Reflections about government have always been at the heart of the discipline, and certainly government cannot be understood without reflecting upon the nature of policy as an end in itself. Consequently, it is especially puzzling that so little attention has been paid to this aspect of politics by political scientists in general and comparative specialists in particular.

In one sense these assertions must be qualified. Students of American politics, unlike their colleagues in the crossnational areas, have recently renewed their interest in the policy process. A spate of books and edited works has appeared with the avowed purpose of filling this profound gap in the existing literature.[3] Thus a new field is apparently emerging within the discipline of political science, a field which should have been of great interest from the beginning.

Perhaps this blossoming interest in the policy process is based on the realization that little sustained and systematic attention has been given to the policy process per se. The best political scientists in the United States have devoted their talents to the study of American voting behavior, citizen and elite attitudes, political parties, and state and local politics. Research grants, scholarly publications in the more important journals, and academic prestige seem to have been related mostly to work in these fields. Since that is where the action has been, the most innovative minds have given their talents to areas other than the national policy-making process —and even less attention has been given to the crossnational policy-making process.

In addition, sociocultural factors may have inhibited American scholars from devoting their interests to the policy process. The behavioral mood and its emphasis on microphenomena has been oriented essentially toward individual actors and the way they behave. As such, behaviorally trained researchers are uniquely qualified to develop and test hypotheses relating to individual and group attitudes. Accordingly, we have learned how political ideologies and attitudes are developed, how people become alienated from the political process, and why they cast their ballots as they do. Similarly, behavioralists have developed sophisticated techniques to handle large quantities of data. Thus, armed with research designs and questionnaires, American political scientists have aided in the effort to understand individual and group attitudes.

However, the reaction against traditional studies in micropolitical science has often neglected an important phenomenon—political institutions. Consequently, there is a tendency to abstract individuals from their institutional contexts and to treat them as independent entities. Thus, the impact of institutions upon individual behavior has been ignored in too many cases. For example, we know that political parties are more than mere aggregates of voters and the groups which support them. Parties are institutions which shape the values and behavior of individuals who consistently come within their orbit. Thus, it is important to identify those groups and individuals which favor a given political party, and it is also necessary to comprehend the role of party organization in such things as getting out the vote, and its effect on the behavior of the more active membership. An increasing number of writers in the field are turning toward the organizational aspects of parties, but they are a minority.[4]

Institutional arrangements obviously have a profound impact on politics. For example, a party system may be disciplined or undisciplined, and the executive and legislative branches of government may be fused or separated; and these conditions are extremely important in determining power relationships. If an American president ever gains a disciplined majority in Congress, he will be far stronger than any predecessor. Similarly, procedural and legal rules favor certain individuals and groups at the expense of others. Clearly, the rules under which congressional committees operate have served to protect interests favorable to the status quo. Nonetheless, a concern for micropolitical pressures obscures that fact and we tend to ignore the obvious as a result. Political institutions are, however, crucially important since they define the limits and levels of political battle and establish controls which first legitimize and then resolve conflict in favor of certain participants. We cannot begin to understand political man unless we understand the institutional context within which the individual operates.

An antiinstitutional bias may help account for the current tendency to view decision making and policy making as essentially similar in nature, or to regard them as synonymous processes. Viewing decisions in this way inevitably narrows the observer's range of concentration to include only the limited role of the individual in face-to-face relationships. Thus interacting individuals—executives, committees, groups, legislators, etc.— become the primary concern of political inquiry, and institutions as molders of human behavior recede into the background. Phrases such as "disjointed incrementalism" and words like "choice" become operational concepts for the study of behavior in committee-like environments.[5]

Sociocultural influences may work in other ways to inhibit meaningful research on the policy process. Specifically, a reverence for empiricism may have deterred some scholars from studying a field so obviously fraught with empirical difficulties. The study of politics in the American states often considers the relationship of policy outputs (e.g., welfare support) to socioeconomic conditions, party competition, and the like. Conversely, scholars have seldom dealt with the ways in which particular policies are initiated and implemented (the so-called conversion process). This is not surprising because in the first instance the policy process appears to defy generalization and because it is difficult to impose order upon such a complex subject. Complexity in turn encourages wariness and at this point the behavioral mood becomes decisive. Behavioralism values empiricism

to a high degree and emphasizes techniques amenable to rigorous quantifi-
cation; thus the behavioralist often inverts the procedural norms of research. Ordinarily research might be expected to first elaborate a problem
and then to utilize the best techniques available to resolve it. Presently, far
too many studies allow the research technique to determine what problems
are to be analyzed. In that case, method takes priority over substance, and
theory is equated with the manipulation of a few variables. Consequently
sophisticated methods are used to test relatively low-order hypotheses;
means are progressively converted into ends.[6] The results of such research
sometimes appear trivial from the standpoint of substantive theoretical
concerns, but many practitioners argue that such building blocks are necessary to fully develop theories of politics. C. Wright Mills observed
several years ago that sociology:

> . . . assumes that such studies as these are by their nature capable of being
> "units" which at some point in the future can be "added up" or "fitted
> together" to "build up" a reliable and verified image of some whole. . . .
> Theory becomes the variables useful in interpreting statistical findings. . . .[7]

Since so many American political scientists have inverted means and
ends and since the discipline is largely oriented toward specifically American concerns, comparative politics has developed little theoretical material
relating to the policy-making process to guide students in their work. If
American political scientists have resisted self-conscious theorizing about
the policy process, their comparative counterparts can be as strongly in-
dicted since they have taken their cues from the Americanists. The average
comparative specialist is confronted with such a maze of differing political
and social structures that he may legitimately despair at any meaningful
solution to the problem of the policy process. Some interesting studies
have appeared in the field of comparative politics in the past few years, but
little work has been devoted to the systematic study of the policy process.
There have been first-rate studies of political culture, political socialization, group activity, and party voting. Micropolitical phenomena have
increasingly concerned dynamic crossnational scholars. The interview and
questionnaire increasingly play a large part in comparative studies, and the
comparative area is considered as backward by some political scientists
who concentrate on American studies.[8]

    If we think of the subject areas of political science in general and
comparative politics in particular as a series of concentric circles which
encompass studies of political phenomena least involved with direct government (voting, socialization, etc.) and in which the center includes decision making at the national government level, it is apparent that the center
receives far less attention than the periphery. The area which clearly distinguishes political science from other disciplines has been largely ignored
by its practitioners, and the periphery has gained the attention of most
professionals in the field. The reason for this state of affairs may not be
merely accidental. The relatively easy access to data, the impact of profes-

sional and research needs, and a tendency to value technical precision at the expense of theory building all have combined to produce this situation. The perceptive Jacques Ellul has noted that our society is increasingly wedded to technique and many empirically oriented political scientists have comforted themselves by believing that the laborious confirmation of low-order hypotheses will add up to general theory. That belief is in perfect accord with the norms of a "technological society." [9]

## TOWARD A COMPARATIVE EXPLANATION OF THE POLICY PROCESS

It is possible that we have reached a sort of dead end in political science, and that further advancement will require less work at the periphery and greater concentration on the center. This will necessitate a reorientation, a subordination of data to theory. A new approach will demand greater attention to genuinely theoretical concerns and simultaneously an acceptance of less sophisticated tools to test theories. Such an emphasis may not entail a simple "either . . . or" situation, but it may create a dilemma which will never be completely bridged.

To grasp the nature of the policy process crossnationally, concepts, typologies, and theories of sufficient generality to account for policy-related activities in various kinds of political systems are needed. The work of Theodore J. Lowi is addressed to the American experience but it may nonetheless be useful to comparativists.[10] This study of the comparative policy process is dependent upon many of Lowi's conceptualizations so it is necessary to consider the strengths and limitations of his ideas as they relate to the field.

Lowi argues that the anticipated outcome of individual issues largely determines the pattern of a conflict from the beginning until it is resolved by governmental decision. He suggests there are three types of policies—distributive, regulatory, and redistributive—and each tends to generate its own arenas of power with special sets of actors and conflict resolution points. Distributive policies involve little conflict because they can be broken down into small units, thereby avoiding face-to-face conflicts. Patronage in its largest sense is synonymous with the politics of distribution and so are more specific government decisions dealing, for instance, with rivers and harbors and beautification of highways. In such "give-away" politics the participants are highly stable, because the committee structures of Congress and the executive branch make the decisions.

Regulatory policies, on the other hand, differ markedly because they indulge some individuals or groups at the expense of others; hence, regulatory policies result in face-to-face conflicts. They cannot be disaggregated into small units and dispersed in the manner of distributive policies. Regulatory issues take on the characteristics of the classical interest group struggle, as described so often by theorists of American politics from Bentley through Truman. Congress plays the major role in group competition over the authoritative allocation of values, and the regulatory arena is highly unstable since the participating elements shift according to the issues; i.e., each issue tends to bring forth differing contestants.

Redistributive issues, broadly speaking, revolve around the rich and poor, have and have-not, and working and middle-class interests. The Social Security legislation of the New Deal era and tax bills periodically enacted into law are examples. Like distributive policies, redistributive issues involve a highly stabilized elite structure, with "peak" associations of labor and management and top executive officials making major decisions. Lowi suggests that if C. Wright Mills' "power elite" exists, it is at this level of conflict. Redistributive policies also have something in common with regulatory policies because redistributive issues cannot be disaggregated into smaller units, but redistributive policies allow larger groups to be indulged or deprived; indeed, deprivation is likely to be significantly greater than in regulatory cases.

That, briefly, is the essence of Lowi's theory. It has two major advantages: it offers the possibility of linking policy types with decisional structures, and it provides a sufficient level of generality for comparative specialists who deal with political problems at the systemic level. Nevertheless, the Lowi conceptualizations create some difficulties for crossnational scholars.

For one thing Lowi tends to treat any bills which have the short-run effect of reallocating incomes as redistributive.[11] Indeed, his more recent work indicates that any tax bill is redistributive. However, this classification destroys meaningful and clear-cut separation between redistributive and regulative types, especially for the student of crossnational politics. Lowi points out that two differences between the two types of policies are the greater ease with which regulatory issues can be amended and the fewer controls exercised by the sponsoring committees.[12] Nevertheless, even in the case of the United States his technique raises a problem, for tax bills in the United States House of Representatives have almost always been brought to the floor under the legislative device known as the "closed rule." Since amendments by House members may be severely proscribed in such instances, few amendments are passed over the objections of the sponsoring committee or offered on the floor of the House. Therefore, the closed rule has as much as anything else to do with the determination of issue types. If this is true, the only meaningful remaining distinction between redistributive and regulative issues is the more open, coalition-building qualities of the latter as contrasted to the more quiet, behind-the-scenes decision-making qualities of the former.

One way to preserve a clear-cut distinction between types is to limit redistributive issues to class-conflictual policies; that is, to battles of Marxian proportions occurring between major worker and business interests. If one conceptualizes redistributive issues in this manner, one may be more confident of their differences from other types. Thus certain political battles which appear class-based no longer do so when strong and overt class conflict is attributed to the type itself. For example, Lowi uses the enactment of Social Security as a prime instance of redistribution. So it was somewhat; but President Roosevelt's decision to water down the redistributive qualities to make the bill more palatable to the middle classes, the length of time spent in bureaucratic infighting behind the scenes, and the long period the bill remained locked in congressional committee all had the consequence of reducing the perceived class impact by the time the bill was finally enacted. Therefore, although the long-term effects were possibly redistributive in character, the issue was fought out in other than redistributive terms in the short run. Thus, conceptualizing the problem in terms of class warfare is likely to result in different conclusions than conceiving of the problem, as Lowi apparently does, from an implicit budgetary model involving what he refers to as the "disaggregation" of units.[13]

A more basic problem for students of comparative politics, however, arises if the major difference between redistributive and regulative issues is reduced to quiet executive and bureaucratic bargaining versus more freewheeling legislative coalition building. For example, because the highly centralized British system with its disciplined parties resolves various types of issues (as defined by Lowi) roughly in the same manner, we encounter a problem in separating clearly and analytically regulative and redistributive cases from one another. If a parliamentary majority exists, executive committees work in the background and decide various types of issues, and Parliament dutifully ratifies their decisions. Important legislative battles often take place within caucus between ministers and backbenchers from the same party, and not between parties on the legislative floor. Party lines are not so easily crossed, and individualistic backbench behavior on the part of ordinary MPs aimed at the scuttling and amending of government bills is not so readily tolerated as in the United States.

Consequently, if one follows Lowi's typology to the letter, differentiating many regulative and redistributive bills from each other in parliamentary regimes proves difficult. This situation apparently led J. P. Nettl to question the applicability of the Lowi scheme to regimes such as the British one since Great Britain is characterized by a highly centralized decision-making apparatus.[14] Perhaps, however, we should not be so pessimistic, for with certain modifications the Lowi typology proves quite useful for crossnational scholars if modified in the following way:[15]

(1) Distributive policies display little, if any, conflict and are settled quietly in executive and/or legislative committees. Party discipline is unaffected.

(2) Sectorally fragmented policies display moderate conflict among interests representing primarily economic sectors and are resolved on the legislative floor by coalitions of legislators bargaining with ministers or other bureaucrats who oversee the particular sectors. Party discipline remains relatively strong in most cases.

(3) Emotive symbolic policies display wide conflicts of deep intensity over "way-of-life" issues in which governments refuse to stake out positions and in which individual legislators reject leadership controls over their actions. Party discipline is virtually nonexistent.

(4) Redistributive policies display wide conflicts of deep intensity between classes and are settled by "peak" associations of labor and management negotiating with presidents and prime ministers (legislatures are relatively quiescent). Party discipline is relatively high.

The logic underlying this typology is that differences in the scope and intensity of political disputes bring forth special kinds of political actors and special kinds of political institutions for resolving these debates. Put in a slightly different manner, there are four possible arenas of conflict— or stabilized conflict patterns—encompassing particular kinds of conflict, men, and institutions.

The discussion that follows examines each of these four types of policies—distributive, sectorally fragmented, emotive symbolic, and redistributive—in a variety of political settings through case studies of each type of policy in Great Britain, the United States, Canada, West Germany, and France. But to derive a complete picture of the relationship between policy types and the different kinds of conflicts, political actors, and governmental institutions involved in each case, the basic political arrangements in each system must first be considered. Therefore, chapter 1 briefly describes the major political institutions of Great Britain, the United States, Canada, West Germany, and France. This chapter provides the reader with an overview of the diverse political settings within which policies are made and across which those policies can be compared. Then, in chapters 2 through 5 each of the four types of policies is examined in detail and the nuances of each are illustrated through specific case studies. Finally, the discussion is concluded by exploring some of the theoretical implications of this study.

## NOTES

1. A significant recent exception is Martin Landau, "The Concept of Decision," in James B. Christoph and Bernard E. Brown, eds., *Cases in Comparative Politics,* 2nd ed. (Boston: Little, Brown and Co., 1969), pp. 18–32.

2. This statement is only slightly stronger than some recent comments by Raymond A. Bauer, "The Study of Policy Formation: An Introduction," in Raymond A. Bauer and Kenneth J. Gergen, eds., *The Study of Policy Formation* (New York: The Free Press, 1968), p. 4.

3. E. g., see Charles E. Lindblom, *The Policy-Making Process* (Englewood Cliffs, N.J.: Prentice-Hall, Inc., 1968); Yehezkel Dror, *Public Policymaking Reexamined* (San Francisco: Chandler Publishing Co., 1968); Austin Ranney, ed., *Political Science and Public Policy* (Chicago: Markham Publishing Co., 1970); and James E. Anderson, ed., *Political and Economic Policy-Making* (Reading, Mass.: Addison-Wesley Publishing Co., 1970); and Thomas R. Dye, *Understanding Public Policy* (Englewood Cliffs, N.J.: Prentice-Hall, Inc., 1972).

4. For a strong statement on this point, see Theodore J. Lowi, "Decision Making vs. Policy Making: Toward an Antidote for Technocracy," *Public Administration Review,* May/June 1970, pp. 314–25.

5. As we suggest below, the nature of the issue—i.e., the numbers of people and intensity of feeling—determines which institutions will resolve particular disputes. Hence, many so-called key decision makers may well not even resolve certain kinds of issues. For examples of decision-making theories, see Landau, "The Concept of Decision"; David Braybrooke and Charles E. Lindblom, *A Strategy of Decision* (London: The Free Press, 1963), pp. 81ff; Herbert A. Simon, *The New Science of Management Decision* (New York: Harper and Brothers, 1960); Richard C. Snyder, "A Decision-Making Approach," in Roland Young, ed., *Approaches to the Study of Politics* (Evanston, Ill.: University of Illinois Press, 1958), pp. 3–38; and James A. Robinson and R. Roger Majak, "The Theory of Decision-Making," in James C. Charlesworth, ed., *Contemporary Political Analysis* (New York: The Free Press, 1967).

6. Jacques Ellul, *The Technological Society* (New York: Vintage Books, 1964); also, Lowi, "Decision Making vs. Policy Making."

7. C. Wright Mills, *The Sociological Imagination* (New York: Grove Press, 1961), pp. 65–66.

8. Robert T. Golembiewski et al., *A Methodological Primer for Political Scientists* (Chicago: Rand McNally and Co., 1969), p. 229.

9. Ellul, *The Technological Society,* pp. 8ff.

10. See Theodore J. Lowi, "American Business, Public Policy, Case-Studies, and Political Theory," *World Politics,* July 1964, pp. 677–715; also, his "Decision Making vs. Policy Making."

11. Lowi, "American Business." For instance, in 1964 he tends to emphasize the "impact" of issues upon people whereas by 1970 he apparently gives greater importance to the kinds of bills considered.

12. See Lowi, "Decision Making vs. Policy Making."

13. Ibid.

14. See J. P. Nettl, *Political Mobilization* (New York: Basic Books, 1967), p. 105.

15. For a discussion of the utility of types of social science, see John C. McKinney, *Constructive Typology and Social Theory* (New York: Meredith Publishing Co., 1966). Our typology of the policy process is addressed to the patterned flow of issues. It focuses upon unfolding conflicts and institutions as well as key political actors. Consequently, it is not a typology of opinion. The reader must therefore resist the temptation to conceptualize, for example, an emotive symbolic policy in terms of discrete individuals and then proceed to argue that the issue may be emotive symbolic for some, redistributive for others, etc. We are concerned with patterns, not individual opinions.

# 1

# AN OVERVIEW OF POLITICAL INSTITUTIONS

TO comprehend the typology and the case studies related to the policy-making process, one must have at least a rudimentary understanding of the basic political institutions of various Western democracies. Although a major aim of comparative politics is to achieve ever higher levels of generality in explaining political phenomena, this task is exceedingly difficult without a grounding in the experiences of particular nations and governments. Therefore, in this chapter brief sketches of the major political institutions of Great Britain, the United States, Canada, West Germany, and France are presented.

The various case studies included in this book are drawn from nations which adhere to political democracy but differ from one another in rather significant ways. For example, a few have developed a relatively high degree of political consensus, while others have traditionally experienced deep ideological and social cleavages. Similarly, some possess two-party systems and hence the ability to form governments based on majorities, whereas others have been characterized by multiparties and coalition government. Again, certain nations differ markedly in executive-legislative relationships; that is, both parliamentary and presidential types of government are included as well as a somewhat mixed variation (Fifth Republic, France). All in all, there are rather sharp divergences in experience and practice among Western nations.

## GREAT BRITAIN

The British form of government has long had its share of scholarly admirers in the United States, from Woodrow Wilson to E. E. Schattschneider and James McGregor Burns and others within the "responsible party" school. Supporters of the British system have delighted in its coherence and ability to govern, particularly as evidenced by the concept of government responsibility before Parliament. The British cabinet stands or falls as a collective body. In the highly unlikely event that the House of Commons votes it out of office, the prime minister has two choices. He may submit his resignation; in all probability, however, he will dissolve the House and call upon the populace to resolve the issue. Responsibility is therefore assured, for the sovereign voter theoretically knows whom to credit with either troubles or satisfaction he may derive from the current government.

The clear lines of responsibility and accountability running from government to voter are undoubtedly facilitated by the British two-party system. Unlike many nations on the Continent, Great Britain has been blessed with cabinets composed entirely of Labour or Conservative party members. Consequently, it has been unnecessary to include several parties in each cabinet, thereby blurring the lines of accountability. And unlike the American two-party system, Britain's does not experience those periodic deadlocks between president and Congress which too often result from being controlled by different parties representing different constituency interests.

From the British standpoint, the United States and such Continental nations as Italy and France (at least in the Third and Fourth Republics) confuse or avoid responsibility because they divide power among the legislative and executive branches or because government coalitions, which may include small, centrist parties, are unlikely to reflect dominant feelings in the country. Neither America nor the Continental multiparty systems, to use Bagehot's term, "buckle" legislative and executive branches in a meaningful, harmonious relationship. But in Great Britain, Parliament and cabinet are securely welded through common party ties and party discipline, the cabinet being the leadership of the parliamentary majority party. Major decisions are made within cabinet or parliamentary caucus with ultimate decisions binding all members of the majority.

The prime minister, furthermore, is the true leader of his party and government. With many patronage prerogatives, controls over parliamentary agenda and debate, and the right of dissolution, he occupies an exalted position of authority within Parliament. Unlike his executive counterparts in many other nations, he has little need to worry about powerful legislative committees emasculating his program, since rigorous discipline usually keeps his followers in line.

Of course, there are periodic denunciations of cabinet government as little more than disguised dictatorship. The prime minister's imposing powers of patronage through his right to appoint his fellow cabinet ministers, ministers of state, parliamentary secretaries, and external party organization leadership and shadow governments (in the case of the Conservatives) are certainly clear evidence of his strong position. True, in making selections, he must carefully consider the wishes of powerful factional leaders, and to this extent his freedom of choice is limited. Nevertheless, as many as one-fifth of the majority's parliamentary membership

may receive some sort of patronage dispensation from the leader. Similarly, as head of a disciplined party, the prime minister can count upon the
loyal support of his backbenchers. As a result, the right of the legislature
to bring a government to its knees through a vote of no confidence is
largely a dead issue in present-day Britain, since no party is likely to vote
against its own leadership and risk facing the opposition with a divided
majority at election time.

The fear of disguised dictatorship, unresponsive to the wishes of the
people and its representatives in the legislature, is directed toward other
aspects of cabinet government as well. Although many thinkers question
the growing powers of the prime minister and his cabinet at the expense
of Parliament, more fear the enhanced role in policy making of the permanent higher civil service. Unlike its American counterpart, the British
bureaucracy is protected from undue pressure. Each minister can place
himself between high civil servants and the elected members of Parliament
since a minister assumes personal responsibility for his own ministry. For
both bureaucrat and minister, of course, there are advantages. The bureaucrat retains anonymity, integrity, a reputation for impartiality, and, in
general, a prestigious position as servant of the Crown. He also finds it
simple to remain aloof from partisan warfare. The minister, on the other
hand, gains loyalty from the higher civil servant and security from the
knowledge that he is getting advice unencumbered by partisan loyalties.

Although it has been argued that question time in Parliament provides
an excellent way to air criticisms of administrative malfeasance, the British
legislature has few of those checks upon the bureaucracy available to its
American counterpart: the investigatory power, the practically unlimited
ability to bring administrators before congressional committees, and the
practice of continual oversight. Such checks are shunned on the grounds
that they endanger cabinet responsibility before Parliament and, ultimately, the people.

While one need not conclude that the British political system is in any
way undemocratic in essentials—after all, its rulers are subject to periodic
elections—it is clearly a centralized democracy in terms of executive decision making. Because much policy is certainly forged behind the scenes by
ministers, bureaucrats, and the interest groups, Parliament tends to resemble a mere ratifying body. In this sense, it seems most tame when compared
to the rambunctious American Congress.

Ordinary parliamentary backbencher initiatives occur less frequently in
Great Britain than in the United States because Great Britain's doctrine of
collective responsibility, a disciplined party system, and a well-developed
executive committee structure place a damper on backbencher independence. Hence, the British MPs do not find it a simple matter to vote their
personal convictions or those of their individual constituencies. As a result,
the more open system of bargaining and coalition building, a part of life
in the American Congress, is much less blatant in the House of Commons;
but the fundamental process itself is surely evident.

## THE UNITED STATES

That the American political system seems much more open and free-wheeling than Great Britain's is not surprising, given the disciplined majorities which unite legislative and executive branches in the latter. In the United States, however, constitutional checks and balances and a separation of powers may actually facilitate conflict between president and Congress, even in those instances when the same party, be it the Democrats or the Republicans, dominates each branch of government. Moreover, unlike the British prime minister, the chief executive in the United States cannot dissolve Congress; nor can he, like his presidential counterpart in France, submit a bill to referendum or suspend Parliament for six months. Nor does he have the legislative controls over debate, timetable, and agenda available to leaders in European parliamentary systems. Such powers are mostly the prerogative of congressional committees. In addition, in parliamentary regimes (or partly parliamentary, as in present-day France) there is a built-in need for a majority[1] and a modicum of party unity within that majority because dissidence can lead to the loss of office at worst and unwanted elections at best. In the United States, however, president and Congress can each survive an onslaught from the other without being threatened with irreparable loss of power. Hence, in the United States there is less need to keep political battles more subdued and less vocal.

Fundamentally, however, the tensions between Congress and president derive to a great extent from the different types of constituencies each represents. The House of Representatives and Senate tend to overrepresent rural and small-town interests (the Senate to a lesser extent since its urban electorate is of greater importance), whereas the president, due to the electoral college vote, gains disproportionately from the larger states and big-city ethnic interests. It is, of course, possible that a highly popular president may occasionally mitigate the effects of differing constituencies by making his support necessary to members of Congress. Nevertheless, his "coattails" are not nearly so beneficial as they might be were he not limited by a system of staggered elections in which the House, Senate, and president face the electorate every two, six, and four years respectively.

This point becomes more salient when the power relationships within Congress are examined. Thus, it is more accurate to speak in terms of congressional committee-executive relationships than legislative-executive relationships. Congressional committees are to a great extent dominated by politicians from the one-party, more status quo-oriented areas of the nation. The key legislative elements with which the president must therefore contend are the committee chairmen, who have risen to positions of power because of seniority. Obviously, their districts hardly resemble the constituencies which the chief executive must woo. Committee chairmen have authority over the creation and disbanding of subcommittees; they determine who can or cannot testify before their committees; they can decide when and if committee meetings will be conducted; they can and often do exercise stringent controls over agenda. In general, the key power of the congressional committee in the American system is not only the framing of laws but also the right to investigate, compel executive officials to testify before Congress, appropriate funds, and exert a continuing oversight of administration. Such powers have led more than one department, bureau, or agency to make its peace with the committee which oversees its operations—quite often at the expense of its nominal executive leader, the president.

Undoubtedly, if the president could count upon a unified and disciplined party, his life would be much easier simply because, as leader of a disciplined political organization, he could anticipate loyalty to the party rather than mere seniority to be a chief criterion for membership on powerful committees. Similarly, a congressional party characterized by disciplined voting would hardly embarrass a president through continual oversight and investigations. Since major decisions, including the staffing of key committee positions, would be made by national leadership, it is highly probable that the congressional committees and the president would work much more in harmony. As a result there would be greater coordination of administration by the president.

It can therefore be concluded that a possible consequence of party disunity and indiscipline in the United States has been the decentralization of decision making down into the congressional committees and into middle-level agencies and bureaus rather than upward into the higher reaches of the presidency. In this respect it is useful to view the American political process in the image of numerous triangles individually encompassing three institutional legs: interest group, congressional committee or subcommittee, and bureaucracy. Each of these imaginary triangles embraces within its special functional area the defense of certain interests. If, through common needs, the three legs of a given triangle are closely aligned and if the group (or groups) represents a sufficiently powerful electoral or political force (as in agriculture or in military procurement), then a president's ability to enforce his will upon that part of his own bureaucracy is considerably reduced.

This state of affairs is especially likely to exist when powerful constituency groups and friendly congressional committees or subcommittes find it beneficial to depend upon one another for mutual support. In such instances the constituency interests find departments, agencies, and bureaus only too willing to avoid discord with Congress and groups alike. To take a single example further considered in chapter 3, it was found that tobacco state senators and representatives sat on the subcommittees and committees which legislated on tobacco problems, and committee members, not to say tobacco associations, had considerable sway with the Tobacco Division of the Agriculture Department. When such close linkages occur, presidents often find it exceedingly difficult to bend the bureaucracy to their own needs.

# CANADA

The major national political institutions of Canada are modeled along distinct British lines. Its orthodox parliamentary form of government stamps Canada as not only a part of the Commonwealth but a nation largely dominated by people of British extraction. As in Great Britain, legislative authority is vested in Parliament, although by the terms of the British North America Act (which originally brought the various British colonies into a single unit in 1867) and subsequent judicial interpretation, the Canadian legislature and the provincial governments share certain powers far more than their counterparts in the British Isles. Similarly, in Canada as in Great Britain it is the lower house (House of Commons) rather than the upper house (Senate) which prevails in the legislative process. While the BNA Act does give the Senate rather extensive formal powers, the upper house has in fact functioned as a ratifying body for legislation deriving from the House of Commons and has confined itself mostly to the task of tidying up bills deriving from the latter.

One should not, however, exaggerate the importance of the Canadian House of Commons. Although it is surely dominant in relation to the Senate, the Canadian House of Commons plays a distinctly secondary role to the prime minister and the cabinet, since it is they who dominate for the most part the legislative and policy-making process. Thus, backbenchers apparently have few formal powers in the House of Commons. For example, they are prohibited from proposing increases in expenditures—that right is conferred upon the individual ministers—and they have small expectation that their private members' bills will ever reach the floor for consideration. In each of these vital areas it is the ministers themselves who decide which particular initiatives are to be taken. Cabinet leadership is also strengthened by the tight party discipline so prevalent among the major parties in the House. Ordinary MPs therefore are largely dependent upon parliamentary caucus meetings as a place to air their grievances. Just how influential such meetings are is difficult to judge since they are held in secret.

The process by which the prime minister and his cabinet are chosen in Canada resembles the British practice. As representative of the queen, the governor general when seeking a potential prime minister calls upon the particular party leader he expects to be most capable of forming a majority in the House. The duly appointed potential prime minister in turn selects his own cabinet, its membership being taken from the House of Commons (by custom a senator may be included) and reflecting the factional and party balance at that particular moment.

Like their British counterparts, Canadian parliamentary parties have long been characterized by great cohesion and discipline in the House of Commons. Yet unlike Great Britain, Canada cannot count upon a persistent party majority in the legislature; therefore, instead of a two-party system, it has what Professor Leon Epstein calls a "two-plus party system."[2] Either the Liberal party or the Progressive Conservative party (PC) is capable at times of gaining an absolute majority of seats, but in recent years it has been necessary on occasion to call upon a third party, the more leftist New Democratic party (NDP) for support of or at least acquiescence to a minority government (that is, a government not representing a majority of all members in the House). Occasionally, as in 1958 under John Diefenbaker, when the Conservatives won an absolute majority, or, as in 1968 and 1974, when the Liberals triumphed under the leadership of Pierre Trudeau, a coalition government has been unnecessary. However, in the intervening years between these two lopsided party victories, the NDP has often held the balance of power in the House of Commons.

The impression should certainly not be left, however, that Canadian political institutions are mere replicas of British ones. The ethnic factor, for example, is especially important in Canadian politics. At times ethnic conflict between an English-speaking majority and a French-speaking minority centered in the province of Quebec has severely tested the bonds of Canadian unity. In this respect Canadian voting behavior is characterized more by ethnic and regional loyalties than by class ones. Indeed, outright class voting may well be the lowest among any predominantly English-speaking country in the Western world.[3] Thus the Progressive Conservatives and Liberals, the two major parties, are each composed of a disproportionate number of English-speaking and French-speaking supporters respectively.

Similarly, party organizations themselves are weakly articulated, and in fact provincial and federal organizations are relatively independent of one another both in terms of carving out policy positions and in terms of recruitment into positions of party leadership. Furthermore, a party may be strong at the provincial level but quite weak at the national level (e.g., the Social Credit party), and careers to an extent are made either at the national or local levels alone. Such arrangements diverge rather strongly from British and European models.

Consequently, provincial governments are hardly mere appendages of the federal government. Although the British North America Act does not formally grant the provinces the powers given to the states in the United States Constitution, the provinces in reality have developed as strong entities. Thus, they control a larger array of economic, welfare, and education programs than do the American states. Nothing could be farther from the British and most European practices.

## WEST GERMANY

The nations considered above are highly stable democracies, unencumbered for the most part by traditions of political oppositions which threaten the constitutional order. This cannot be said for West Germany and France. Each of these nations has been faced historically with grave threats from extremists on left and right. Germany has been especially subject to political division and turmoil. Unification of most German-speaking peoples came only in the latter part of the nineteenth century; prior to 1871 Germans had been divided into many different kinds of political orders. Little other than the church and the Holy Roman Empire held these diverse states together in feudal times. But even that fragile unity was cut asunder by Martin Luther's revolt against the church and the subsequent growth of Protestantism in the northern areas. Thus, the divisions of religion were superimposed upon prior political divisions. Later, following the French Revolution of 1789, Napoleon's invasion of the German states did result in the imposition of some unity, but the major consequence was more to awaken the fires of German nationalism than to sow the seeds of liberalism as implied in the ideas of the French Revolution.

When German unity did finally take place in the latter half of the nineteenth century, it was achieved not under more Westernized Austria but rather under the hegemony of more Eastern-oriented Prussia; and Prussia was geared to nationalism, militarism, and a centralized and bureaucratic Germany, not to an emerging bourgeois liberalism already pressing for major political and social change throughout Europe. Led by an arrogant *Junker* aristocracy which manned the key military and civil service positions, by 1871 Prussia had unified most German-speaking peoples under its leadership.

Furthermore, Prussia was not wedded to free market concepts on the order of the British model. An emphasis upon military power and national might led its leaders to support cartels and in general to engage in monopolistic practices; in return a protected German industry supplied the leaders with the tools of war. In Great Britain and France, an independent, politically confident bourgeoisie made its influence increasingly felt. In Germany, however, industry, particularly prior to 1933, was led by men who reflected the status needs and hierarchical relationships of older, more traditional values. As a result, industrialization did not change German society; more accurately, it was fused with, and shaped by, preindustrial values.[4]

World War I ended Prussian hegemony. The new Weimar Republic established in its place a democratic constitution which was supported by more liberal forces, especially the Social Democrats. But democracy was never really given a chance to operate. When harsh reparations were demanded from the victorious Allies following the German defeat in World War I and democratic elites, not the authoritarians of Wilhelmenian Germany, were forced to pay the bill, opposition propaganda utilized this humiliating treatment as a pretext to struggle against the regime. In addition, the gravest inflation and the worst depression in memory hardly gave the Weimar Republic an opportunity to gain legitimacy. And out of this humiliation and turmoil arose a political movement of the extreme right, the National Socialist party (Nazis). The extreme left as represented by the Communist party gained in popularity. These parties made parliamentary democracy unworkable because their strong representation in the legislature enabled them to shake the various coalition governments to their foundations. The fragility of coalitions in turn led to a belief among many Germans that democracy as a system was simply unworkable.

That the Weimar Republic would fall under such conditions is hardly surprising. In 1933, Nazi Adolf Hitler was designated chancellor by an aging President Paul von Hindenburg. Utilizing emergency powers handed over to him by the president, Hitler quickly destroyed his political opposition and soon created what can only be called a totalitarian political system in which basic freedoms were ruthlessly suppressed. His policies of expansion in foreign affairs finally led to World War II and another German defeat. Once again the dream of unity had been shattered, for postwar Germany was divided into Western and Eastern zones, one side controlled by the American, British, and French occupation forces, the other side by the Soviet Union. Out of this partition arose two regimes, the democratic Federal Republic of Germany and the Russian Communist-led German Democratic Republic.

## The Federal (Bonn) Republic

Following World War II, in September 1948, a constituent assembly met once again to attempt the creation of a viable German democracy. Undoubtedly, the turbulent political history of Germany weighed heavily upon the delegates. With the Weimar experience planted firmly in their minds, many delegates were determined that the new attempt at democracy would not only assure the democratic forms but that it would also create a government sufficiently strong to ward off the threats of extreme right and left alike. To insure these ends, the Bonn constitution, while recognizing the role of political parties in politics, reduced the power of the two strongest Weimar institutions, the president and *Bundestag* (lower house), and strengthened the position of the chancellor. The latter, however, remained constitutionally responsible to the lower house. The notorious Article 48 of the Weimar constitution, which had allowed President Hindenburg to rule by emergency decree and to delegate power to the chancellor to suspend civil liberties and to govern without the support of a parliamentary majority, was eliminated. (In 1968, however, new emergency laws were added to the constitution under which civil liberties could be restricted in certain circumstances.) In addition, the Bonn constitution deprived the president of an independent political base, since he was to be indirectly elected for no more than two five-year terms by a special convention composed of members of the *Bundestag* and an equal number of representatives of the state legislatures.

It was felt that a major reason for government instability in Weimar lay in an unholy alliance of the extremist parties in the legislature which were unable to come to an agreement among themselves, but could easily vote more moderate governments out of office. Thus, just as the founders of the French Fifth Republic would do some ten years later, the Bonn framers sought to legislate political stability into existence. Their solution to the problem of instability was the "constructive vote of no confidence" by which no chancellor could be overthrown until his opposition could come up with an alternative chancellor of its own.

Indeed, not only was the chancellor strengthened at the expense of the president, but the role of a traditional institution, the *Bundesrat* (upper house), was enhanced. Composed of representatives of the *Land* (state) governments in proportion to population, the *Bundesrat* is essentially a congress of appointed state ministers who vote on instructions from their governments. As such, it is designed to represent states rather than parties, since each state casts its votes as a unit. The constitutional powers of the *Bundesrat* reflect traditional notions of German federalism which emphasize direct participation by the provincial governments in national policy making and administration rather than distinctly separate powers for each jurisdictional level of government. Thus, the *Bundesrat* was given an absolute veto in certain policy areas which most affect the *Laender* (states) but only a suspensive veto over other types of legislation.

Subsequent developments in West Germany were highly favorable for a strong democratic government. The first chancellor, Konrad Adenauer (1949–63), was a somewhat authoritarian personality whose long tenure insured continuity and stability in the initial development of the Federal Republic. He was aided by the growth and success of his own political party, the Christian Democratic Union (CDU) and its Bavarian affiliate, the Christian Social Union (CSU). The CDU/CSU controlled the largest number of seats in the *Bundestag*. A party with a slightly right-of-center orientation, the CDU/CSU formed coalition governments with a number of smaller parties. It gradually expanded its electoral appeal at their expense. These smaller parties, with the exception of the Free Democratic Party (FDP), all eventually declined and lost national representation. The FDP's independence and freedom to maneuver were compromised somewhat since its electoral support was then heavily middle class and conservative; hence, it was unable to form coalitions with the major opposition party, the Social Democrats (SPD). However, in 1969, the FDP joined in coalition with the SPD, thereby providing the first real alteration in governmental power since the founding of the Federal Republic. The new, more progressive domestic policy positions of the FDP combined with continued support for advanced foreign policy initiatives to cause internal strains. The defections of a number of old-time parliamentarians certainly contributed to the need for an early election of 1972. However, the election apparently consolidated a new and more unified position for the FDP as the balancing force in German politics, encouraging foreign policy initiatives and attempting to brake any leftist ventures in domestic economic arrangements.

Consequently, the party alignments have no doubt had much more to do with continued democratic stability in West Germany than the formal constructive vote of no confidence. It has had some importance as a device for chancellors to employ against their own party members within the *Bundestag:* Adenauer and his successor, Ludwig Erhard, both challenged disgruntled CDU deputies to use it if they could only agree on a successor. However, a formal vote has been attempted only once, in the summer of 1972, when Rainer Barzel, the CDU/CSU opposition leader, unsucessfully attempted to oust Willy Brandt as chancellor.

The *Bundesrat* also developed somewhat differently than the founders had expected. Because busy *Land* ministers found it difficult to divide their time between local work and periodic trips to Bonn to legislate on national affairs, their seats in the upper house came increasingly to be occupied by their civil servants. The consequence was the growth of what can only be termed a bureaucratically oriented legislative institution. The high prestige given legal training and the civil service in Germany has worked to the advantage of the *Bundesrat* in its relations with the lower house, particularly in the drafting of legislation and in the conference committees of the two houses. In general, the *Bundesrat's* orientation has been more committee centered and less conflictual than that of the *Bundestag*. Efforts are usually made to avoid open challenges to the *Bundestag*, and to define issues as technical questions requiring legal expertise. Due to its role, the government coalition parties usually make an effort to insure a favorable partisan balance within the upper house. This means that *Land* government elections have important national overtones. At present, with the exception of the U.S. Senate, the *Bundesrat* is the most influential upper house of any of the countries being considered in this book.

Perhaps at this point a word should be said about the committee structure in the German parliament, for in general it is of far more importance in the drafting and amending of legislation than are the committees of the parliamentary systems of Great Britain, Fifth Republic France, or Canada. Allocations of seats on the committees are determined by proportional representation and, unlike in the United States, the chairmen need not belong to the largest party in the house. In the civil service milieu of the *Bundesrat,* as mentioned, the committees have been turned into decisive instruments of influence. Because in part such a high value is placed on expertise and specialization, the *Bundestag* has also been affected by bureaucratic norms; hence, the values dear to the civil service have influenced the lower house as well (many members also derive from civil service backgrounds). Indeed, time spent in committee exceeds that of other major democracies. Not surprisingly, as in the United States where legislative committees are particularly strong, Bonn politicians with highly personal or constituent interests in the legislation of certain committees have sought seats on those committees in order to have an influence on legislative outcomes. It is unusual for the political parties, who determine committee membership, to remove elected members from their posts.[5]

Thus, in a formal sense German executive-legislative relationships give a greater impression of pluralism than do those of Gaullist France, Great Britain, or Canada, although such does not appear to be the case in the United States and the Third and Fourth French Republics. It is the impact of the legislative committees in part which gives such an impression. On the other hand, this impact is more than balanced by the powerful position of the chancellor as well as by a strong tradition of party discipline in the legislature.

## FRANCE

Unlike the United States, Great Britain, or even Canada, France has faced a chronic problem of political instability. Many scholars, including not a few French commentators, profess to see an approaching demise of deep ideological fissures in modern industrial democracies. Particularly when such analyses are derived from a class-oriented or general socioeconomic perspective, it does appear that greater class mobility, the growth of numerous and varied interest groups, the reduction of differences in life-styles and consumption patterns, the rapid growth of white-collar groups, and the decline of warfare between proletariat and bourgeoisie have reduced the potential for great clashes. According to this interpretation, Marx might be relevant today for newly developing nations, but he is no longer applicable to the more mature democracies.

Despite the undeniable fact that its social and economic structures have been greatly modernized since the end of World War II, France still seems susceptible to large-scale social conflicts such as the explosion in May 1968 between students and workers on one side and middle-class Gaullists and their supporters on the other. Unlike industrial disputes in Anglo-American societies, those in France focus less frequently on specific wage-price controversies. As a result discords between proletariat and capitalists often degenerate into generalized debates over the nature of the regime itself. On more than one occasion the comfortable middle and upper classes have been frightened by anarcho-syndicalist and Communist influence within the working-class movement. The Communist party in particular has retained the steadfast loyalty of the workers and has consistently polled around 20 percent of the total vote in France. Since they could hardly include Communists in their coalitions and hence obtain a majority of the left in the National Assembly, other left-wing, but democratic, parties could play little role in representing the socially discontented. If the democratic left joined governments, it was reduced to hopeless compromise; if it accepted the consequences of its doctrine, it was relegated into political exile by centrist and rightist parties.

In weakening the democratic left, Communism helped to poison the social and political climate by preventing meaningful change while at the same time appearing to many Frenchmen as a permanent insurrectionary force. The representatives of the proletariat have professed a fear of authoritarianism and fascism from the political right. Indeed, fears of military coups, for example, have long been part of the political scene. In fact, threats to the republic have come from right and left alike. Military and clerical elements on the right have often given less than overwhelming loyalty to the various republics, while a Communist party dominant over most workers and unions has posed a potential threat to stability for many years now.

In addition, each side—left and right—has been historically character-ized by differing conceptions as to how authority should be legitimately exercised. Thus, the left has perceived that the best protection against threats to the republic lies in a reduction in the power of the executive branch of government and an enhancement of the prerogatives of the legislative assembly, whereas the right has been intent upon expanding executive authority as the best method for assuring order.

Therefore, representing differing socioeconomic groupings, ideologies, and conceptions of authority, groups on the left and right have maintained uneasy relationships for almost two centuries. Not surprisingly this differ-ence in perspective has produced much disagreement about how the ills of the French polity should be alleviated.

From a sociological point of view, in other societies potential class conflicts may be confined within more localized boundaries, but in France such conflicts may become more quickly nationalized in scope simply because its institutional life is so thoroughly centralized. To take an exam-ple, a student rebellion at a major American university need involve no more than a board of trustees or at most the state machinery, but a similar revolt in France is likely to draw the national government immediately into the fray. In that nation a university crisis can hardly be kept from the office of the minister of education and therefore probably from the cabinet itself. Thus, whereas responsibility can usually be avoided by American national officials, a similar squabble in France can hardly be diverted from the topmost positions in French society.

In general, then, disputes in France are more easily directed toward the French state. If the debate becomes sufficiently crucial to the belligerents, the republic itself may well be threatened; and in this century France has experienced more than its share of such conflicts—and republics as well. In more decentralized and pluralist societies, however such antagonisms may be more easily managed at a lower level, thereby never becoming crucial for the society as a whole. Therefore, one might speculate that in the more pluralist orders many grave tensions are less likely to become nationalized in scope.

These social and political tensions within the French polity have led to periodic alterations in the constitutional order. Since the case studies in the following chapters will include issues drawn from three of these republics —the Third, Fourth, and Fifth Republics—it is useful to consider briefly certain similarities and differences among them. The Third and Fourth Republics contained many constitutional resemblances, but the Fifth Republic departs in practice from the two previous regimes in certain significant respects.

## The Third Republic (1875–1940)

Although the Third Republic had a relatively long life by French stan-dards, it was still characterized by political instability. Executive authority was made weak almost from the beginning because presidents were allowed small constitutional scope within which to operate. Their principal duties involved ceremonies, appointments, and nominations. The nominating function was especially noteworthy, since the president was called upon to nominate a potential prime minister who in turn would be acceptable to a majority of deputies in the lower house of the legislature. In this sense, then, the system functioned somewhat as an hereditary monarchy, minus the security of heredity and status, of course.

Despite its rather formidable constitutional powers, the presidency was soon placed in a position subordinate to that of the legislature. Following an 1877 electoral contest a conservative president, Marshal Marie Edmé Patrice MacMahon, dissolved the Chamber of Deputies in a dispute with its radical membership and he was forced to resign (1879). Thereafter, the president lacked the power of dissolution and the lower house assumed a growing importance. But this weakening of the presidency did not lead to a strengthening of the cabinets and premiers. Third Republic governments were usually of short duration, perpetually threatened with overthrow by hostile groups of deputies. Whereas cabinets in present-day Britain, West Germany, or the Fifth Republic have generally retained disciplined majority support in their legislatures, tight controls over legislation throughout the initiation and committee stages and therefore dominance of agenda and debate and resistance to interpolation, Third Republic governments enjoyed none of these advantages of security or authority.

Since there were so many parties in the Chamber of Deputies, the role of the small center groups became crucial in the formation of governments. But since the cabinets were created from these small and diverse parties, and since the resulting majorities had so few permanent links binding them together, any disagreement was easily translated into a government crisis. Indeed, according to the calculations of David Thomson, during the 70 years of the Third Republic, some 50 prime ministers and 500 different cabinet ministers took part in the exercise of governmental power.[6] Under such changing conditions, governments lacked authority, much less decisiveness. As a result power passed to disparate groups of deputies and to the standing committees, each of which was dominated by highly particularistic interests. Important and innovative government bills therefore either died in the Chamber of Deputies or were emasculated in committee or on the floor.

Originally the conservatives of that period had hoped that the Senate, as well as the presidency, would serve as a bulwark against the democratic inclinations of the Chamber; hence, they made it a coequal branch so far as the passage of legislation was concerned. Its veto, hopefully, would place restraints upon the overly enthusiastic Chamber of Deputies. Accordingly, it was elected indirectly, with the small towns and rural communes receiving disproportionate weight in comparison with the large cities (this disproportionality was modified somewhat in 1884). Furthermore, senators were required to be at least forty years old and were given long terms of office (nine years). Terms of office were staggered to prevent the effects of massive changes in electoral opinion. Contrary to the expectations of the constitutional writers, however, as the Senate evolved it did not find itself in perpetual disagreement with the lower house, for in actual practice the two houses worked rather well together.

A basic problem for the stability of the Third Republic resulted from the total absence of a majority party during the life of the regime. Indeed, it could be argued that the weak presidency, premier and cabinet flowed from this inability to find a majority in the legislature. In present-day France, for example, the Gaullists have governed with near majorities (1962–67) or actual majorities (1968–73) for most of the past decade. As a consequence, a high degree of unity of purpose was established under the presidencies of Charles de Gaulle and Georges Pompidou. It is difficult to believe that their moral qualities were superior to many of their Third Republic predecessors. True, there were differences in the presidential powers of each republic, but one can hardly underestimate the importance of a coherent majority for executive leadership. Thus, when the president asserted his rights during the Third Republic, he immediately found himself confronted by a hostile Chamber of Deputies, as Marshal MacMahon learned. This absence of a majority also weakened the prime minister and his cabinet. Any government which sought to control or thwart a major interest group soon found itself doomed to oblivion.

The factions and deputies themselves could not govern, but they were unwilling to surrender any of their prerogatives for the sake of governmental coherence. As a result cabinets were short-lived, often brought down over truly insignificant issues. Since several parties were included in governments, any given debate might lead to a sudden resignation by one of the parties in the coalition. Hence, the prime minister had to be quite careful in his actions. Indecisiveness and nondecision making were therefore built into the political system.

## The Fourth Republic (1945–58)

Established immediately following World War II, the Fourth Republic continued in the tradition of its immediate predecessor with multipartyism, legislative dominance, and a weak executive. Not surprisingly, it was unable to cope with certain postwar difficulties which would have made life uncomfortable for even the strongest of governments. A rampant inflation, the growth of rebellion in the French colonies, and a Communist party more popular than ever because of its role in the Resistance were sufficient in themselves to encourage political instability. The leader of the Resistance forces and first premier of the new republic, General Charles de Gaulle, had hoped to create a strong executive independent of the lower house and the parties; but the traditional groupings, now aided by the growth of new parties, quickly asserted themselves following the end of hostilities. In disgust de Gaulle resigned as premier in January 1946, and went into temporary political exile. In 1947, however, he sought to return to power through the creation of a new political party, the Rally of the French People (RPF).

It is hard to imagine a higher degree of instability than that of the Fourth Republic in terms of executive leadership. The system was nominally a parliamentary one, but far removed from the stable parliamentary governments found in the other nations discussed here. None of the parties was strong enough to command a majority in the all-powerful National Assembly; and two groups, the French Communist party and the Gaullist RPF, were committed for very different reasons to the destruction of the system itself. Together they had enough votes to make life quite uncomfortable for the various governments of the day. The result was government by a number of small centrist-oriented parties, each jealous of its own prerogatives, and all too eager to bring down any cabinet which failed to do its bidding.

Indeed, the average life span for each of these cabinets was only about five months, although most of them fell not by a vote of no confidence, but rather because some angry coalition partner decided to leave. Ironically, the unending stream of new governments produced a much less profound change than might appear at first glance, since all too often many of the same ministers in a fallen cabinet returned to power in the succeeding one. These returns occurred because the various center parties, due to their narrow and tenuous majorities, had little room to maneuver between the large Communist and Gaullist parliamentary groups; hence, there were simply not many different possibilities open to forge a new coalition. As a result, and despite apparent instability, some governmental continuity was nevertheless achieved. In fact, coalition partners might even colonize certain ministries as, for example, the *Mouvement Républicain Populaire* (MRP) did in the case of the Foreign Ministry.

The problem for a prospective premier who would form a coalition was that any number of issues drove deep wedges into any given cabinet. For example, the Catholic MRP could support the Socialists in economic policy, but the two groups came to a parting of ways whenever the issue of state aid to church schools was raised. Similarly, the Radical party might join the Socialists on the church-state issue, but the Radical position on welfare and social issues often found the party in alliance with the conservative *modérés*. The latter in turn were generally proclerical, laissez-faire (except where direct state aid to peasants and businessmen was involved), and hostile to many social policies espoused by the more leftist parties. Such a posture was likely to bring them into conflict at any given time with Radicals, Socialists, or the MRP. On any given day in the National Assembly, the various parties which composed governments in this period could be found at odds with one another.

## The Fifth Republic (1958– )

When General de Gaulle and his followers returned to power in May 1958, following a revolt in Algeria by settler and army insurgents against the discredited Fourth Republic, they were determined to restore the power of the state so that France might once again assume its place among the powerful nations of the world. The Gaullists quite naturally blamed the weakness and corruption of the Fourth Republic upon the dominant position of the National Assembly, an institution which seemed to create and destroy governments at will.

General de Gaulle's remedy for France's ills lay in the creation of a new constitution which had as its basis a strong executive to contain a rambunctious legislature. To the Gaullists, Fourth Republic instability was not caused so much by the views and behavior of ordinary Frenchmen, or even by French politicians, as by institutional arrangements which gave the lower house (the National Assembly) the right to vote governments up and down at will. Thus, since the problem was deemed as a legal one, the remedy as well was a legal one.

General de Gaulle had set forth the outlines for a new constitution as early as 1946 in his famous speech at Bayeux, when he called for a strong president independent of the whims of the parliament. In 1958, with his trusted disciple and constitutional expert, Michel Debré, he put his wishes into practice. Therefore, according to the new Fifth Republic constitution, a president, as the physical embodiment of the state and "arbiter," was given extensive powers, including the right to negotiate treaties, to dissolve the National Assembly, to submit bills to national referenda, to appoint the prime minister (and on his recommendation, the members of the government), and to suspend the constitution itself for a limited period in the event of a national emergency. Imagine an American president with the power to dissolve Congress and call for new elections or with the prerogative of overriding a recalcitrant Senate and House by submitting his proposals to the public for ratification. Indeed, the one area in which the French president may have been in a weaker position than his American counterpart lay in his indirect election by an electoral college of notables. Even this potential limitation—potential because de Gaulle's authority and prestige hardly required constitutional justification—was rectified in October 1962, when the general, acting on what may only be termed unconstitutional grounds, submitted to referendum a bill allowing henceforth for the direct election of the president of the republic.

An aggrandizement of the presidency was not the only way by which the National Assembly was reduced in stature in the Fifth Republic. To ensure that the Assembly remained more docile than in the past, the upper house, the Senate, was given the power to veto and amend legislation emanating from the lower house. Senators were elected indirectly by deputies, general councillors, and municipal council delegates. Each one was to serve for nine years, and the terms were staggered. In the case of division between the two houses, however, the government position was paramount, for it had the right to resolve the dispute according to its own discretion. Finally, the new constitution declared the incompatibility of ministerial portfolio and National Assembly membership. Thus, upon assuming a government position, the individual deputy was required to resign his seat. Gaullists had long argued that such a reform would discourage potential ministers from conspiring against cabinets.

The Fifth Republic constitution was not designed so much to give power to the president as to make him something of a modern Caesar. In fact, there is strong evidence that Michel Debré, the principle author of the new constitution and first prime minister in the Fifth Republic, believed that General de Gaulle wished mainly to observe the political wars from Olympian heights as an "arbiter," intervening only intermittently in the decision-making realm of domestic politics. Indeed, it was expected that de Gaulle's interests lay for the most part with the great concerns of foreign policy. Consequently, what can only be called parliamentary government was expected to take care of the more mundane concerns of day-by-day government.

That parliamentary government was what Debré had in mind may be suggested from Article 20 of the constitution. There it plainly states that the prime minister "directs the policy of the nation." Apparently Debré expected the parliamentary aspects of the regime to become predominant once de Gaulle lost himself in foreign policy concerns or departed from the scene. However, when the general opted for a nationally elected president in 1962, Debré dutifully fell into line in support of a presidential regime.

At any rate, the de Gaulle-Debré creation is a hydra-headed executive with built-in potential for conflict between president and prime minister. So far this conflict has not occurred for two major reasons: the authority and prestige of de Gaulle as well as the early development of a disciplined majority party in Parliament, the Union for the New Republic (UNR). So dominant was de Gaulle during his presidency that the prime minister became little more than a glorified staff aide to the president, and Prime Minister Georges Pompidou (1962–68) admitted to the National Assembly that he himself could continue to function in a meaningful manner only so long as he had the confidence of General de Gaulle. Not even Michel Debré had gone so far during his premiership (1958–62) to state the case for presidential supremacy. Similarly, the Gaullist party was tightly disciplined, and it proudly displayed its unconditional loyalty to the president. Consequently, through his hold on the party, de Gaulle closely controlled both cabinet and National Assembly.

From the standpoint of policy theory, the French constitutional system is an interesting one. Because two forms of government are combined within the same political order, one might well ask if the pattern of the policy process deviates substantially from that of the more "pure" parliamentary and presidential types found in Great Britain and the United States. Moreover, a major problem for the French polity becomes the proper apportionment of power in a system where prime minister and president each can claim constitutional legitimacy in major decision-making areas. So far this potential conflict over the proper domain for each has been kept within bounds for the simple reason that the same political faction has dominated the presidency, the premiership, and the National Assembly for much of the Fifth Republic. But now that the Gaullist party has lost its absolute majority in the lower house and has lost the presidency to Independent Republican Valéry Giscard d'Estaing, a new situation may arise. In the future it is possible that coalition government will return to France. After all, each executive leader, president and premier, may well represent quite different political factions in the future. If and when that day arises, the institutions created by de Gaulle will be tested to the limit.[7]

## CONCLUSIONS

The nations and regimes considered in this chapter have one significant trait in common—namely, a democratic political system. In certain significant ways, however, they differ markedly from one another.

(1) *They vary in terms of social and political cohesion.* The United States, Great Britain, West Germany (at present), and Canada have not had to worry greatly about antiregime or antidemocratic political parties and movements within their societies. Both the United States and Canada have experienced racial and ethnic tensions, but presently these tensions pose little threat to political stability. France, on the other hand, has long been hampered by periodic threats from the political left and right.

(2) *They vary in terms of their legislative-executive powers.* The United States and France of the Fifth Republic have presidential regimes which are insulated from overthrow by legislative bodies. Presidents in each of these countries may claim to represent democratic majorities since they, as well as the legislatures, must present themselves to the populace in national elections. Although the French chief executive, unlike his American counterpart, may bypass the legislature entirely by submitting bills to national referenda, he may find his dominant position threatened sometime in the future. The Fifth Republic constitution created not only presidentialism but also a parliamentary form of government in which the prime minister and his cabinet are held responsible to the parliament. The result is a dual executive whose contradictions are not readily apparent at this juncture. Conversely, the other political systems considered in this chapter are—or were, as in the case of the French Third and Fourth Republics—orthodox parliamentary regimes based upon the concept of government and ministerial responsibility to the legislature.

(3) *The ability of the legislature to exercise meaningful control over the executive varies strongly among these regimes.* In Great Britain and Germany the governments have undoubtedly held the initiative, whereas in the Third and Fourth Republics of France the deputies were ascendant and the National Assembly easily threatened the political lives of fragile government coalitions through votes of no confidence. Similarly, the need for several parties to form government coalitions and the potential disagreement over any number of issues meant that the resignation of any particular group continually loomed as a distinct possibility. Canada occupies an intermediary position. In periods following PC or Liberal sweeps (as, for example, in 1958 and 1968) in national elections, its cabinets have controlled solid

majorities, but during other years it has been forced to resort to minority rule.

(4) *They vary with respect to party systems.* Both the United States and Great Britain have long been characterized by viable two-party systems in which each of the parties has alternated in power. The Bonn Republic has approached two-partyism, for the CDU and SDP have continually retained an overwhelming share of the national vote. Nevertheless, both have been forced to share power with the small FDP. Although the Gaullist party in 1968 did win an absolute majority of all seats in the National Assembly, it has nonetheless been forced throughout most of the Fifth Republic to govern with the aid of the Independent Republicans. The March 1973 loss at the polls and the defeat of Gaullist Jacques Chaban-Delmas in the May 1974 presidential campaign suggest that the Gaullists are losing their majority position. Finally, Canada has two major parties, either of which is capable of winning an absolute majority of all seats in the House of Commons. At times, however, neither party has controlled a majority of all seats.

In the overview just concluded, the emphasis was placed upon distinctions between various democracies through such characteristics as relative stability, presidential or parliamentary forms, or party systems. Future chapters, however, will deal in more general terms with the ways in which policy is made or the manner in which issues flow from the time they are initiated until they are settled. It will be argued that certain patterned flows tend to repeat themselves in various democracies no matter what the peculiarities of their respective institutional frameworks. For example, Great Britain and the United States differ markedly in the institutional arrangements, but policy flows display rather similar characteristics in both countries.

The policy process should be conceptualized as an independent variable which affects other structures and processes rather than as a mere resultant of ongoing activities occurring within and between major political institutions. This outlook suggests a treatment of policy types in terms of their influence upon institutional behavior, not the other way around. The typical comparative text in the past has devoted a chapter to the policy processes in a given nation or nations in which discussion was centered on cabinets, legislatures, courts, and bureaucracies as policy-making structures. Included were considerations of the relative influence of each institution, the individuals and groups which gain access to them, and the relative controls exercised over and by key decision makers. On the whole such approaches have been more descriptive than theoretical. Conversely, the aim of this work is to focus upon the comparative policy process in such a way as to make generalizations (i.e., theoretical statements) which can cut across the rather diverse nations and institutions discussed in this chapter. To that end the policy process should be thought of as a concept to be treated somewhat independently of these institutions. One should think, therefore, in a comparative and theoretical way about the flow of issues themselves, although keeping the institutional aspects firmly in mind at all times.

## NOTES

1. See Leon D. Epstein, *Political Parties in Western Democracies* (New York: Praeger, 1967), p. 322.

2. Leon D. Epstein, "A Comparative Study of Canadian Parties," *American Political Science Review,* March 1964, pp. 48–49.

3. Robert R. Alford, *Party and Society* (Chicago: Rand McNally and Co., 1963).

4. E.g., see Ralf Dahrendorf, *Society and Democracy in Germany* (Garden City, N.Y.: Doubleday & Co., Inc., 1967), pp. 33–64.

5. Arnold J. Heidenheimer, *The Governments of Germany,* 3rd ed. (New York: Thomas Y. Crowell Co., 1971), pp. 175–76.

6. See David Thomson, *Democracy in France Since 1870,* 4th ed. (New York: Oxford University Press, 1964), p. 112.

7. Indeed, it appears that the forces of disintegration have already begun to set in. When the March 1973 elections were completed, the Gaullist party proper, the Democratic Union for the Fifth Republic (UDR), had lost 89 seats. Although the UDR in coalition with two other parties still gave "Gaullism" a temporary majority in the National Assembly, it seems that, contrary to the predictions of many noted observers, the UDR is hardly likely to achieve the long-term role of a British-type Conservative party. For a discussion of the reasons for UDR weakness, see T. Alexander Smith, "Gaullism and the French Voter," *Political Science,* September 1968, pp. 52–63. For an optimistic view of the future, see especially the well-known work of Jean Charlot, *The Gaullist Phenomenon* (New York: Praeger Publishers, 1971).

# 2

# THE POLITICS OF
# DISTRIBUTION

A S E. E. Schattschneider has cogently argued, to define an issue is to
determine—or at least to go far in determining—the scope of conflict.
Some people wish to keep the scope narrow; others want to make it more
public. Thus, arguments about free enterprise or socialism in reality resolve
around the question of how much socialization of conflict can be tolerated.
It follows that the man or group able to manage the conflict in his or its
own interests will likely emerge the winner; obviously, he who can define
the issue has a significant advantage over his opponents.[1]

In the distributive arena conflict is largely absent. To use Schattschneider's word, it is "privatized." The policies supported by individuals
or groups have been defined in such narrow terms that face-to-face disputes among participants over political questions do not take place. Those
who make claims upon the polity are mostly indulged; no one is deprived.
Such well-known phrases as "pork barrel," "mutual backscratching," and,
in the broad sense, "patronage" capture the essence of distributive politics.
In a more intellectual vein much so-called "incrementalism" is also essentially distributive politics.[2]

In fact the politics of patronage is practiced so widely by political man
that it hardly excites us at all until dishonesty and corruption happen to
be discovered. It therefore includes the great bulk of little-noticed administrative and legislative outpourings over time. The actives in distributive
politics generally include a very small number of individuals whose failure
to gain indulgence leaves them angry with only a few other individuals,
probably those in official positions. The issues are so personalized that
creating interest on the part of large groups for the welfare of the deprived
is almost out of the question. The lawyer who fails to get the title work
he thinks his due from the state or the party contributor who is denied a
road through his property must pressure certain political officials to realize

their claims; and, as a result, their hostility is likely to be directed toward specialized individuals. Thus, the impact of such issues is particular, not general.

Examples of distributive policies are numerous: rivers and harbors, roads, the traditional tariff, licensing practices, beautification, defense procurement programs, many private members' bills. They seem to be particularly pervasive in agriculture. In fact, included below are two such cases from Great Britain and West Germany, for there is no better field than agricultural politics for illustrating the nature of distribution. They may be found also in the many government bureaucracies which regulate business and labor, ostensibly in the interest of the public. Over long periods of time the interactions between regulator and regulated become mutually beneficial, and a stabilized relationship develops. These interactions are essentially noncompetitive, resulting from the distributive nature of the issues at hand. Thus, as many studies in the United States show, regulatory agencies have served the interests of the regulated so well that a real question sometimes arises as to who is regulating whom. The important thing to remember, however, is that the relationships tend to be highly individualized and/or personal.

One finds essentially the same phenomenon in European societies. Thus, Joseph LaPalombara in his study of Italian interest groups discovered that the big business-oriented *Confindustria* was on exceptionally good terms with the Ministry of Industry and Commerce. Henry W. Ehrmann found similar patterns of behavior existing in France between the technocrats of business and government. In addition, much of France's postwar nuclear development policy appears to have been of this sort. It would seem also that Samuel H. Beer's discussions of "quasi-corporatism" in Great Britain have leaned heavily upon issues in which conflict has been mitigated through the employment of distributive means. For example, the extensive use of governmental committees composed of civil servants and group representatives is significant in this regard in that bargaining is low keyed, lacking in tension, and often quite informal.[3]

Interestingly, when such writers discuss the interactions of governmental bureaucracies, they often call attention to situations in which the expertise of the group is needed due to the technical nature of the questions raised.[4] This should not be surprising since they are describing for the most part interactions that produce distributive-type politics. After all, a basic characteristic of distributive policies is that competition between interested parties can be avoided by defining the issues so narrowly that face-to-face confrontations do not take place. Presumably most technical legislation requiring expertise fits this requirement since relatively few individuals are knowledgeable, involved, and interested in the prospective legislation. For this reason participants can more easily be indulged without bringing potential opponents into the battle.

To think in distributive terms may call for a reassessment of certain conclusions with regard to this kind of legislation. For example, Professor

Harry Eckstein's argument that increasing levels of consensus in Western democracies have shifted demands from the legislative halls to the executive departments—since the demands themselves are largely technical, not ideological—may be somewhat misplaced.[5] Significantly, the study in which he makes this argument deals with the British Medical Association (BMA), an organization highly likely to make specialized and technical demands of a distributive type. In other words, rather more important than the level of consensus may be the particular types of issues raised by the BMA. Therefore, whereas it may be true that a consensus on general policy will affect the intensity and scope of demands made upon the political system in general, it does not necessarily follow that case studies such as those on the BMA can explain the supposed shift in power from legislative to executive bodies per se. Since only distributive policies for the most part have been considered, the conclusion may be based upon insufficient data. On the other hand, it can be argued that the number of distributive policies has probably increased relative to other types of policies in stable and highly complex industrialized Western societies.

To place the distributive type of policy in proper perspective, it is important that one be aware of two attributes in particular that seem to characterize this type so well. For one thing, since they are so highly individualized and/or specialized, distributive issues are unlikely to excite political parties sufficiently to encourage them to engage in battle on the legislative floor. Second, due to the issues' narrow specialization, their technical nature, or the lack of partisanship that they engender, committees can play a dominant role in handling them. Consequently, distributive policies are settled by executive and/or legislative committees.

In this respect, the degree of control exercised by executive committees relative to legislative ones over distributive issues seems to depend upon the type of party system (that is, the number of parties) and the absence or presence of party discipline in the legislature. For example, in Great Britain the executive monopolizes distribution whereas in the United States it must share it with congressional committees. Similarly, in present-day Italy,[6] Fourth Republic France,[7] and Norway,[8] for instance, distribution is shared between bureaucratic and legislative committees. The reasons seem clear enough. In Great Britain there exists both party discipline and a majority party. In Italy, Fourth Republic France, and Norway, multipartyism and coalition government are the rule. On the other hand, like Great Britain, the United States possesses a majority party system, but neither Democrats nor Republicans display great discipline in Congress. As a result, party leaders have been unable to gain disciplined followers; and in the absence of this discipline, influence flows elsewhere, namely to the congressional committees.

Nor, conversely, is discipline in the absence of a majority party likely to enhance executive committee control over distributive issues. For example, assume that party membership on legislative committees is allocated roughly according to proportional representation among the parties in the legislature. In this situation it is likely that in the process of accommodating themselves with fellow members' needs or in seeking to enhance their personal role or that of their committee, members would be led to favor some degree of committee autonomy. Such an attitude hardly seems far fetched given legislators' desire to seek membership on committees where their own or constituents' interests are involved, given the need for specialization and expertise, and, finally, given members' natural desire to enhance their own role and that of their committee in the legislative process. Therefore, it would hardly be surprising if committee members found themselves at odds with their party leadership.

In the presence of a disciplined majority, however, it is much more difficult for these centrifugal tendencies to develop. After all, the government presumably has greater controls over the legislative timetable and agenda; disciplinary procedures can be more easily enforced; and the penalties for obstruction by backbenchers of the government's program can be all the greater, since in the last analysis they are forced to stand for reelection on its performance. At any rate, the presence of a disciplined majority gives the government the tools to dominate committee decision making—i.e., distributive policy making—because it can more easily utilize its own committees of ministers and bureaucrats.

Events taking place in France may help confirm or deny this hypothesis. Because throughout much of the Fifth Republic a disciplined majority has governed the National Assembly (unlike the case of the Fourth Republic when parliamentary committees held much power in a multiparty system), distribution has been performed mainly in executive departments. This dominance has not gone unnoticed, for there have been repeated denunciations in the press and elsewhere about the rule of technocrats. However, if the UDR continues to lose its preeminent position by further electoral or legislative defections, then legislative committees may well come to play once again a key part in distributive policy making.

## CONCLUSIONS

In sum, it is suggested that distributive policies possess the following major attributes:

(1) They are characterized by little, if any, conflict.
(2) They involve few or no confrontations between groups since participants, whether they be persons, firms, bureaus of government, or whatever else, do not significantly compete with other interests in seeking aid from the government.
(3) They are unlikely to affect party discipline.
(4) Key decision makers are legislative and/or executive committees.

Although lacking the normal excitement of other types of policies, distributive issues undoubtedly occur with greater frequency than any other type and make up the overwhelming bulk of government activity.

# GREAT BRITAIN

*Annual Price Reviews in Agriculture*

To a far greater extent than their numbers warrant, British agricultural interests have played a major role in decisions affecting them as a major section of the economic life of that nation.[9] As in the United States, demands for material support have been linked to the virtues that the rural way of life allegedly upholds and are regarded as effective forces against the sinister threats posed to that way of life by the expansion of urban centers. If these claims are true, it follows that it is the duty of society to assure that farming remains a viable force in modern life since rural values protect man against many of the more debilitating temptations of the city.

This glorification of rural values is, of course, a familiar one to most Americans. The British farmer, however, has developed another and much more practical argument upon which to base his case for special treatment by the state. A recurring balance-of-payments problem has continually plagued British policy makers. This difficulty in keeping the country's imports and exports in balance or, to be more exact, a tendency to import more than it exports, has enabled farmers to argue that the sustained growth of agricultural products will reduce the nation's need for food imports from such nations as New Zealand. Therefore, an increase in food productivity will help to solve the balance-of-payments problem. Since the American economy is not nearly so dependent upon the vagaries of the international system as is the British economy, it has been much more difficult for U.S. farmers to make this argument.

The major organizational structures involved most closely with politics in Great Britain differ rather markedly from those found in the United States. Thus, an American would find that agriculture is much more centralized in Great Britain. In that nation the National Farmers Union (NFU) represents almost 90 percent of all farmers, whereas American farmers have historically been divided into at least three major groups, the Grangers, the Farmers Union, and the American Farm Bureau Federation. Moreover, the individual American farmer is much less likely to be a member of a farm organization than is the Britisher. Finally, American agricultural groups have been far less centralized than has the National Farmers Union. Since this high degree of participation and centralization prevails also in British business and labor organizations, one is led to speculate with Professor Harry Eckstein and others that such a pattern may be compelled in part by the highly centralized nature of the British state machinery, particularly its party system, its cabinet, and its unitary form of government.[10]

Political scientists in the United States for years have been critical of the preferred position of American agriculture due to its success in winning large subsidies from the government in Washington, but many among them might be surprised to learn that since World War II, subsidization of the British farmer has occurred at higher levels than across the Atlantic.

This fact seems rather perplexing at first glance, for Great Britain has fewer farmers as a percentage of its population than does the United States; therefore, irate voters from rural constituencies should not in theory give the British parties undue fright, although there is some evidence that government leaders more than backbenchers fear that hostility on the farms might all too readily make a governing party a minority in the next election. Similarly, there is little evidence that "responsible government" and a disciplined two-party system have more successfully resisted the demands for preference from special interests than has the American system with its lack of party discipline, its powerful legislative committees, its separation of powers, and federal form of government. Indeed, admirers of the British system have tended to argue that party discipline protects ordinary MPs from lobbyists to a far greater extent than in America, where the absence of discipline presumably enables powerful constituency interests to exert much influence over legislators unable to retreat into the protection of party discipline.[11]

With regard to agriculture in particular, the outcome in the United States has been the establishment of an intimate triangular relationship between the Agriculture Committees of the Senate and House, the executive bureau or agency, and the local farming committees. This relationship, discussed in general in chapter 1, has apparently served to inhibit any meaningful elaboration of a national farm policy in the public interest since the president and national party leadership are to a large extent eliminated from the decisional process.

The image of a triangle, so helpful for an understanding of the American policy process, is of little use in comprehending the British case, however, since one corner of the triangle, the legislative committee, is missing. Thus, in Great Britain executive committees composed of ministers and/or permanent civil servants for the most part monopolize a function which their American counterparts must share with legislative committees. As suggested previously, this consequence in all probability derives from the existence in Great Britain of a disciplined two-party system in which leadership is pushed to the topmost levels of the executive and away from the legislature and its committees.

## The Desocialization of Agricultural Politics

For most of the past thirty years at least, agricultural policy in Great Britain has been overwhelmingly distributive in nature. Originally the British farmer was typically Tory in his political leanings, but his leaders in the NFU have long since given up narrow partisanship. When Labour came into power following World War II, it showed little inclination to legislate contrary to NFU interests; and in fact the party of the urban worker was, if anything, more receptive to farmer demands than was the Conservative party. Although the Labour party had originally favored land nationalization and had been perceived as the party of urban labor, the agriculture minister of the first Labour government following the war, agriculture minister of the first Labour government following the war, Tom

Williams, nevertheless quickly made himself a favorite with the NFU leaders. Moreover, the inexperience of the new government with agricultural problems gave the NFU a decided advantage in its dealings with the Labourites, for the government found itself forced to rely upon the NFU for expert advice. Although the NFU had initially adopted a neutral position with some trepidation, it soon discovered that this desocialization of of politics brought positive benefits.

A major consequence of the decision to desocialize the issue was to remove agriculture from the purview of Parliament and from the more orthodox form of political conflict. Distributive politics became the established method for resolving problems, and the NFU confined itself to behind-the-scenes negotiations with whatever government happened to be in power at the time. Spokesmen for the farmer gave no small amount of justification for this "above politics" stance. They resolutely contended that it was improper for agriculture to go behind the government's back to reach agreements with the opposition or to play the latter off against the government. If it became necessary to disseminate information outside the prescribed (i.e., government) channels, then the information should be distributed in the most thoroughly nonpartisan manner. In the opinion of the NFU leadership, this position was taken only in the national interest, so if the farmers found it useful to make appeals to outside forces—namely Parliament and its representatives—then the appeal itself must be directed towards both sides of the aisle, Labour and Conservative alike. Memoranda, position papers, and other political propaganda were therefore carefully submitted to each of the major political formations. The preferred stance, however, was to remain aloof from party politics altogether.[12]

This desocialization of the agricultural issue has mostly excluded agricultural issues from partisan debate and parliamentary scrutiny altogether, a tendency which naturally enough has worried the exponents of more open and democratic forms of politics. But it may be contended that the British Parliament with its disciplined two-party system is simply unequipped to deal with distributive-type politics; and so long as agricultural policy in Great Britain is defined in desocialized and distributive rather than in discordant and conflictual terms, it is difficult to perceive how the pattern will change. Moreover, since the House of Commons generally has been given little information regarding NFU and government decision-making initiatives, one can see why it has been most reluctant to intervene.

Of course, this is not to say that occasional irritations between the NFU and the government have not come into public view. For example, in 1944, 1956, 1963, and 1965 there were some publicized disagreements between the farmer and the state; and, with British attempts to adapt to the Common Market and the imposition of a common tariff, we may expect to see more agitation from a sector which is undoubtedly inefficient when compared to, say, French agriculture. Nonetheless, the general pattern of agricultural politics in Great Britain has been one of quiescent bargaining within Whitehall. This style of politics has long been favored by government and NFU leadership alike, although grassroots farmer discontent has occasionally forced the NFU to assert its leadership role by criticizing the government publicly.

## British Agriculture as Distributive Politics

Many commentators have remarked upon the particularly close relationship established between the civil service in Whitehall and the NFU following World War II. Referred to in various places as a "closed circle," a "special relationship," or even an outright "partnership," this unity of civil servant and rural representatives has created an ideal environment for distributive politics. Indeed, the most minute decisions relating to the total agricultural budget and allocations to various commodities or products have been determined each February at committee meetings known as Annual Price Reviews.

Not only the agenda, but the atmosphere of Price Review meetings has been highly favorable to distributive politics. For one thing, negotiations have been conducted by Agricultural Ministry and NFU officials alone. In the period immediately following the war, NFU negotiators were more likely to be generalist in orientation, men who themselves had strong ties with the farm. After a few setbacks to farmers because a lack of sufficient data had placed them in a weak position vis-à-vis ministry officials, the NFU upgraded and expanded its staff and research functions. With increasing specialization, expertise, and permanence of leadership, NFU officials came more and more to resemble their opposites in the higher civil service. In turn, this greater similarity among organizational types encouraged each side to view its needs from a common perspective, a perspective quite favorable to norms which emphasize specialized and limited concerns. Perceiving the agricultural problem in this manner, officials, both private and public, therefore helped to create a policy conducive to the development of a continuing series of highly specific and discrete decisions in which alternative interests of contradictory views were defined out of existence by a nonconflictual definition of the problem. Whether out of sheer apathy, fear of electoral retaliation, or genuine sympathy for rural life, the unwillingness of other interests to challenge NFU claims probably helped to ease tensions within Price Review sessions, since the negotiators had greater room within which to maneuver and less to fear from outsiders in the bureaucracy and Parliament. In any case, this system of distributive politics has served farmers quite well.

In still other ways, each side has continued to make special efforts to accommodate the needs of the other. Thus, a habit developed early by which the NFU formally endorsed the outcome of each February Annual Price Review, thereby emphasizing its role as the sole spokesman for the farmer and as a direct participant in governmental decision making. The consequence was to merge still further the state and the interest group. The success of these negotiations from the farmer's standpoint may be gleaned from the fact that in only one year between 1945 and 1960—1956—did the

NFU find it necessary to repudiate explicitly a Price Review agreement, although it is true that its endorsement in certain other years has been less than enthusiastic.[13] Since the British farmer has generally been quite easily aroused to action by falling agricultural prices, it may be assumed that he has on the whole found the Price Review mechanism to his liking.

This distributive pattern of policy making received its statutory basis in the Agricultural Act of 1947. Interestingly enough, the act itself was worded in such a vague manner as to give negotiators each year practically unlimited power to bargain and haggle for the subsidization of a large array of agricultural products. Thus, the act said that agricultural policy should look to the best ways for increasing "efficiency," but it gave little guidance as to how best to achieve it. Actually, the wording was purposely left vague precisely because it was felt by the drafters that rapid changes in agricultural conditions called for giving administrators the utmost flexibility. As Peter Self and Herbert J. Storing put it, the statute "provides a broad framework of objectives and standards whose actual efficiency depends upon their administration."[14]

The principal effect of the Agricultural Act of 1947 was to give to the minister and his civil servants practically unlimited authority to do what can only be called legislating agricultural policy, since not only can subsidies be negotiated on a yearly basis, but the terms of reference of the act are themselves so general and unclear as to defy the possibility of specific legal controls over administrative discretion. And as the NFU is a major participant in the decision-making process, one can easily understand the considerable farmer influence at Whitehall. Operating within the broadest limits, committees have made agreements over subsidies behind the scenes and then laid them before Parliament in the form of Orders which could have been theoretically vetoed by either house, but which in reality have been seldom challenged.[15]

The specific processes involved in distributive policy making at Annual Price Reviews have remained a closely guarded secret, and even a special select committee on agriculture in the House of Commons has been unable to learn very much; if a parliamentary committee is denied information, one may readily understand the difficulties in store for a mere student of politics. Self and Storing do say that negotiations within the Ministry of Agriculture go through two relatively distinct stages: one stage at which a total sum of money is agreed on, followed by a subsequent one in which the relative shares are parceled out. This conclusion has nevertheless been denied by a ranking civil servant who obliquely suggested in 1968 in an appearance before a legislative committee that "there is a complex here, a single ball of wax, from which it is difficult to pull out one single element."[16]

One is therefore left largely in the dark as to the specifics of agricultural decision making. A *Times* journalist, David Wood, has maintained that the February 1969 Price Review was concluded between NFU and Agriculture Ministry officials in the first instance, but was then followed up by tense ministerial committee meetings (sessions in which heads of government departments participate) in which the ministers of agriculture, the treasury, the board of trade, and economic affairs reviewed the initial proposals deriving from the Department of Agriculture. However, at this time the minister of agriculture, Cledwyn Hughes, failed to convince his colleagues from other departments to support agriculture's proposals, and he was subsequently defeated in full cabinet as well when he tried to achieve a reversal of the ministerial committee decision. This refusal to allow Agricultural Ministry proposals to go virtually uncontested each year has been on the rise for the past few years and shows few signs of abatement.[17] Despite the spirited battle behind the scenes, the conflict in this case remained throughout in essence a privatized one, carried on in Whitehall and outside the parliamentary seat of Westminster.

A more typical pattern of post–World War II decision making in farming is the Annual Price Review of 1955. This particular decision on the subsidization of various commodities was seemingly resolved within the Ministry of Agriculture and, unlike the Price Review of 1969, resolved without opposition from other departments of the government bureaucracy. Thus, in February 1955, farmers were awarded an increase in guarantees and subsidies of some 28 million pounds a year. This handout from the state was not justified by the ministry in terms of rising costs on the farms, but rather as a means to "compensate for exceptionally foul weather" of the previous year.

This generous increase in subsidization took place at a time when it had become increasingly evident that surpluses were rapidly accumulating and might soon become an insurmountable problem. Subsidies had grown sharply between 1948 and 1953 and had been justified on the grounds that ever higher levels of production were needed to alleviate the perennial balance-of-payments difficulties and to lower food prices at home. Once defined, however, the issue was not easily redefined, especially since the nonconflictual nature of an issue in which the costs to other groups were not immediately apparent did not readily lend itself to exploitation by antifarming interests. Besides, 1955 was an election year, and to deprive farmers as a specific group might invite retaliation at the polls and hence the loss of some seats to the Tory government in power at the time.

At any rate, in 1955, although there were in the opinion of the *Economist* too many pigs, the guarantee was nevertheless increased by the government; although milk consumption had fallen off, the price was raised, adding to the national surplus. Oats and barley were also guaranteed higher prices, and direct grants were allocated to calf-rearing farmers, to those farmers who ploughed up grassland, and to those who utilized limes and fertilizers. Indeed, between 1953 and 1955 the proportion of money going to agriculture rose from 200 million to 250 million pounds.[18] This was distributive politics at its best—or worst, depending on one's point of view.

*Conclusions*

The mechanism of the Annual Price Review therefore has historically been an excellent forum for the definition and practice of distributive politics. In creating its own experts to negotiate with their opposite numbers in the Ministry of Agriculture, the NFU has contributed still further to the perpetuation of distributive politics in the agricultural field. Through conscious decision—by the adoption of an "above politics" attitude calling for strict nonpartisanship—the NFU has for the most part excluded the divisions and conflicts inherent in party and parliamentary battles from the agricultural agenda. Thus, in opting successfully for a highly restricted scope of conflict, the NFU has usually eliminated potentially competing groups from any consideration; or at least its ostensible nonpartisanship and quiet methods of operation in Whitehall have usually enabled it to avoid direct confrontations with other major interests. The result has been that decisions affecting farmers have been relegated to the governmental bureaucracy, not to the House of Commons, for resolution. On the other hand, the very lack of clear guidelines given to the bureaucracy in the Act of 1947 has instead given NFU and ministry officials almost unlimited freedom within their area to distribute subsidies and guarantees to the farming community in any way they see fit.

Professor Lowi has referred to this delegation of legislative authority in the United States as "interest-group liberalism."[19] It is his view that this "policy without law" has given pressure groups with specialized concerns a decided advantage over the bureaucrats who are supposed to regulate them for the public benefit. Civil servants are placed on the defensive because, in developing legislation, Congress has often failed to spell out in detail its intentions. Hence, the public servant in the field is left to his own devices, unable to fall back upon clear law as a protective device; and since his interactions are most likely to occur with the very interests he ostensibly regulates, it is hardly surprising that there is more meaningful participation in policy making by interest groups than by legislative bodies in many instances.

Significantly, Lowi refers to agricultural decision making as an area where this derangement of public power has proceeded farthest and where the triangular relationship between legislative committees, bureaucracy, and interest groups has been especially strong. In his opinion these relationships throughout government have done much to erode public authority, produce social and political turmoil, and sow distrust in the decade of the 1960s. In the larger sense, therefore, he has produced not only a study of interest-group liberalism but a theory of democratic stability, or of political instability, if one prefers.

The preceding pages would suggest, however, that agricultural policy in Great Britain is characterized by interest-group liberalism as much it is in the United States. In turn, this suggests that the reasons for political instability have little to do with interest-group liberalism as such, for, after all, Great Britain is easily one of the most stable democracies in the Western world.[20] Be that as it may, the vague and ambiguous Agricultural Act of 1947 and the Annual Price Reviews each February have encouraged the fullest possible participation in the public domain by a private group.

# THE UNITED STATES

## *The 1930 Smoot-Hawley Tariff Act*

Debates over the merits or demerits of the protective tariff have long formed part of the American political scene.[21] The salience of the tariff as a political issue has been largely dependent upon the vagaries of the political party battle. The Republican party established itself as the major champion of protectionism beginning with its creation immediately prior to the Civil War. Conversely, the Democratic party became associated in the public mind as the defenders of free trade. Conventions of each party periodically reconfirmed that image. Only in recent years, as the party situation itself has become somewhat more fluid with regard to protectionism, has that view of the factional conflict begun to undergo a change. Thus, in 1962 when President John F. Kennedy made his famous plea for a free trade policy which would enable the United States to meet the challenge of the growing European Common Market, proponents of the bill could be found on both sides of the political aisle. In the intervening years the Republicans had become more liberal on trade matters whereas the Democrats had become somewhat more protectionist. This was especially true in the Southern states, earlier champions of free trade within the Democratic party; with the region's burgeoning economic development in recent decades, the South had become increasingly receptive to protectionism as a doctrine.

In reviewing the historical record, one must not attribute too much party discord to tariff issues. Actually, until the presidency of Franklin D. Roosevelt the protectionists were numerous enough in both major parties to be firmly in control of such matters. Thus, the Republican majority was clearly under the sway of protectionism, and Democratic opposition to that dominance was sporadic, timid, and mainly confined to the party's Southern wing.

## *Background*

The first tariff in the United States was enacted during the presidency of James Madison. Unlike subsequent tariffs, however, the purpose of this one was not to restrict imports but to raise money for the federal treasury. This method of financing was resorted to especially during periods of international conflict. Thus, during the Wars of 1812 and 1860, Congress found it necessary to raise tariffs still higher and to increase the number of items on the list in order to finance the war effort. Once established, however, such tariffs were quickly perceived by their beneficiaries in business and industry as a right, as almost a part of the natural order of things.

One major justification advanced by protectionists in this period was that infant industries needed a high tariff wall behind which to grow until the day arrived when they could compete successfully against the more mature industries of Europe. As private interests increasingly discovered that the tariff was a very useful device to protect themselves from foreign competition, they placed pressures upon Congress to maintain and extend protective legislation, even if the necessity for federal revenues had not declined in the meantime. For its part, Congress found that it was far easier simply to multiply the number of recipients of protection rather than to attempt a reduction in benefits to those already favored. Once begun, this process could be expanded indefinitely, which in fact is what has happened over the years. In 1816, for example, the tariff statute covered only 4½ pages, but by 1930 it had grown to some 200 pages.[22]

In all probability the linking of the tariff to nationalism in the public mind gave to protectionism an assured legitimacy which continued to exist well into the twentieth century. In particular, it was argued throughout the nineteenth century that a powerful Great Britain was bent upon strangling in its infancy a small but emergent American industrialism by flooding American markets with cheap goods from abroad. The War of 1812 with Great Britain and pro-Southern British sympathies in 1860 only strengthened this belief. Similarly, the South during the Civil War was antiprotectionist, and indeed had justified its secession in part on the grounds that high tariff walls imposed upon it by the North invited retaliation in foreign markets against Southern agricultural products. It seemed to many non-Southerners that since their enemies had been free traders, a belief in protectionism was in the finest patriotic tradition.

Nevertheless, certain forces ultimately undermined protectionism, or at least eroded support for the tariff as the chief device for import regulation. As the United States grew into an industrial giant, many leaders began to understand that exports were increasingly necessary to American well-being; if foreigners could not sell their goods to this nation, then they would hardly have the dollars to purchase products from the United States. In addition, methods superior to the tariff for restraining imports came into fashion: quotas, special subsidies, currency controls, and the like. Finally, sources for revenue other than the tariff came into existence, such as the personal income tax.

The Great Depression accelerated the decline of the tariff. In 1934, the Reciprocal Trade Act was passed. Committing the United States henceforth to freer trade, Congress instructed the president of the United States to engage in negotiations with other nations for the purpose of mutual reduction (or mutual increases) in tariff rates. The act was periodically renewed during the various Democratic administrations, but it received strong bipartisan backing in 1953, when the Republicans under President Dwight D. Eisenhower extended it once again. Free trade was no longer a monopoly of the Democratic party, but was now also supported by most Republicans as well.[23]

The Smoot-Hawley Trade Act of 1930 was the last but most comprehensive piece of pure protectionist legislation enacted by an American Congress. When it was first initiated in 1928, protectionists seemed to be in full control of political events. Few would have dared believe that in a very short time they would be in retreat before new forces of internationalism. Protectionists certainly were far from complete failure in achieving gains after the enactment of the Reciprocal Trade Act of 1934. Yet they were never again so uniformly successful as in 1930.

## The Elements of Privatized Conflict

Because the Smoot-Hawley bill was contested in legislative committee, the main decisional components from beginning to end were contained within the House Ways and Means and Senate Finance Committees. Indeed, President Herbert Hoover in his annual message of 1929 emphasized the dominant role of Congress in this respect, and he apparently never sought thereafter to implant his own views upon the pending legislation. Similarly, when the bill was reported out of committee, it met little opposition on the floor. Thus, throughout the life of this bill neither presidential nor legislative floor activity was evident to any large extent. That a bill of such importance could be so limited in conflict potential and in terms of bureaucratic or presidential initiative must seem strange to non-Americans used to ministerial dominance of the legislative process. Were a similar bill to arise in Great Britain, the major focal points of resolution would in all probability be administrative committees within the executive branch. But in the United States a lack of party discipline and strong party leadership has helped to create a situation in which the committees of Congress play a role in policy making seldom observed elsewhere.

Between 1928–30 there were several elements present to insure that the tariff question remained relatively quiescent, confined to committee negotiations. These elements were: (1) ideological harmony over tariff matters; (2) time limitations placed upon committee consideration of the bill; (3) the lack of publicity given to the hearings; and (4) the utilization of certain procedural devices in committee which thwarted discussion of questions concerning the general usefulness of the tariff.

In the first place, the ideological ingredients necessary for a major battle were largely absent in Smoot-Hawley. It takes at least two antagonists to fight, but in this period of American history both major parties were too wedded to protectionism to struggle over the issue. In fact, Smoot-Hawley itself was a mere revision and extension of another piece of protectionist legislation, the Fordney-McCumber Act of 1922. In both instances the Democrats passively acquiesced to Republican dominance, although in 1930 Congressman Cordell Hull did write a rather sharp minority report in the Ways and Means Committee. This degree of harmony was possible because members of each party basically accepted the view that enactment of tariff legislation was economically sound, proper, and patriotic, although, of course, they might disagree over details. To such men there was no question of a debate between the spokesmen for protection on the one hand and the defenders of free trade on the other. The only hope for free trade proponents resided in their ability to convince the political powers that their particular needs did not in themselves violate the principle of protectionism. This they sought to do by acknowledging dutifully their support of the tariff in general while at the same time attempting to convince the legislative committee membership of their right to specific aid. But the logic of a situation in which nationalism and protectionism were merged assured them little comfort from legislators over the long run.

Since the tariff and nationalism were equated in the minds of many Americans in this period, it is easy to understand why contrary opinions were given such short shrift, much less legitimacy. But if pervasive protectionism among the populace was not sufficient to keep the issue essentially privatized, the tactics of the legislative committee elites were surely calculated to achieve that effect. The chairmen of the two committees, Senator Reid Smoot and Congressman Willis C. Hawley, not to mention the Democratic and Republican party leadership, acted upon the belief that protracted discussion of the tariff question could only arouse latent groups to enter the fray. The longer the issue remained unresolved, the greater the available opportunities for creating discord among various kinds of protectionists: those who had been excluded in the past from coverage; those who felt their own tariff levels to be inadequate; and, finally, those who simply had an interest in free trade. In general, the greater danger to consensus derived not so much from importers as from secondary producers. The latter might easily perceive a potential threat to their profit margins from a tariff placed on goods they were forced to purchase (either at home or abroad).

The committees sought in various ways to reduce any possibility for a conflict which might be potentially disruptive either to party consensus or to the legislative timetable. Therefore, specific plans were made to place time limits upon the bill. To that end the length of the sessions was sharply circumscribed. On December 5, 1928, the Ways and Means Committee authorized public notice of hearings to commence on January 7, 1929. Consideration of tariff legislation would be limited to four months, or some thirty-five actual days of hearings. As it was, completion of testimony took forty-three days. The Senate completed its hearings on July 18, 1929, and sent the bill to the floor for a vote on September 4, 1929. It was the intention of the congressional leaders to force the bill through Congress prior to December 1929, when Congress reconvened in regular session. Levies were placed upon an estimated 25,000 separate items covering almost 200 pages in a short period of time, demonstrating the feverish pace at which the two committees worked.[24]

There was also a rather clear absence of publicity given to the sessions. The notice of the hearings was merely posted, leaving interested parties to fend for themselves as best they could. No attempt was made to invite witnesses to testify—in particular, witnesses of opposing views—for such testimony might have encouraged dissension. Since few firms had paid lobbyists, staffs in Washington, experience in dealing with legislators and bureaucrats or even the help of alert congressmen eager to bring the pending legislation to the attention of their constituents, it is not surprising that testimony was limited to far smaller numbers than otherwise might have been the case. The posting procedure tended to favor those with the necessary knowledge about Washington politics, and such interests were overwhelmingly favorable to the tariff. Since this lack of information automatically excluded many groups from the competition, the potential for discord was further reduced. Interestingly, however, in the end almost 1,100 people did in fact find a way to testify.[25]

In addition to ideological consensus, a lack of publicity given to the tariff issue, and the speed with which the hearings were conducted, the procedural devices utilized during the course of the committee sessions also helped to keep the conflict within narrow bounds. Persons requesting to testify were placed on a waiting list, their order of appearance determined according to the time at which particular items of interest to them appeared on the committee agenda. Individual testimony was therefore limited to specific items on particular days and at certain hours. This restriction was ruthlessly enforced by a "rule of relevancy" by which the chairman was empowered to cut off debate on any subject other than that relating to the specific items and paragraphs under discussion. The effect was to limit the possibility of a broad-gauged attack on the tariff as such: since a witness could appear only when the particular item or paragraph of interest to him was under consideration, and since he could, furthermore, talk only to that one point, then it was obviously quite difficult for free traders and others to mobilize coalitions among themselves. They were limited to items; they were prohibited from discussing the tariff as an issue.

## Peace Among the Indulged

Although Congress through its committees and party leadership refused to define the tariff issue in the potentially discordant but clear-cut terms of free trade vs. protectionism, the committees themselves were faced with a problem of justifying their support for specific tariff rates.[26] If protectionism were deemed a legitimate political doctrine by most participants, there remained the difficulty of determining not only which particular industries merited rewarding, but also at what levels the rates should be set. In creating legislation, the committees also had to guard themselves against the charge that the largest contributors to the campaign chests of the Republican party would receive the greater benefits. The House rule was for the bill to be written by a fifteen-man committee of the majority; and such men, as Republicans, surely did not wish their party accused of favoritism in the case of a few well-placed firms.

In order to give an appearance of fairness and yet remain true to the protectionist principle (itself inherently unfair to some industries), Congress employed a comparative costs formula for the determination of tariff levels. Through the formula Congress attempted to base tariff rates upon the comparative differences in the costs of production between American firms and their foreign competitors. It was widely believed that foreign labor was much cheaper than American labor and therefore there was a stark possibility that cheaply produced goods manufactured abroad would flood the American market, bringing on unemployment and business failures. The tariff therefore would give firms in the United States an opportunity to compete with other nations on a more equitable basis.

If one accepted not only this protectionist definition of the issue, but the utility of the comparative costs formula as well, a fundamental dilemma still remained: how was one to gain a true knowledge of costs of production in other countries? Could congressional committees with their limited resources ever effectively understand comparative costs even with the help of the Tariff Commission (an organization which included experts on tariff matters)? This was doubtful because even if they were able to master the complex subject matter they were still limited by their commitment to swift enactment of tariff legislation. Given the time limitations placed upon the committees, any serious consideration of comparative costs was for all practical purposes excluded from the agenda at the outset. As might be expected, the committees made little effort to gain an essential knowledge of differences in costs of production among the nations.

The hearings provided scant opportunity for a dispassionate analysis of the tariff in terms of the usefulness of the comparative costs formula or its impact on the American economy. Conspicuously absent was any of the give-and-take of spirited debate, for committee members were apparently unwilling to challenge testimony supplied in the sessions. As a result the committees made no effort to achieve a balance between pro and antitariff groups. In fact, protectionists dominated the hearings to such an extent that alternative opinions went unrepresented in the committee rooms. Presumably more information might have been garnered had economists or lobbyists with pronounced antitariff feelings been invited to submit testimony; and an invitation would surely have been justified under the circumstances. After all, protectionist sentiment was clearly dominant at the hearings; protariff spokesmen were naturally favorable to as high a level of support for their own industries as possible; and, finally, lobbyists would place their own needs in the best possible light.

There was a rather clear tendency to accept at face value the data provided by protectionists. No effort was made to check out the many rumors repeated by lobbyists that dire threats were posed in the immediate future to certain American industries by foreign imports. The committees hardly could have done much in the way of gathering information anyway since the severe time limitations precluded a useful investigation into such rumors.

The committees made sure that those industry spokesmen who did testify at the sessions felt as comfortable as possible. Embarrassing or penetrating questions designed to trip up witnesses were scrupulously avoided, and little effort was made to check on the authenticity of the lobbies' data. The potential beneficiaries of the protective tariff were therefore given every benefit of doubt. Indeed, the atmosphere surrounding the sessions was not that of petitioners making pleas before a powerful state. The reality was an affair among mutually sympathetic allies in which the representatives of business and government negotiated with one another as friendly equals. And among these equals committed to as little conflict as possible, a desocialized outcome was assured.

Despite the manifest intentions of committee members and the various petitioners for protection, there was always the potential danger that aggrieved parties would upset the harmonious relationships. Although importers obviously had a most vital interest in expanded international trade, ironically they did not pose the real threat to consensus. Certain weaknesses inherent in their situation reduced their bargaining power. First, importers were mainly confined to one region of the nation, the Northeast. Consequently, their ability to bring sufficient pressure upon Congress was limited to their influence with senators and representatives from the East. Second, most importers did not employ large numbers of workers, so economic hardship resulting from a loss of foreign markets was unlikely to expose legislators to electoral retaliation. Domestic producers, on the other hand, were likely to employ many more workers and to be scattered throughout the nation.

Nevertheless, the major obstacle to political peace did not rest with the importers; rather, it was the secondary producers who posed the greatest threat to an accord simply because they might well be compelled to pay higher prices for goods protected by the tariff schedule. Thus, not only would they be prohibited from purchasing cheaper goods abroad but in addition, the domestic products they bought, now protected by a tariff wall, would be more costly as well. Since the secondary producers, as primary manufacturers, were among the larger firms in terms of production and employment, they were a potential adversary to those domestic firms clamoring loudest and receiving protection from the state.

The evidence suggests, however, that in the discussions over Smoot-Hawley, secondary producers on the whole displayed little agitation, much less a successful defense of what one would think were their interests. Their lack of strong resistance may have been influenced in part by their position in relation to the tariff. Unlike the primary producers, they were not directly affected by the threat of foreign goods entering American markets. Similarly, the burden placed upon secondary producers by the tariff schedule was not so readily understood, since it was the goods they bought, rather than the products they actually sold, which were most influenced by the tariff. The farther removed one's own product is from the direct impact of the tariff, the less likely he is to be concerned about the ultimate harm it may have upon his economic well-being. Similarly, by curtailing sharply the supply of money, the largely independent U.S.

Federal Reserve Board may contribute to a downturn in the economy, but the person thereby unemployed is far more likely to blame the president, Congress, or the capitalist for his misfortune.

For an understanding as to why so little real conflict occurred over the Smoot-Hawley bill, one should not underestimate the sustained effort made by the Committees on Ways and Means and Finance to keep both importers and secondary manufacturers relatively contented or at least neutralized. The importers' inherent political weakness plus the basic illegitimacy of the free trade doctrine were probably sufficient to keep them from making trouble. Because the secondary manufacturers had potentially more economic and political power, however, they created a different sort of problem altogether for consensus-prone committee decision makers. The legislators' response to the threat of dissension was to buy off the opposition by simply extending coverage of the tariff to as many interested parties as possible, in some instances to firms which had not even requested aid. Since this practice could hardly be rationalized on economic grounds, an extension of protection to so many firms and industries was justified not only as patriotic but also as the essence of consistency, fairness, and impartiality. In some cases the extent of coverage was carried to such lengths that certain firms included in the tariff schedule employed only a handful of workers. In other instances, if it were concluded that various industries might be hurt by a tariff, then the committee simply added them to the list of protected industries. This practice may have been bad economics, but it was good politics, for the effect was, as Schattschneider put it so well, to "disorganize the opposition" before it could begin to think seriously about mounting an attack.

The legislative desire to accommodate apparently influenced lobby spokesmen. The various lobbyists sought consistently to avoid antagonizing one another through a strategy by which each interest made its special demands independent of other interests. Described by Schattschneider as "reciprocal non-interference,"[27] this type of politics involved more than a mere "live and let live" approach to political activity. Expressions of good will were so pervasive at the hearings that various lobbyists felt compelled to demonstrate that while they indeed had special requests to make with regard to pending legislation, they in no way wished to jeopardize the rights of others. Protectionist spokesmen incessantly repeated that while it was quite proper for an individual to seek protection for himself, he ought to do nothing to prevent others from doing the same. Even the large farm associations one might have expected to oppose protection for industry adopted a thoroughly conciliatory stand on industrial questions. This harmony among the lobby spokesmen served a major function: it helped to stabilize the number of participants taking part in the sessions, and this limitation in turn gave greater advantages to those few firms and industries already engaged in the bargaining process. On the other hand, dissension among the various industrial spokesmen might have increased the amount of publicity given to the tariff question and therefore incited previously latent interests to action. Quiescence thus enhanced the possibilities for gain among groups already involved in the negotiations.

## Conclusion

Compared with most of the British agricultural decisions considered earlier, the tariff discussions of 1929–30 may seem somewhat more noisy. Yet the fact remains that the Smoot-Hawley bill excited little real debate among those taking part in the struggle. When the bill was signed into law in 1930, the Congressional Digest demonstrated the extent of its interest by devoting a total of seventy-one words to its passage.[28] The congressional committees, the party leaders, and the various lobbyists who appeared at the hearings all made strenuous efforts to avoid partisan disputes over a program which had something for everyone who knew his way around Washington well enough to make himself heard. Thus, once an individual had made his request for inclusion in the tariff schedule, attempts were made more often than not to accommodate his interests (assuming he did not intend to discuss the virtues of free trade). As the clerk of the House Committee on Ways and Means suggested at the time of the hearings, all required of any citizen was a letter to the committee requesting an appearance when his particular item and paragraph came up for discussion in committee.[29] If it is generally true, as the more cynical say, that politicians can rise above principle when the occasion demands, it may be no less true that they can just as easily rise above conflict.

# WEST GERMANY*

## Agricultural Subsidization

When it comes to the politics of agriculture, most free market economies forego the virtues of competition and free trade in favor of protectionism. Certainly this has been the case in West Germany despite fervent rhetoric about the free market and neoliberal economic principles. As in the United States and Great Britain, agriculture has enjoyed a special position in the distribution of economic services and benefits by the government.

## Background

A subsidized and protected agricultural sector has a long history in Germany. Protective legislation such as price supports and import-export regulation was begun under the Second Empire in the late 1800s, and continued during the Weimar Republic. In the Nazi government controls became total in their impact. After World War II, West German agriculture found itself at a disadvantage in adapting to a modern industrialized economy. Productivity was below that of other economic sectors because farm costs were higher relative to yield, and farm income lagged behind that of other occupational categories. In addition, several aspects of the traditional

---

* Prepared by Margot Nyitray.

agricultural organization, such as scattered land holdings and a large number of very small farms with poor soil conservation and use, inhibited modernization and increased efficiency.[30] Disadvantages also extended to the social level, including increasing rural isolation in a rapidly urbanizing society as well as poor education. Farmers were becoming a socially marginal group as their percentage of the work force declined from 75 percent in the 1900s to less than 10 percent in the 1960s. A general consensus existed on the need for government assistance to farmers. This was supported by ideological valuations of the virtues of the rural way of life, as in the United States and Great Britain, as well as by practical arguments about the importance of agricultural self-sufficiency for national strength.

Prior to 1933, German farmers were split into a variety of interest organizations based on regional, economic and religious divisions. After the experience of compulsory unity under the Nazis, and due in part to the decline in religious conflict and the split with the Eastern Zone, German agricultural interests in the Federal Republic were able to establish a highly centralized unitary organization to represent their interests. The *Deutscher Bauernverband* (DBV) has more than 1.2 million members. With 90 percent of those in full-time agricultural work as members, the farmers have the highest degree of organization of any West German interest group. Although there are a number of other specialized agricultural interest groups such as the *Deutscher Raiffeisenverband e.V.*, a federation of German agricultural cooperatives concerned with economic aid, and the *Deutsche Landwirtschaftsgesellschaft* which is concerned with technological developments, all groups are united in the Central Committee of German Agriculture. At the local and state levels, there is considerable overlap of officials between these groups and the DBV, and the DBV has always controlled the chairmanship and general manager's position in the Central Committee. Within the DBV itself, of course, certain state associations of farmers, particularly in Bavaria and Lower Saxony where agriculture is predominant, have contributed crucial strength to the national organization. Other factors, including the traditional ideological importance of the rural "estate" and its social isolation, have also contributed to the high cohesion of West German farmers. Their marginal social position has also led to a high degree of status anxiety which has been used on more than one occasion by the DBV leadership to reinforce unity.[31]

The DBV has to be considered one of the most influential interest groups in West German politics. It has been very successful in representing the farmers' demands for governmental aid to remedy the disadvantages of the agricultural sector and to insure farmers of an adequate income. Its success is in part a consequence of its position in relation to voting blocs and the competitive position of the political parties. Unlike the British National Farmers Union, the DBV has not been politically neutral. It has generally used its strategic position within the bourgeois parties to gain its aims, although in recent years, it has also worked occasionally with the SPD in the legislature. At least since the late 1950s, farm issues have become more salient for the Social Democrats because of increased SPD efforts to widen the party's base and cut into the rural vote. While the SPD has had only limited success in attracting farm votes, all parties have quite similar positions on rural issues. Thus, all of them support government aid, although the SPD places more emphasis upon the social problems of the farm worker while the CDU/SCU exhibits concern for price improvement.

Farmers have the highest voter turnout (93 percent) of any occupational group in West Germany. Yet surveys indicate a very low level of overall political information and interest among them, which suggests that voting behavior is based almost entirely on appeal to group interests and leadership cues. Despite the fact that there are many other occupational groups larger in numbers, such a highly cohesive and organized bloc of voters is important to any party which can attract them. In the past, the farmers have largely voted for the bourgeois-conservative parties, and they continue to express traditional farm distrust of the socialists. Most farmers, especially the Catholic small farmers in the South and Southwest, have voted for the CDU/CSU, although in 1969 the NPD cut into this vote. The FDP has received the support of some large Protestant farmers in the North and wine-growers in the Southwest. It is only in the most recent elections that the SPD has been able to cut into CDU/CSU support in some rural Protestant districts.[32]

Table 1

Farmers' Party Preference

| Party | CDU/CSU % | FDP % | SPD % | Others, No Vote, Unknown % |
|-------|-----------|-------|-------|----------------------------|
| 1953 | 61 | 13 | 5 | 21 |
| 1956 | 67 | 9 | 9 | 15 |
| 1961 | 72 | 11 | 6 | 11 |
| 1965 | 67 | 7 | 8 | 18 |
| 1969 | 59 | 4 | 7 | 30 |

Source: 1953-65, H. G. Schlotter, *Die Willensbildung in der Agrarpolitik* (Munich: BLV Verlagsgesellschaft, 1971), pp. 207-8; 1969, Hans D. Klingemann and F. U. Pappi, "Die Wahlerbewegungen bei der Bundestagswahl am 28 September 1969," *Politische Vierteljahresschrift* 11:1 (March 1970) 124.

This voting behavior has been transformed into direct participation in the legislature through what is usually referred to as the "Green Front." A remarkably stable percentage of *Bundestag* members have been agricultural representatives, including many important officers of the DBV who have been or are CDU/CSU representatives. One of the vice-chairmen of the CDU/CSU parliamentary party is always an agriculture representative, and the farm group is the largest organized faction within the CDU/CSU caucus. DBV and other agricultural organization officials as well as other representatives of rural districts are also organized within the FDP in the *Bundestag.* [33]

These groups have worked for the selection of agriculture ministers who would represent their views. During the period of CDU/CSU coalition governments, they were generally highly successful. While not always entirely satisfied with the actions of Heinrich Lübke, the first agriculture minister and subsequent president of the Federal Republic, the farm organization members found his successor, Werner Schwarz, a former DBV officer, certainly more to their liking. Indeed, in the SPD-FDP coalition governments since 1969, an FDP representative of the farmers has been agriculture minister. The DBV has thus enjoyed a good relationship with the Ministry of Agriculture (technically, Food, Agriculture and Forestry). While not much information is available about the lower levels of the bureaucracy, there has generally been close contact and mutual interest in many areas. In addition, the government's administrative rules of procedure suggest ministerial consultation with appropriate interest groups and specify that these should be national organizations, thus giving the DBV (or other such groups in different areas) a semilegal status within the executive process.

The organization of the *Bundestag* and the autonomy of its committees have much importance for the Green Front. As in the American Congress, the *Bundestag* Agriculture Committee has served as a means of protecting farm interests. Since 1949, an absolute majority of the committee's members in each session have been representatives of agriculture. Many of them have been current DBV officials, and the chairman of the committee for many years was Bernhard Bauknecht, vice-chairman of the DBV.

### The Reduction of Conflict: Distributive Principles in Agriculture

The distributive pattern of politics in West Germany falls somewhere between those of Great Britain and the United States. A great number of issues are resolved through negotiations within the executive with little publicity, much less legislative involvement. Additionally, in the *Bundestag,* and particularly in the Agriculture Committee, the Green Front has found a highly effective second line of defense. It has sought to keep distributive-type agreements reached in the executive and in legislative committee from becoming the object of floor fights; and it has attempted to improve the DBV's bargaining position with the lower bureaucracy when there is resistance to its demands from the ministry. In a very real sense the committee has helped to prevent potential opposition groups from moving most issues into another, more pronounced, area of conflict. Committee consideration tends to take place in an atmosphere of expertise. The concern has not been with the question of priorities or the principle of agricultural aid programs, but with technical questions about the best distribution of benefits. The committee versions of agricultural policy bills have generally been approved by unanimous vote on the floor of the *Bundestag*.[34]

In 1950–51, a series of agriculture market regulations (*Marktordnungen*) were passed unanimously to provide price supports for various farm products: beef, grain, sugar, and milk. Although only government economic measures which were neutral in their effects on the market were supposed to be acceptable to the prevailing economic philosophy, these measures created no conflict or controversy. They were simply justified as necessary to market stability and the adjustment of agriculture to a modern economy. Under most of this legislation, fixed maximum and minimum prices were set annually by the legislature or by executive order. Import and supply offices (*Einfuhr-und Vorratsstellen*) were established in Frankfurt to maintain the price level by buying and selling and by regulating imports. Because the price levels were determined by political decisions, primarily within the Agriculture Ministry in consultation with the DBV, these offices worked fairly automatically to maintain prices. If the world price was lower than the German level, import duties were imposed (since 1963), and if the world price was higher, these offices bought up the German surplus.[35]

The best illustration of the DBV's success in the distributive area of politics was the passage of the Agriculture Law (*Landwirtschaftsgesetz*) in 1955.[36] As previously noted, there was general agreement in the early 1950s on the need to provide government aid to agriculture; what limited conflict there was concerned the more technical question of which economic policy instruments to utilize. Neoliberals, including many government bureaucrats and agricultural economists, believed that the chief cause of agriculture problems arose from structural hindrances to adaptation and competition in the free market. They generally favored extensive structural aid programs which would recombine the smallest farms, make better use of technology and improved soil management, form agriculture credit and marketing organizations, improve rural education, and relocate industries to rural areas to provide alternative employment for those forced off unprofitable farms. The Economic Council of the Agriculture Ministry published several reports which supported the arguments for structural reform. In 1953 and 1954 the Adenauer government, and Agriculture Minister Lübke in particular, stated the government's goals as improvement of agriculture structure, reduction in costs, and an increase in productivity in order to equalize agricultural and other economic production.

Meanwhile, the DBV was working on farm problems from a different perspective. While not opposed to long-term aid for structural improvements, it was naturally less inclined to focus on long-range programs that would produce few immediate benefits to its members and indeed lead eventually to a reduction in their numbers. Instead, the farmers' association emphasized that farm problems were natural and unavoidable due to dependence on climate, the length and uncertainty of the production period, harvest variations, and the comparatively poor storage capacity of farm products. As a consequence, it urged equalization subsidies in the form of a general parity system to stabilize agricultural prices, secure an adequate living standard, and protect agriculture from import competition. By 1954, the DBV had developed draft legislation which would organize a profit-cost parity system and obligate the government to employ various economic measures to remedy the disparities. In presenting its program the DBV was aided greatly both by its ability to define the issue simply as a technical question of procedures to remedy agricultural disadvantages, and by the issue's lack of salience for other potentially affected economic interests. Thus, the possible opposing coalition of business and labor interests likely to be affected by higher farm prices was never activated.[37]

Because the government was slow to respond to DBV demands, the Green Front took the legislative initiative in the *Bundestag*. In early 1954, the CDU/CSU and FDP parliamentary parties introduced legislative drafts which, while avoiding the term parity, clearly reflected DBV proposals. The SPD had no clear position beyond vague support for additional governmental aid. The draft legislation required the government to use economic measures to insure that there was a restoration of parity between agricultural profits and necessary expenditures figured on an annual basis. It was presented not as an alternative to the government's structural program, but as a supplement to it which would provide farmers with a measure of economic security during the extended period when structural reforms were gradually taking effect. Again, this was important to the DBV's success in defining the issue as nonconflictual, since consideration was then focused on the technical questions of procedures to provide parity rather than on general agricultural problems and their causes.

The draft legislation was referred to the Agriculture Committee and to a special parity subcommittee composed of members of the Economic and Agriculture Committees. In the initial consideration by the parity committee, the limited conflict centered on technical questions. The parity committee became a forum for bargaining between the government economic experts, represented by the Economics Committee members, and DBV representatives. The main questions concerned the procedures to be used for calculating annual profits and particularly costs, and the specification of government responsibility. No other economic groups exerted any real political opposition to the farmers during the course of committee discussions. Due to government economists' objections to some of the technical provisions in the DBV proposal, the committee revisions reflected some modifications of procedures. For example, the original draft called for a calculation of disparity on the basis of average farm production. Using the average was likely to have some effect on the amount and rationality of the aid, since it would ignore the variations between very poor and better-off farms. The committee revised the procedure to include separate calculations for different types and sizes of farms. In addition, it proposed a calculation of farm costs which did not include estimates of wages to family members or interest on capital investments as suggested by the

DBV, although the committee draft suggested that the government consider these additional costs in preparing measures to deal with calculated disparities.[38]

Before final consideration by the full Agriculture Committee, the government issued other proposed revisions. Aside from some additional technical changes, the only general concern dealt with the specification of economic instruments. The government raised a constitutional question about the wisdom of listing economic measures which would bind the government to future legislation and thus possibly conflict with the constitutional provision that gave the chancellor responsibility for establishing policy guidelines. While the technical revisions were accepted without much change, the Agriculture Committee retained the paragraph which listed the general policy means to be used to provide aid: trade, tax, credit and price policies.[39]

As reported out by the Agriculture Committee for final floor consideration, the bill represented a quiet victory for farm interests and the DBV. Since questions relating to the goals and priorities of government subsidies were never raised, potential opponents were never aroused. Rather, the final draft reflected agreements reached between the DBV and the government on technical questions. The key to DBV success was therefore the desocialization of conflict through a technical definition of the issue which avoided arousing the opposition of other economic groups with powerful representation in the *Bundestag.*

The bill was passed unanimously without any changes on September 8, 1955. The state agriculture ministers can play an important role in the *Bundesrat* but there was little need for them to intervene since the bill was acceptable. Discussion in the *Bundesrat* centered on some of the technical questions and the issue of constitutionality; but the committees considering the legislation did not press these concerns or recommend calling a conference committee, and the bill thus became law on September 9, 1955. The Agriculture Act of 1955 achieved a far-reaching institutionalization of farmers' demands within the bounds of distributive politics. Aid measures passed in accordance with it since 1955 have improved the absolute position of agriculture without, however, erasing the disparity with other occupational categories.

## The Green Report and Green Plan: The Annual Distributive Process

The 1955 legislation requires the federal government to submit an annual report on the position of agriculture to the *Bundestag* and *Bundesrat* —the Green Report (*Gruener Bericht*)—as well as a comprehensive statement of measures which will lead to an equalization of profits and costs and bring the economic position of farmers into line with other socioeconomic groups. This annual agriculture subsidy budget is called the Green Plan (*Gruene Plan*).[40] In the plan, subsidies have been divided since 1964 into three types of measures: (1) structural improvement subsidies to ameliorate the effects of problems such as the scattered location of farm land and poor working and living conditions; (2) income subsidies to improve the income position of farmers; and (3) subsidies which provide for credit reductions for farmers. Federal aid within the Green Plan has increased from approximately 600 million deutsche marks in the first year (1956) to over 2 billion deutsche marks in the late 1960s. Expenditures throughout the 1950s grew faster than the total budget and have kept up with increasing expenditures in the defense and social policy fields.

The Green Report is prepared annually by a special bureau (*Abteilung VI, Referat* 7) within the Agriculture Ministry which maintains formal and informal contacts with the DBV. However, since the overall government budget is prepared by the executive in the fall, whereas the Green Report is not submitted until February 15, the relationship between the Green Report and the Green Plan is somewhat indirect. During the government's budget discussions in the fall, the Green Report is not yet available and therefore proposed Green Plan total expenditures are determined not on the basis of the new agricultural situation, but on an increase from last year's expenditures. In the general cabinet determination of the federal budget, this gives an advantage to the Agriculture Ministry over the Finance Ministry, which is more likely to be concerned with economy in government spending. The actual measures proposed in the Green Plan reflect the close relationships between the Agriculture Ministry and the DBV, and they represent some balance between farmers' demands and bureaucratic concern with economic flexibility and rationality.[41]

The total lump sum for the Green Plan is an item in the general budget, rarely challenged in the legislature. The specific Green Plan, however, is submitted separately, and the Agriculture Committee has considerable influence on distribution of aid within the limits of the overall sum. The Agriculture Committee can avoid conflict with the Budget Committee and politicization of the question so long as it does not attempt to increase the total sum for agricultural aid. The general set of proposed instruments, which are the result of executive-DBV agreements, is also usually left unchanged by the committee. However, it has been quite effective in shifting money from one kind of program to another within the Green Plan, usually by increasing the amounts for income subsidies which have a more immediate effect and are favored by the DBV. Thus, the committee serves as a second stage of distributive politics in which government programs may be readjusted to favor farm interests to a greater degree than occurs within the executive branch. Finally, the Green Plans have not been challenged on the floor and the usually unanimous approval by the *Bundestag* is an indicator of the politics of distribution. The *Bundesrat's* role has centered on a consideration of technical administrative problems since the *Laender* Agriculture Ministries are responsible for the implementation of much of the federal legislation.

### The Advent of the Common Market and Increased Conflict

The founding of the European Economic Community did not solve, and in fact probably deepened, the problems of the German agricultural sector.

While the initial rhetoric implied a free European agricultural market, the results have been increasingly in the direction of replacing separate national protection with an international protectionism. The establishment of the Common Market therefore seems to have brought about at least two changes. First, various groups favoring European integration as well as business interests affected by trade decisions have been aroused. Second, those issues which have become politicized, and have thus created a sectorally fragmented type of conflict, may increasingly be resolved within the executive by coalitions of ministerial representatives of the various interests rather than within the legislature. This is because the final decisions are made by international agreements in the EEC Commission and the domestic political decision is determined by the executive through the West German negotiating position, with the *Bundestag* having only a limited advisory role. On these issues, the Green Front in the legislature may decline in importance as the influence of relationships within the executive increases.

The conflict which arose in West Germany over the establishment of a common European grain price may indicate this trend. Since the German price level was the highest of the six Common Market countries , any international agreement was bound to lead to a decrease in German grain prices. Because the DBV was able to use its influence to block a coalition of business and political interests in the Economics Ministry and Foreign Office from proceeding with German participation in negotiations, for a number of the years the farmers' organization was successful in preventing an EEC decision. Eventually a compromise was reached which was quite favorable to the DBV, although the final EEC agreement was less so. In addition, once the EEC decision was made, the DBV was able to move successfully back to distributive politics and secure without opposition *Bundestag* passage of legislation which provided for extensive domestic compensation for losses resulting from the intended grain price decline.[42] Thus, the DBV has been successful even when issues shift to sectorally fragmented politics. It has also been able to work well within the legislature with both the SPD and the CDU/CSU. Nor has the recent shift in party power and the change to a SPD-FDP coalition government led to lessened influence of farmers in distributive politics. Party programs are quite similar on agricultural issues, and the DBV is still frequently able to avoid conflict by using its relationships in the Agriculture Ministry and control of the *Bundestag* Agriculture Committee to define many domestic agriculture policy issues in nonpolitical, technical terms.[43]

In the meantime, of course, agriculture remains a continuing and perhaps increasing problem area both within the West German economy and for the Common Market. The distributive subsidy policies so effectively pursued by the DBV have only bypassed and not really contributed to a solution of the serious structural problems which continue to exist, and the socioeconomic isolation of the farmer remains. Efforts to shift the blame for these handicaps to foreign countries have only increased the difficulty of reaching Common Market agreements as well.[44]

*Conclusions*

Unlike the British NFU, the DBV political strategy has not been a nonpartisan one. Through the Green Front, the *Bundestag* Agriculture Committee, and its close relationship with the Agriculture Ministry, the DBV has been able to use its cohesion as a voting bloc to reinforce the general consensus on aid to agriculture and to define issues as technical and nonconflictual. Thus, it has usually avoided arousing potential opposition. As in Great Britain, the general legislation passed in 1955 gave considerable discretion to the government in the selection of aid measures, which in turn allowed room for the utilization of DBV influence within the executive. This was reinforced by DBV control of the powerful Agriculture Committee in the *Bundestag.*

Thus interest group liberalism has proceeded apace in West Germany as in Great Britain and the United States. The potential for instability arises not from the distributive process itself but from the fact that decisions made by such means have reflected the short-term interests of the DBV without solving the serious long-range problems in agriculture. One consequence of such distributive outcomes may be increased tension and anxiety within a socioeconomic group (farmers) which has to some extent in the past been responsive to right-wing radicalism.

## CONCLUSION

Policies of the distributive type are found with more frequency than any other policy type considered in this work. Yet because they arouse so little overt or partisan conflict and involve such limited numbers of people working in committee-like situations, they are in many ways the most difficult kind to research. After all, little is written about them despite the fact that they are pervasive in political life.

The three case studies in this chapter have described distributive issues in Great Britain, the United States, and West Germany. Although each type, of course, displays the basic attributes of the distributive policy, there are nevertheless certain apparent national differences. In particular, one major crossnational difference appears to be a much higher degree of centralization of the distributive process within the reaches of the bureaucracy in Great Britain than in the United States. In the latter, because the committees of Congress play an especially powerful role, the executive must share this power to a much greater extent with the congressional committees. West Germany falls somewhere in between, although in all probability it is much closer to the British than to the American pattern. It might be noted in this respect that the DBV paid much more attention to the legislative committees than did the British NFU. This in turn may have helped determine the different strategies employed by each: nonpartisanship by the NFU, restrained partisanship by the DBV. Thus, since the NFU did not really have to worry very much about the House of Commons and since it could depend upon the legislature's acquiescence to the cabinet, it could more easily advocate an above-the-battle approach, one especially calculated to appeal to civil servants who dislike overt partisanship anyway. Conversely, in West Germany the tendency for the DBV to maintain such close contacts with the legislative committees, particularly as a second line of resistance, suggests that the committees play a large part in the politics of distribution. But having emphasized such differences, it should not be forgotten that in each case it was committee and not legislative floor activity which was most important in dealing with and resolving the issue.

Finally, a speculation is in order: if true "power elites" exist in various Western nations, it is on such issues that they work their will upon the general public. In fact, it is quite possible that through distributive politics such an elite may hold sway in many democracies, for the overwhelming number of issues are probably distributive in nature. In general, the more specialized the subject matter, the greater the likelihood that the decision-making forces will be highly concentrated and specialized in their interests. It is here that one might look for power elites for the simple reason that the subject matter limits the numbers of citizens concerned with the issue. Even such concerns as devaluation and exchange rates, which do have a profound impact on our lives, cannot motivate many people to political concern, much less action. Government may be elitist, therefore, because most issues are specialized. Conversely, it follows that such an elite will find more difficulty in getting its way when issues become sufficiently "hot" to excite large-scale involvement. In most of the cases considered here and in the next three chapters, it can be said that the nominally or reputedly more powerful elements often failed to emerge victorious. Put another way, large-scale involvements lessen the possibilities for narrow elitist controls; but since ordinary men give so little attention to political questions, it is highly unlikely that decision-making processes can be opened up quantitatively by very much.

## NOTES

1. E. E. Schattschneider, *The Semisovereign People* (New York: Holt, Rinehart and Winston, 1960), pp. 2–8, 20–21.

2. See, for example, David Braybrooke and Charles E. Lindblom, *Strategy of Decision* (New York: The Free Press, 1963). It should be noted that a widely regarded study utilizing the concept of incrementalism is devoted to budgetary problems which, as one might expect, are largely distributive in nature. See Aaron Wildavsky, *Politics of the Budgetary Process* (Boston: Little, Brown and Co., 1964).

3. Joseph LaPalombara, *Interest Groups in Italian Politics* (Princeton: Princeton University Press, 1964), pp. 258–70; Henry W. Ehrmann, "French Bureaucracy and Organized Interests," *Administrative Science Quarterly*, March 1961, pp. 534–55; Lawrence Scheinman, *Atomic Energy Policy Under the Fourth Republic* (Princeton: Princeton University Press, 1965); Samuel H. Beer, "Pressure Groups and Parties in Britain," *American Political Science Review*, March 1956, pp. 6–9.

4. In addition to the works cited in footnote 3, see Harry Eckstein, *Pressure Group Politics: The Case of the British Medical Association* (London: George Allen and Unwin Ltd., 1960).

5. Eckstein, *Pressure Group Politics*, pp. 18–19.

6. At least this conclusion may be drawn from LaPalombara, *Interest Groups in Italian Politics*, pp. 248–49.

7. Philip M. Williams, *Crisis and Compromise: Politics in the Fourth Republic* (Garden City, N.Y.: Anchor Books, 1966), pp. 255–91.

8. James A. Storing, *Norwegian Democracy* (Boston: Houghton Mifflin Co., 1963), pp. 86ff.

9. For a thorough study of agricultural politics in Great Britain one should consult Peter Self and Herbert J. Storing, *The State and the Farmer: British Agricultural Policies and Politics* (Berkeley: University of California Press, 1963); also, see their "The Farmers and the State," *The Political Quarterly* 29 (1958): 17–27; and J. Roland Pennock, "Agricultural Subsidies in England and the United States," *American Political Science Review*, September 1962, pp. 621–33.

10. Eckstein, *Pressure Group Politics*, chap. 1.

11. For a consideration of these points, see Pennock, "Agricultural Subsidies in England and the United States."

12. S. E. Finer, *Anonymous Empire: A Study of the Lobby in Great Britain* (London: Pall Mall Press, 1966), pp. 38–39; and Self and Storing, "The Farmers and the State," pp. 20–21.

13. See Self and Storing, *The State and the Farmer*, p. 63.

14. Self and Storing, "The Farmers and the State," p. 21.

15. Pennock, "Agricultural Subsidies in England and the United States," p. 628.

16. Donald R. Shell, "Specialist Select Committees," *Parliamentary Affairs*, Autumn 1970, p. 401.

17. *The Times* (London), March 17, 1969.

18. See *The Economist*, March 19, 1955, pp. 979–80; and Pennock, "Agricultural Subsidies in England and the United States," p. 629; also, E. M. H. Lloyd in *The New Statesman and Nation*, March 5, 1955, pp. 312–14.

19. Theodore J. Lowi, *The End of Liberalism: Ideology, Policy, and the Crisis of Public Authority* (New York: Norton, 1969).

20. In this respect one might do well to read Arend Lijphart, *The Politics of Accommodation: Pluralism and Democracy in the Netherlands* (Berkeley, Calif.: University of California Press, 1968).

21. Information for this case study was derived from E. E. Schattschneider's classic study of the tariff, *Politics, Pressures and the Tariff: A Study of Free Private Enterprise in Pressure Politics, as Shown in the 1929–1930 Revision of the Tariff* (New York: Prentice-Hall, Inc., 1935).

22. Schattschneider, *Politics, Pressures and the Tariff*, p. 22.

23. For a more thorough account of changes in tariff doctrine over time, see Raymond A. Bauer, Ithiel de Sola Pool, and Lewis Anthony Dexter, *American Business and Public Policy: The Politics of Foreign Trade* (New York: Atherton Press, 1963), pp. 11–79. For a chronology of major tariff legislation prior to the Smoot-Hawley Act, see *Congressional Digest* 8 (June–July 1929) 162–63.

24. Schattschneider, *Politics, Pressures and the Tariff*, p. 17.

25. Ibid., p. 36.

26. Ibid., p. 88; also, in general, see pp. 126–45.

27. Ibid., pp. 135–36.

28. *Congressional Digest* 9 (December 1930): 316.

29. Clayton F. Moore in *Congressional Digest* 8 (June–July 1929): 165.

30. For a general description of the economic situation and policies, see Heinz Dietrich Ortlieb and Friedrich-Wilhelm Dorge, *Wirtschafts-und Sozialpolitik* (Opladen: C. W. Leske Verlag, 1967), pp. 112–16.

31. For a description of the various farmers' groups and their organization, see Rupert Breitling, *Die Verbaende in der Bundesrepublik* (Meisenheim: Verlag Anton Hain K. G., 1955).

32. H. G. Schlotter, *Die Willensbildung in der Agrarpolitik* (Munich: BLV Verlagsgesellschaft, 1971), pp. 207–8.

33. Gerhard Loewenberg, *Parliament in the German Political System* (Ithaca: Cornell University Press, 1967), p. 110; and Paul Ackermann, *Der Deutsche Bauernverband im Politischen Kraeftespiel der Bundesrepublik* [Tübingen: J. C. B. Mohr (Paul Siebeck), 1970], pp. 70–71.

34. Karl-Heinrich Hansmeyer, *Finanzielle Staatshilfen fuer die Landwirtschaft* [Tübingen: J. C. B. Mohr (Paul Siebeck), 1963], pp. 90–93.

35. *Getriedegesetz,* November 4, 1950; *Zuckergesetz,* January 5, 1951; *Milch-und Fettegesetz,* February 28, 1951; *Vieh und Fleischgesetz,* April 25, 1951. For a description of this legislation and the operation of the import offices, see Ortlieb and Dorge, *Wirtschafts-und Sozialpolitik,* p. 114; and Hansmeyer, *Finanzielle Staatshilfen fuer die Landwirtschaft,* pp. 162–67. For their current activities, which have been altered somewhat by EEC agreements, see Friedrich Nobis, *Die Bundesministerium feur Ernahrung Landwirtschaft und Forsten* (Frankfurt: Athenaeum Verlag, 1966), pp. 107–8.

36. The most thorough description of the development and passage of this legislation is in Viola Graefin von Bethusy-Huc, *Demokratie und Interessenpolitik* (Wiesbaden: Franz Steiner Verlag, 1962), pp. 1–35.

37. Hansmeyer, *Finanzielle Staatshilfen fuer die Landwirtschaft,* pp. 72–74.

38. Both the Industry and Trade Council (DIHT) and the Bank Deutscher Länder expressed some general opposition to permanent subsidies as contrary to neoliberalism, but they did not attempt to exert any political pressure. The BDI issued a joint statement with the DBV which supported a parity system. Bethusy-Huc, *Demokratie und Interessenpolitik,* pp. 18–26.

39. Ibid., pp. 30–37.

40. These two documents have been combined since 1968.

41. For the sections within the Agriculture Ministry responsible for preparation of the Green Plan, see Nobis, *Die Bundesministerium fuer Ernahrung Landwirtschaft und Forsten,* pp. 60–61, 79.

42. Ackermann, *Der Deutsche Bauernverband im Politischen Kraeftespiel der Bundesrepublik.*

43. Schlotter, *Die Willensbildung in der Agrarpolitik,* pp. 218–21. For a study of a sectorally fragmented agriculture issue in which the DBV worked with the SPD and the unions against a coalition of business interests within the CDU/CSU and FDP, see ibid., pp. 349–79.

44. Alfred Grosser, *Germany in Our Time* (New York: Praeger, 1972), p. 183.

# 3

# THE POLITICS OF SECTORAL FRAGMENTATION

**A**LTHOUGH it has often been defined by other terms, the sectorally fragmented type of policy is quite familiar to political scientists. Indeed, the rather numerous case studies dealing with interest-group behavior are likely to be subsumed under this type, for to speak of "interest-group" or "pressure-group" activity tends to conjure up a vision of economic groups such as firms, trade associations, or even peak associations fighting one another or pressuring government officials in order to gain a larger slice of the public pie. Although its more prominent spokesmen from Arthur Bentley through David Truman and Charles Hagan would themselves hardly limit its range to economic groupings—they would include *all* group activity—it has often been limited in this way by students of comparative politics.[1]

Nevertheless, within the framework of the typology of this work, it is not feasible to equate interest-group or pressure-group politics with sectoral fragmentation. The typology presented here grows out of an emphasis upon different scopes and intensities of conflict and the tendency for such conflicts to be worked out around certain kinds of political actors and institutions. To analyze the policy process from a purely interest-group perspective would not be helpful in drawing the necessary distinctions. While groups of one sort or another, no matter what the levels of conflict, are likely to be involved in almost any given issue, it is important to understand that conflicts and their respective impacts vary enormously. For example, one study in Chapter 2 showed that economic interest groups took an active part in the tariff issue, but subsequent chapters will demonstrate that economic interest groups have also been active in disputes of a far more conflictual nature. Although the groups were similar in type, the political climates within which they were operating could not have been more different. Therefore, to speak of the politics of "sectoral fragmenta-

tion" rather than of "interest-group" or "pressure-group" politics delin-
eates not so much a type of group as a type of conflict. Put another way,
an attribute of the sectorally fragmented policy is pressure-group activity,
but all such activity is not necessarily of a sectorally fragmented type.

Sectorally fragmented policies are characterized by competition in
which the contestants face one another through direct confrontations.
Thus, they diverge sharply in this respect from the distributive type.
Unlike distributive policies, since they tend to be defined in such a way
as to preclude the satisfying of all participants, they involve a struggle
regarding who is to be indulged by government. For example, government
decisions to cut the subsidization of alcohol distilled from beets, wine, and
apples or to raise the amount school teachers contribute to a superannuation fund can be expected to arouse agricultural and teacher associations
alike.[2] The same reaction may be expected from attempts to enact a law
requiring cigarette advertisers to place health warnings on packages, food
packaging laws, or fair trade bills, anticartel legislation, and certain tax
reforms. Such legislation cannot usually be satisfactory to all parties concerned; its impact is direct and injurious to specific interests (or at least they
believe this to be the case).

Because sectoral issues are defined in discordant terms, a growth of
conflict is bound to emerge; and because someone feels he is going to be
deprived, the resolution of the dispute takes a different form from that of
distribution. The executive and legislative committees, which are able to
operate so effectively in nonconflicting situations, find it extremely difficult to contain sectorally fragmented issues. An aggrieved party which is
refused help from a committee is hardly expected to continue working
through existing channels. The grievance will be taken elsewhere; and
elsewhere is the floor of the legislature, the place where group struggles are
settled. Indeed, the fact that the legislature must resolve such disagreements amply demonstrates that bargaining relationships have evaporated
at another point.

Nevertheless, there is a built-in limitation upon the expansion of this
kind of conflict. The deprivations, it will be recalled, tend to be specific
rather than general in their effects. This implies that broad class, economic,
and social interests are not so likely to be activated. Hence, it is not the
so-called "peak" associations such as the Confederation of British Industries in Great Britain or the National Association of Manufacturers in the
United States which enter the fray; rather, the participants tend to be
individuals, groups, and associations associated with particular sectors of
the economy. To take an example, an anticartel law is not going to be
opposed by all industries, but in fact may be favored by quite a few firms.

Similarly, the political activists vary with the given issue in sectorally
fragmented cases. Cohesion among participants tends to be fluid and
short-lived. In David Truman's sense, groups unite around "shared interests," but once the issue is settled, the various parts of the coalition disinte-
grate and go their separate ways. This pattern differs rather markedly from

the distributive policy type in which the key participants are with regularity members of specialized committees.

Finally, there is another rather important point to be made with regard to many sectorally fragmented policies. Not only are they resolved on the legislative floor, but also ordinary ministers and their subordinates often take a major part in conflict resolution. This pattern becomes especially apparent in parliamentary regimes such as Great Britain and the France of General de Gaulle, where disciplined party government is the norm. In such nations the lack of widespread and open conflict within the legislative majority, the appearance of absolute party unity, and, in general, the relative quiescence which seemingly surrounds the issue may give the observer an impression that he is seeing something other than sectoral fragmentation at work. Indeed, he might easily conclude that he is looking at a case of mere distribution. Nonetheless, ministerial activity (or the activity of those immediately below a minister in the hierarchy) is a good sign that sectoral fragmentation is taking place. The reason is that these issues involve sectors, and ministers are usually concerned with sectoral interests. Whenever such interests are activated, it is the minister who must respond in the government's name. In fact, he may himself activate those very interests, for it is he, after all, who must cajole, negotiate with, and react to party and group elements which wish change. While a prime minister or president may well take a lively interest in what the minister is doing, it is nevertheless not the chief executive who is likely to be most active on behalf of the government. If it may be said that distributive policy making is committee work, and that redistributive policy making is presidential or prime ministerial bustle, then the sectorally fragmented type represents to a great extent ministerial action plus legislative floor activity.

## CONCLUSIONS

Sectorally fragmented policies differ from the distributive ones discussed in the last chapter principally through their ability to excite much larger numbers of people who in turn divide against one another mainly over sector-related disagreements. Sectoral policies may display in particular the following attributes:

(1) They show moderate levels of conflict, the extent of which is determined both by the size of the socioeconomic sector and by the number and kinds of interests closely related to that sector.

(2) Major participants include not only interest groups and their legislative supporters, but ministers and other government bureaucrats concerned with the particular sectoral interests under consideration.

(3) Party discipline is on most occasions relatively strong, although at times some breakdown in discipline may well occur.

(4) Such issues are settled on the floor of the legislature.

# GREAT BRITAIN

### The Resale Price Maintenance Bill

Resale price maintenance (RPM), known as "fair trade laws" in the United States, is the device by which manufacturers can require retailers to sell their goods at set prices. It allows the manufacturer of a product to determine the ultimate price charged the consumer. In doing so, it raises serious questions with regard to public policy. From the standpoint of the supposedly sovereign consumer, it results in higher prices; but to the marginal businessman it may be the difference between his going broke or staying in business. Since large retailers may be wholesalers as well, they can more easily reduce their costs. Indeed, they are unlikely to support RPM for the simple reason that their competitive advantages over smaller retailers may be lessened. All things considered, such laws raise thorny problems for political decision makers. In abolishing RPM one may increase efficiency, reduce costs, and thereby aid the consumer, but at the same time its demise may lead to the elimination of small businessmen and therefore to increased hardship and even unemployment.

### Background

RPM is an old practice in Great Britain, going back as far as the early part of the nineteenth century when book publishers began issuing new titles at uniform prices.[3] By the end of the century small shopkeepers had begun to organize in earnest, and in 1896 the first successful price maintenance group, the Proprietary Articles Trade Association, was created to advance the interests of chemists.

In the twentieth century the problem of RPM periodically burst upon the political scene. In 1919 and 1931 the question was taken up, but only after World War II did it become a more or less continual issue. In 1947, Sir Stafford Cripps, on behalf of the Labour government, announced the creation of a committee to investigate the effects of RPM. The Lloyd Jacob Committee, as it was called, took much testimony; and in March 1949, it reported to Harold Wilson, then president of the Board of Trade. In essence the committee concluded that RPM in itself was not necessarily bad, and that therefore its use by individual manufacturers should not be proscribed. Nevertheless, the committee did not look with favor upon huge trade associations which had built up elaborate systems to enforce RPM through fines, stop-lists, and secret codes. As a consequence, it advocated the dismantlement of "collective" RPM.

After some delay the Labour cabinet decided to accept the major recommendations of the Jacob Committee. The cabinet, however, felt the more prudent approach was to avoid overt coercion of industry. As a result, businessmen were encouraged to take steps on their own to free themselves from dependence upon the trade associations. In other words, reason and persuasion were to be used by a Socialist government to encourage business to give up its reliance upon the collective enforcement of RPM.

It was not to be the Socialists who abolished collective RPM; that task fell to the supposedly probusiness Conservative party. The Tories have always been pulled in two directions so far as economic policies are concerned. One tradition, essentially laissez-faire and bourgeois, emphasizes the positive benefits resulting from vigorous economic competition. The role of the state therefore should be a limited one of establishing rules which facilitate economic competition and freedom, of eliminating restraints against economic freedom. But another more paternalistic and aristocratic tradition sees no particular virtue in economic competition; therefore, it has no difficulty in supporting the small shopkeeper against the large manufacturing interests. After all, it makes good electoral sense, for smaller businessmen are among the strongest Tory voters.

After the Conservatives returned to power in 1951, the free enterprise tradition gained ascendancy, partly because the militancy of the pro-RPM advocates began to produce its own opposition and in part because the practice itself was breaking down in certain sectors of the economy, notably in the grocery trade.[4] It was then apparently less dangerous to oppose its abolition. Moreover, the Board of Trade was manned by officials firmly hostile to RPM, and they kept the issue before the public. The Tories enacted the Restrictive Trade Practices Act in 1956, which, while giving its major share of attention to the problem of monopolies, struck hard at the price-fixing practices of the trade associations. It was the court which would ultimately be given the power to abolish RPM agreements.

After the general election of 1959, the Conservative president of the Board of Trade, Reginald Maudling, erected an internal fact-finding committee within his ministry to gain pertinent facts about resale price maintenance. From his perspective, this approach had two advantages: it reduced pressures from pro-RPM backbenchers and it gave him time to gain new information which could help bring an end to the practice. The committee sent 8,000 questionnaires to manufacturers, wholesalers, and retailers to ascertain the true facts of the case. But by the time the information was gathered, Maudling had been replaced by Frederick Erroll.

Erroll, as Maudling before him, was committed to the abolition of resale price maintenance, but on two separate occasions an anti-RPM bill was shelved in cabinet because of significant opposition. Interestingly enough, the major pressures on the cabinet derived from Tory backbenchers, which suggests that backbench influence over policy-making leadership can be a very important determinant whenever enough MPs are involved. Whereas some backbenchers argued that the Tories should champion industrial efficiency and lower consumer prices by abolishing RPM, still others claimed that the party should not risk losing the vote of the "small man" (i.e., shopkeepers). This latter group included a large number of highly pragmatic men, who in many cases opposed RPM on purely economic grounds, but believed the issue would destroy party unity and weaken the party in the constituencies; hence, they wished to avoid the issue altogether. Such opposition was strong enough throughout the premiership of Harold Macmillan to thwart the anti-RPM forces.

When Sir Alec Douglas-Home succeeded Harold Macmillan as prime minister in October 1963, the stage was set for the great battle which would finally spell the end of RPM in Great Britain. To replace Erroll, Sir Alec chose ambitious Edward Heath as his new president of the Board of Trade, and also gave him the portfolio of secretary of state for industry, trade, and regional development. Heath, whose star had been on the rise since his sterling efforts at holding the party together during the Suez crisis and had also been the British negotiator in the abortive attempt to enter the Common Market, was a major power within the cabinet. The fact that he also held another portfolio gave the Board of Trade a much enhanced status within the government. The RPM abolitionists therefore could count upon a new hearing under the guidance of Heath, who was highly receptive to economic arguments favorable to efficiency and competition. This time they would win, but before they did, the conflict would produce the greatest schism within the Conservative party since the Suez crisis in 1956, and possibly since opposition to the government of Neville Chamberlain led to a backbencher revolt in 1940.

Edward Heath for the moment preferred to avoid a debate over resale price maintenance since the issue was so contentious within the Conservative party, and he was especially reluctant to antagonize his fellow party members only a few months before a general election. But when J. T. Stonehouse, a Labour MP, introduced a private member's bill for abolition, and when Conservative John Osborne came forward with a proposal to regulate trading stamps,[5] Heath could no longer stand above the battle without being accused of indecisiveness and timidity. Heath introduced a bill which forbade manufacturers to set minimum resale prices and to withhold supplies from the dealer who refused to follow quoted prices. Conversely, manufacturers could maintain and enforce maximum prices, recommend and advertise resale prices, and withhold supplies from "loss leaders" (dealers who sell goods below cost so as to attract customers to other goods).[6] Areas affected in particular included cars, electrical goods, television, drugs, cosmetics, books, cigarettes, sweets and ice cream, cameras, and to a lesser extent, stationery, ironmongery, furniture, clothes, leather, clocks, toys, and tools.

## The Development of Conflict

The major dispute over resale price maintenance took place within the majority Conservative party. In deciding to abstain on the vote, the Labour party was content simply to enjoy the misery of its opponents. True, some Labourites were favorable to RPM, but it was the Conservatives who suffered most from internal disagreements. Since many Tory MPs thought of the shopkeepers as a basic interest entitled to strong consideration, they couched their support in terms of an ideological defense of the virtues of the small businessman and his way of life. But a more important consideration for many politicians probably lay in the small business groups' potential for electoral retaliation. This was undoubtedly the reason that the earliest Tory opponents of a projected RPM law in 1964 were the ones who tended to derive from the more marginal constituencies.[7] It was pointed out at the time that some 480,000 shopkeepers would be affected by the bill. For both ideological and practical reasons, then, various members of the Conservative majority had reason to resist its passage into law.

Specific parts of the Heath bill in themselves were sufficiently controversial to create divisions within the Tory majority. In particular, clause 5 —which would have forced manufacturers to appeal to the Restrictive Practices Court for exemption from the law—was galling to certain lawmakers who argued that a presumption of guilt by businessmen was implied. They therefore demanded that RPM be assumed as in the public interest until the court had ruled otherwise. The effect of such an amendment, of course, might have been the retention of resale price maintenance in the absence of specific complaints to the judiciary, thereby emasculating the bill's true intent.[8]

In a similar vein, some Conservatives complained that the Restrictive Practices Court would be overburdened with appeals from individuals to retain resale price maintenance which in turn might lead to a breakdown in the court's administrative effectiveness. Heath countered that there was little danger of such an eventuality since, first, most pleas would be presented by trade associations, not individuals, and second, the judges would lay down precedents applicable to categories of manufactured goods.[9]

Finally, Heath's tactics and personality did little to reduce tensions within the Conservative party. Some Tories resented his timing in introducing so divisive a bill immediately prior to an expected national election campaign. His refusal to compromise on clause 3 (dealing with loss leaders) and clause 5 also drew criticism. He received angry denunciations as well from backbenchers who claimed they had not been properly consulted in the entire matter; consequently, they complained that it was much more difficult to resist pressures from irate constituents.[10] Indeed, Heath's rather dogmatic defense of free market principles made him the butt of bitter jokes by hostile politicians with more mundane concerns. In recalling Heath's role as chief negotiator in the futile British attempt to enter Europe in 1963, it was said that the move had failed because there was no room in Europe for two de Gaulles—the general and Heath.[11]

## The Limits of Conflict

RPM probably represents a somewhat more conflictual case of sectoral fragmentation than is normally found. In particular the demonstrations which took place in several cities as well as a rather severe breakdown of party discipline in the House of Commons were rather unusual occurrences for a sectorally fragmented case. Nevertheless, group activity was confined to trade and retail associations rather than to the peak associations, so there were limits to the expansion of the conflict. Such organizations as the National Union of Shopkeepers, National Chamber of Trade, Federation of Wholesale Organizations and many smaller groups took the lead in protesting against the RPM bill by contacting politicians and administrators and by organizing their respective memberships to get in touch with political representatives. Conversely, the National Association of British Manufacturers, the Federation of British Industries, and the Trades Union Congress were relatively quiescent.[12] Similarly, it was the Board of Trade and especially its president, not the prime minister, who directed the government forces and bore the brunt of the attack from opponents of the bill. Indeed, Prime Minister Sir Alec Douglas-Home apparently concerned himself relatively little with the issue, confining himself to one speech on the topic.[13]

What makes the resale price maintenance controversy somewhat unusual, however, is the relatively great lack of discipline within the Conservative party. In a nation where such dissidence is frowned upon, fifty-six Tories (casting twenty-one nays and thirty-five abstentions) refused to support their own leadership at the second reading of the RPM bill.

Confidence in Heath and the Conservative leadership was so eroded that it was necessary to create new channels of communication for resolving the dispute. Communications between government and backbench normally take place through the chief whip and leader of the House, but the backbenchers were so upset over RPM that a special steering committee, including Tories from both sides in the dispute, was created to mediate between Heath and the dissidents.[14]

Nonetheless, compromise was ultimately reached, and the conflict over resale price maintenance was contained without undue danger to the government. On March 11, 1964, the bill was passed into law. How was a larger altercation avoided? To a great extent the ingredients facilitating class warfare were simply not present. As suggested above, the peak associations which tend to represent labor and business as classes were uninvolved in the dispute; hence, more sectoral interests fought to maintain their privileges in the face of government pressure for reform. Similarly, class conflict may have been reduced because the Labor party did not mobilize its troops against the Tory government. If it had done so, the battle might have taken a very different turn. In fact, many Socialist MPs favored retention of resale price maintenance anyway.

There were also factors limiting the scope of conflict within the Conservative majority. First, the fifty-six backbenchers who opposed their own government could not find a single Tory leader to join them in opposition, and surely a successful revolt would have required at least some overt opposition from within the government itself. Second, Heath himself compromised just enough to take much of the steam out of the dispute. In ultimately agreeing to an amendment to clause 3 dealing with loss leaders as well as to a change in clause 5 altering the question of presumed guilt, he demonstrated a willingness to meet his detractors at least some of the way. Clause 5 was changed so that resale price maintenance arrangements, instead of being presumed illegal in themselves, would be registered with the Board of Trade which in turn could take the individual cases before the Restrictive Practices Court. Although the change was quite small, it did seem to alleviate the ruffled feelings of those who had little stomach for open rebellion.[15]

Heath's attempt to take the onus of enforcement off the government and place it instead upon the Restrictive Practices Court was an especially adroit move. Thus, aggrieved interests could appeal to the court for exemption from the new law if it could be proved that the retention of resale price maintenance in their specific cases was in the public interest.[16] Indeed, the Heath bill went so far as to allow individual manufacturers to maintain RPM until their cases had been heard, a process which might take as long as two years before a settlement could finally be reached.[17] The consequence was to shift the burden of guilt away from political authority and on to the Restrictive Practices Court. In turn the court could break the general issue of RPM down into individual items spaced out over relatively long periods of time. Thus, because deprivations would be highly specific, effective mobilization by the opponents of resale price maintenance would be difficult. In a word, the issue could be "distributized" by taking it out of political debate and placing it in committee.

Nonetheless, in fighting to abolish RPM, Edward Heath proved himself a most courageous politician. To those who considered him "too clever by half," he demonstrated a principled obstinacy when faced by powerful interests. If his action concerning clause 5 suggests his willingness to let the court shoulder some of the blame, there was little doubt as to the ultimate outcome. Parliament had written a fairly tight anti-RPM bill, and the court for the most part would be forced to follow its intention. Besides, the judges themselves were reputed to be most hostile to the resale price maintenance arrangements.[18]

Thus, despite the restlessness of backbenchers, the issue was resolved in such a manner as to avoid undue embarrassment to the governing Tories. That the conflict was confined to sectorally fragmented politics was due in no small way to the skills of Heath and to the displacement of the issue upon the Restrictive Practices Court. Nervous backbenchers were therefore hopeful that with time the hostility on the part of small business would be erased.

# FRANCE

## The Value-Added Tax Debate

With an ever-growing need for additional revenue sources in the United States, especially in view of the growing hostility to the property tax, public officials and economists have recently seen fit to consider the feasibility of the value-added tax (TVA) as a method by which alternative sources of revenue may be developed. Although powerful and vocal interests criticized it as regressive taxation whenever the Nixon administration suggested it as a possible source of new revenue, the concept will undoubtedly be revived in the future. In Europe, on the other hand, TVA has been utilized to collect taxes for some time and is accepted. Its range varies from around 12–15 percent in some countries to a high of 33.3 percent on some products in France.[19]

The value-added tax is simply a levy placed on the value added to a product sold on the market. TVA is unique however in that it may be levied on goods throughout the production and distribution process beginning from the time when the material is first removed from the ground, for example, until it is sold to the final consumer. At each stage of turnover, the tax is assessed anew on the basis of the value added to it. From the standpoint of the firm it "is the sales or gross business receipts of the firm minus the cost of previously taxed goods and services purchased from other businesses."[20]

Perhaps the concept of TVA can be made more clear by taking a basic example. Suppose a manufacturer sells a table which he has fashioned out of plain wood to a retailer for $100. The value added is that cost (cutting, paint, finish, etc.) which goes into the alteration of the original product from mere wood into a finished table. If this added value comes to $40, the furniture manufacturer will then subtract $40 from the sales price of $100, which leaves $60. The value-added tax is a percentage of the latter sum. Thus, if the value-added tax is set at 5 percent, the tax on the table amounts to $3. If the buyer of the table improves the value of the table and in turn sells it, he too is subject to taxation.

There can be little doubt that certain individuals and classes benefit disproportionately from the value-added tax at the expense of others; thus, one scholar's opinion that TVA "was almost universally approved by responsible extra-parliamentary opinion on both Left and Right"[21] is somewhat puzzling, to say the least. In fact, one's position and the interests he supports are likely to go far in determining his opinions about a value-added tax. If he is a large industrialist or manager of an efficient firm, he is likely to favor its adoption into public policy. This is a natural posture given TVA's tendency to fall with less burden upon the more efficient producers. This can be shown by considering the earlier example: if the value added is $40, then the tax is $3; but if the value added is only $20, then the burden of taxation is $4.

Because TVA favors efficient interests, it is not surprising that its proponents, in the United States at any rate, have been found disproportionately among spokesmen for large corporations as well as among economists especially wedded to rapid industrial development, capital accumulation, and foreign trade, rather than to considerations of short-run economic equality. In fact, these proponents would replace the corporation tax in whole or in part with TVA on the grounds that it facilitates efficiency, is more equitable, and promotes economic growth.

Conversely, opponents of TVA argue that the tax is detrimental to the welfare of the ordinary consumer. They say that it falls upon the poor who cannot pass the tax along to someone else, not upon the relatively well-to-do. After all, since the tax is attached to each stage of the production and distribution process, it is the ultimate consumer who bears the cost. More-over, anti-inflationists may dislike it because of its tendency to raise the price level, at least in the short run. Therefore, any country wishing to create such a system would be advised to do so when its prices are rela-tively stable. Finally, small businessmen may oppose it on the grounds that it not only raises their prices but that it requires them to perform much unnecessary paper work. Also, being less efficient, they stand to gain less in general from the system.

## Background

The decision of the Pompidou government to extend the value-added tax did not involve creating an entirely new form for raising revenue for the state. TVA in fact had been in existence on sales at the manufacturing and wholesale levels for some time, although its scope had not been espe-cially broad. Nevertheless, attempts to extend it into other areas of eco-nomic life during the Fifth Republic had brought forth strong opposition in the National Assembly. Both in 1959 and 1961 the Debré government had found the resistance intense enough to force a withdrawal of the bill from consideration in the first case and a decent burial in committee in the second instance.[22]

In 1965, the Pompidou government tried again to enact a value-added tax. This new bill expanded the tax into such areas as agriculture, certain services, the crafts, and transportation. It was widely praised for various reasons: it facilitated French competition in foreign commerce and in ad-justing to the Common Market; it replaced an outmoded and complex tax system with a much fairer and simplified method of collection; and it favored modernization by encouraging efficiency and investment.

The bill had a rather long and turbulent life. When it was introduced in June 1965, the National Assembly immediately proposed some 203 amendments to the government. Fifty-nine were accepted by an accom-modating finance minister. When it was next submitted to the Senate, the upper house laid down an additional 159 amendments. After a conference committee of the two houses was unable to come to an agreement, the bill was returned to the National Assembly for a second reading, but by this time it was necessary to suspend the parliament for several weeks because of the upcoming presidential election of December 5–19, 1965. When the parliament returned in a special session on December 21, the mood was a rather different one than at adjournment. Nonetheless, on December 24, the bill cleared its final hurdle and was passed into law.

The most salient aspect of the 1965 TVA debate was the division it created within the Gaullist majority, that is to say, within the Union for the New Republic (UNR) and the Independent Republican party. In an era when UNR deputies were derided as "unconditionals," in this instance at least they were struggling mightily to dilute the effects of their own gov-ernment's bill both in committee and on the floor. It may be argued that divisions within the majority were exacerbated because of General de

Gaulle's less than spectacular showing in the presidential election, for the president failed to obtain 50 percent of the vote in the first round and was forced into a runoff. For the first time since his return to power in 1958, he appeared politically vulnerable, and his followers may have concluded that his coattails would offer less protection against irate local interests. It was at this point that the bill was in its final stages.

Professor Lowi suggests that revenue bills call forth highly stabilized elites to resolve the issues, and that the decision-making system is therefore a rather closed one.[23] He argues that if a power elite does exist, it is in this arena that the elite will impose its own solution. But TVA in fact generated participation at various levels, and on several occasions the government almost lost its initiative to ordinary backbench deputies and senators. The same may be said for the Finance Committee, which under ordinary circumstances should have helped to guide the bill smoothly to its final passage. But its chairman, Louis Vallon, hardly played a major role in controlling TVA's passage into law. As a pronounced social reformer, he wanted a stronger law than the government was prepared to introduce. By the time the amending process had taken its toll, this left-wing Gaullist must have been even more displeased. Moreover, the great peak associations, much less class-oriented antagonists, certainly do not appear to have been involved in any meaningful way, nor were the great parties of left (Communist) and right (Gaullist) pitted against one another in any coherent fashion. Indeed, the Small and Medium-size enterprises (PME), not the National Council of French Employers (CNPF), took the lead in opposition, and both left and right sought equally to water the bill down in favor of special constituency interests. The Finance Ministry was therefore forced to concede time after time to the parliamentarians. In general, much bargaining and debate took place on the floors of the National Assembly and Senate with various individuals fighting to protect their constituency interests. It was a typical sectoral issue as defined above.

## The Elements of Conflict

Why did the French value-added tax debate become so contentious? There can be little doubt that the confrontation whetted the opposition's desire for battle and created a malaise within the majority. Two exogenous factors may have contributed to the heat of the battle. One factor undoubtedly was General de Gaulle's narrow presidential election victory immediately prior to the return of the parliament on December 21, 1965. Until that time the president had appeared all but unbeatable in elections, but when leftist François Mitterrand, a noted symbol of the discredited Fourth Republic, forced him into a humiliating runoff campaign, many a UNR deputy and Gaullist sympathizer drew the obvious conclusion: de Gaulle's coattails no longer appeared so reassuring as in the past. In earlier years "unconditionalism" had carried many an unknown Gaullist deputy into the National Assembly from constituencies where he had little support from local notables. Now it seemed, however, that a good deal of fence mending was in order, so majority members were much less willing to submit tamely to government directives. Therefore, at the very time TVA was clearing its final legislative hurdle, many deputies in the majority were having second thoughts about supporting so controversial a measure. Finally, if deputies' second thoughts about de Gaulle's political strength were not enough of a problem for the Pompidou government in maintaining discipline, it was also faced with steadily growing pressures from major interests within individual constituencies. The fact that the bill had been under consideration for over half a year gave local groups plenty of time to become aware of TVA's impact and hence to force wavering deputies and senators into support for their specific needs.[24]

A second factor aggravating an already tense situation was the government's insensitivity and blundering in pushing the value-added tax through the legislature. Both the National Assembly in June and the Senate in November voiced complaints about being given too little time to peruse the bill properly. Indeed, in December, when the National Assembly first reconvened following the presidential election, the rapporteur-general's statement was distributed only twenty-five minutes before the meeting began. In another instance, when the Senate took a final vote on the government bill, the government, in the person of Minister of State Jean de Broglie, demanded a package vote prior to any discussion of the various articles. The purpose, of course, was to limit any alterations in the bill. An embittered Senate then proceeded to vote against TVA (218–29), although its decision was quickly overridden in the National Assembly (256–192), where the government commanded a majority composed of UNR and Independent Republicans. While such blunders as described probably had little ultimate effect upon the votes of opposition members, they probably did make many parliamentarians within the majority less willing to come enthusiastically to the support of their government.[25]

Nevertheless, even if TVA had arisen under somewhat more propitious circumstances from the standpoints of the government and majority, it still would have evoked more than the usual amount of legislative conflict. Here, after all, was a tax levy, and politicians are extremely wary about increasing taxes. They are especially hesitant where new taxes are concerned. Far better to keep the older ones rather than impose new levies; for citizens grow accustomed to existing burdens, but new demands make them aware that their representatives are taking their incomes and therefore excite hitherto latent interests which may ultimately mete out punishment. Consequently politicians find it much more gratifying to spend the national income than to accept the responsibility for collecting it.

It was because of this potential citizen retribution that opposition to TVA was so diffuse, so evenly distributed among opposition and majority parties. Although the majority never openly cast its vote against its government, important UNR and Independent Republican spokesmen did make every possible effort within the bounds of nominal party discipline to dilute the effects of TVA. At such times pressures built up so heavily upon government ministers that they would accept amendments by their nominal supporters which they had just refused to accept from opposition spokesmen.

The inherent legislative resistance to any meaningful alteration of the tax structure may be seen in the reaction to the government's intention to eliminate the so-called "local tax" as part of its plan for imposing TVA. The local tax, a levy on retail sales, was generally admitted to be unfair, and some critics believed its enactment was responsible for the rise of poujadism, that outburst in the 1950s of rather intense, sometimes violent, activity against high taxes by small businessmen and artisans.

The local tax, which ran to about 1 or 2 percent, did have certain advantages from the standpoint of particular groups. The levy, when collected, was returned to the locality from which it was taken. As such, it was especially congenial to the needs of the more populous and wealthy communes, the big cities, and the tourist areas. On the other hand, it had the distinct disadvantage of not helping the very areas of France which needed help the most: the more underdeveloped, poorer regions. In replacing the local tax, TVA would therefore serve as a device by which the more backward areas of the nation could be brought up to the national average.

Unlike American politicians, many French leaders hold important local positions as well as national ones. Many big city mayors and general councillors as well as ordinary parliamentarians came from the wealthier and more populated communes and, as a result, had a decided interest in seeing the bill defeated. Fearing electoral retaliation and not wishing to give up their controls over local spending programs, these deputies and senators, dramatically calling upon their long years and personal experiences in local government, sought at a minimum to soften the impact of TVA and, if possible, to defeat it altogether. In general, they argued that in eliminating the local tax Paris was endangering the liberties of local governments and therefore dangerously enhancing centralized power. If localities could not control the purse strings, or rather the funds themselves, in any meaningful way, they were destined to see their rights progressively contract. This defense was particularly interesting given the fact that in the past most major groups in government and commerce apparently had nothing but contempt for the local tax.

In these matters, however, logic seldom carries much weight because the imposition of new taxes unsettles older vested interests and creates newer, often more hostile ones. The result is that to the politician the costs of initiative in this field may appear to far outweigh any possible benefits accruing from the change. Perhaps this is why legislatures so seldom initiate meaningful tax reforms and why they so easily gain a reputation for hidebound conservatism, at least when compared with the executive branch. After all, the interests they must defend are likely to be much more specific, less diffuse than those favored by the executive.[26]

General conservatism with regard to any tax reform and a strong reluctance to eliminate the local tax were sufficient to make the Pompidou government's task a difficult one at best. But the many specialized constituency groups lobbying strongly to have themselves exempted from the value-added tax's coverage brought a potent force indeed into the fray. Deputies and senators from all the parties, encouraged by numerous constituents as well as by the powerful PME, sought to gain exemption from the bill or at least a reduction in the tax level. These efforts led to a barrage of amendments in both the National Assembly and the Senate. Farmers, artisans, beer interests, financial institutions, and other groups found their champions on the floors of each house.

The government, led primarily by Finance Minister Valéry Giscard d'Estaing in the National Assembly and Prince Jean de Broglie in the Senate, made every effort to compromise with the rebellious legislators, but at times it seemed as if the bill would nevertheless be emasculated. The government accepted numerous amendments to eliminate some items altogether and lower the tax levels on others. It also agreed, through a leading Gaullist politician, Roger Frey, to return to the localities, from other revenue-producing sources, funds lost through the elimination of the local tax. Even Prime Minister Pompidou in a speech before a caucus of UNR and Independent Republican deputies personally promised that important concessions would be granted to small business. In fact, according to the influential Le Monde, government compromises with the National Assembly majority, the Senate, the Finance Committees of each house, and a conference committee chosen to iron out difficulties between the two houses cost some 1,680,000,000 francs in potential revenue. These retreats only made the opponents of TVA more determined, however, and the government was ultimately forced to invoke package votes in each house in order to prevent further amendments from the floor.[27]

### The Containment of Conflict

Whereas TVA excited the deputies and senators to an extent not often apparent during Georges Pompidou's premiership (1962–68), it nevertheless had built-in limits so far as the scope of conflict was concerned. As expected, groups, firms, and individuals were involved in the settlement, not classes, peak associations, and top executive leaders. Small business interests, represented to some extent by the PME—a constituent unit, albeit an independent one, of the National Council of French Employers —fought mightily to beat down the government proposal, but the CNPF and General Confederation of Workers (CGT) were very quiet. President de Gaulle apparently took little interest in the bill—rather strange considering that so much is written about his highly personalized style of rule. Premier Pompidou himself did not play a major role in the dispute, and he seems to have confined himself for the most part to the single effort to rally the majority caucus to the government. On this issue it was Finance

Minister Giscard d'Estaing and Minister of State de Broglie who spoke for the government and guided the bill to its final passage.

On the other hand, the government made every effort to limit the scope of conflict by allowing numerous amendments to the bill and by agreeing to compensate local units for financial losses incurred as a result of repeal of the local tax. The government's lack of interest in a really strong value-added tax reform may be seen in Giscard d'Estaing's refusal to follow up Finance Chairman Louis Vallon's proposal that banks, insurance companies, and construction concerns be included within the scope of the bill.[28] In short, the government went into battle with a limited bill; it came out with even less.

Finally, although much more activity took place on the floor of the National Assembly than was usually the case in the France of Charles de Gaulle, the government never really lost control of the issue either to the opposition parties or to its own majority backbenchers. Nor did it neglect to assert its leadership when necessity demanded that it do so. When the package vote was invoked at crucial times, the majority dutifully submitted to the government's will. Gaullist deputies sulked and they conspired to limit the effects of the bill, but they never threatened their government's life over TVA. Consequently, the scope of conflict remained within limits.

## Conclusion

One salient point which emerges from the TVA dispute is that, politically speaking, it is probably far easier to live with bad taxes on the books than to legislate new and more just ones. As Americans have often observed, various presidents periodically suggest tax reform and just as regularly Congress issues little real reform. Perhaps the answer lies in the nature of tax matters. One could, of course, point to the American lack of a disciplined majority and the separation of powers. But the French government in the case of TVA certainly had the major advantages supposedly denied to the presidents of the United States: control over agenda and debate in the legislature as well as a disciplined majority of unconditional Gaullists and their supporters. Yet the UNR's and Independent Republicans' formal loyalty did not prevent them from gutting TVA.

Despite much commotion in the legislature with regard to TVA and the local tax, it is interesting how little was said throughout the debate about the needs of the ordinary consumer. Many parliamentarians championed the rights of specific interest groups, but overt defenders of that diffuse abstraction called the consumer were conspicuously quiescent.[29] Indeed, his very diffuseness is probably what precludes the consumer's finding a champion. This observation, though, only demonstrates too well what students of pressure groups have known for some time: specific, not diffuse, interests usually carry the day in legislative battles; and where taxes are concerned, it is highly unlikely that genuine reforms can derive from the halls of legislatures in the absence of an aroused and intense public reaction. If such reaction occurred, however, the fight would likely evoke another type of policy, the redistributive one.

# THE UNITED STATES

*The Cigarette Labeling and Advertising Controversy*

## Background

The possible health hazards in cigarette smoking have been debated in the United States for a good part of this century, but it was only in 1939 that the first major scientific study suggesting a link between smoking and lung cancer was published.[30] Although the question increasingly became a topic of conversation thereafter, it was not given special emphasis until the 1950s, when a series of studies appeared which seemed to confirm the relationship of smoking to various types of diseases. Particularly noteworthy in this respect was a study, first initiated with much publicity in 1951, whose findings were placed before the public in 1954. From that point on the issue became more and more politicized. Congress held hearings in 1957, and individual legislators demonstrated their restlessness by introducing legislation to cope with the problem. Groups within the federal bureaucracy, notably the Public Health Service and the Federal Trade Commission (FTC), as well as such private groups as the American Cancer Society multiplied their criticisms of the tobacco industry. In October 1962, an advisory committee was created by the surgeon general of the Public Health Service to assess the scientific evidence on smoking. The advisory committee included representatives from the cigarette industry as well as from the antismoking interests. Its report, released in January 1964, confirmed the results of previous studies in the field. Finally, in June 1964, the Federal Trade Commission on its own initiative and apparently without consulting Congress issued a ruling which required that a warning be placed on cigarette packages. This move provoked Congress to action, and in July 1965, the Cigarette Labeling and Advertising Act was passed.

Policy making with regard to tobacco has historically been one of distributive politics. Whatever controls exist have been mostly imposed by the industry itself. Moreover, Congress has generously supported the tobacco farmer through price supports. In fact, because several states have been highly dependent upon tobacco for their well-being and because their representatives have occupied key posts within the legislature, the cigarette industry could call upon key support whenever it found its interests threatened. Therefore, when scientists became increasingly concerned over the possible harmful effects of tobacco, they found their possibilities of action extremely limited. Of course, there were prestigious private organizations to support them such as the American Cancer Society and the American Heart Association; there was the Federal Trade Commission only too prepared to act if given the chance; there was the surgeon general and the Public Health Service; but, in general, the major resource of these groups simply derived from the public prestige in which they were held, in the moral forces they represented.

Since outright prohibition of smoking was naturally out of the question, antismoking groups sought to educate the public about the harmful effects of tobacco. Education, however, was a difficult task at best, for when cigarette commercials suggested that smoking was harmless, pleasurable, and even romantic, it was difficult to see how the scientists' message could gain public acceptance. Indeed, cigarette consumption had continued to increase over the years despite repeated warnings by scientists, and the growing number of smokers among the young was an especially alarming phenomenon. Hence, the antismoking forces saw the problem in the short run as one of placing regulations upon advertising in such a way as to force the cigarette advertisers to admit that the habit was unhealthy. Hopefully, men and women would thereby be encouraged to refrain from smoking. The antismoking forces may have been motivated by the highest of ideals, but they had a built-in weakness: they were fighting on behalf of that abstraction called the consumer, too diffuse to be mobilized against highly specific interests, especially interests supporting a pleasurable habit. The individual consumer may have vaguely felt that smoking was not good for him, but he knew too many people who smoked, and they were living quite normal lives; so why should he become excited about such a problem? It was simply an issue to be left up to the individual himself.

The tobacco groups, on the other hand, had a highly specific interest to defend, and for them to lose implied rather severe economic deprivations; hence, they were strongly motivated to maintain an existing distributive form of politics which until now had given them so much. The surgeon general's advisory committee report and the subsequent FTC ruling shocked them into action, and they defended their interests skillfully.

What were the strengths of the cigarette industry? It had several bases of support, to say the least. Economically, tobacco was a key industry in several states, including North Carolina, Virginia, South Carolina, Georgia, and Tennessee. Not only were large amounts of tobacco produced there, but, in addition, the production of cigarettes was a major source of income for these states. Reductions in tobacco consumption therefore could adversely affect large numbers of people. Moreover, advertising revenue for television, radio, magazines, and newspapers as well as expenditures in warehousing and shipping involved large and important groups in the economy.

Not surprisingly, tobacco interests were well mobilized so far as lobbying activities were concerned. The Tobacco Industry Research Committee (later called the Council for Tobacco Research—U.S.A.) was created to distribute money for scientific research. Hopefully, such research would demonstrate smoking to be harmless. Another organization, the Tobacco Institute, Inc., was founded to combat the publicity of those studies which suggested the ill effects of smoking. Quite active at the time of the cigarette-labeling debate, the Tobacco Institute was created by fourteen tobacco producers. Presidents of the various companies sit on its board. It is a well-financed institution, which not only lobbies but publishes periodicals dealing with industry problems. It has had leading political figures in its directorship, notably former Ambassador George Allen and former

Senator Earle C. Clements from Kentucky. Senator Clements was a close friend of President Johnson and key lawmakers. He was a skilled strategist, and he knew the mood of Congress. As such, he was a particularly effective spokesman for the industry.

Such pressure groups and individuals were not about to allow the anti-smoking forces to seize the initiative without a struggle. They developed an array of scientific arguments which served to blunt the thrust of their health opponents. For example, to the scientific argument that smoking and cancer were positively related, they replied that correlation and cause were not the same thing; the statistical relationship may have been merely a chance occurrence not related to medical reasons.

Similarly, the cigarette industry and its spokesmen called upon that old symbol of the American dream, the capitalistic system. Regulation of commercials was proclaimed an interference with the free market by meddling government bureaucrats bent on enhancing their own powers. Indeed, it was maintained that control over tobacco was merely the initial step for future bureaucratic intervention in the economy. Besides, they argued, to limit cigarette consumption might well lead to a severe unemployment problem and an unfavorable balance of trade. Finally, assuming such drastic steps were in fact necessary, it was only fitting that they be taken by the representatives of the people, namely Congress, and not by the faceless bureaucrats on the Federal Trade Commission.

The fundamental strength of the tobacco industry, however, was not in its moral, economic, and scientific arguments. On the contrary, its power derived mainly from the friends it could count upon within the state machines and particularly within Congress. It could make its influence felt to a great extent because so many industries depended directly or indirectly upon tobacco and furthermore, because tobacco growth was concentrated in particular states. Because these states were mainly one-party and under Democratic control, representatives and senators from these areas often ranked rather high in terms of congressional seniority. Indeed, tobacco state interests have been extremely potent in the various committees and subcommittees of the Senate and House, and they have been particularly well represented in the powerful committee chairmanships. Those members not dependent upon tobacco interests would reflect carefully on the potential costs to their own constituency needs before opposing such powerful figures. As a result, there was little doubt that Congress as an institution was highly sympathetic to tobacco demands.

In the case of the federal bureaucracy the relationships are somewhat more complex. It has long been a norm of American politics that each major interest should have its own direct representation within the topmost positions of government. As a result there are Departments of Labor, Commerce, and Agriculture. The Department of Agriculture's role has been to represent faithfully the farmers' economic concerns—or at least the concerns of certain sectors of farming. In fact, farming interests, through research, education, and price-support programs, have been brought into such close association with government that the line between public and private domains has been blurred almost completely. This has led some critics to conclude that public policy is in reality made by private interests. This has become especially apparent in the development of local committees of farmers to administer many of their own programs. This tendency of direct group participation has gone farthest in the field of agriculture, but the general tendency is apparent in other areas as well.

It is not surprising, therefore, that the Department of Agriculture has failed to question the specific needs of tobacco growers either for reasons of health or in the interest of greater administrative coherence within the executive branch of government. The lack of governmental coordination of programs is an interesting phenomenon in this respect. The Department of Agriculture has long resisted any attempts to reduce the supply of tobacco by cutting or eliminating price supports or by curbing commercial activity on behalf of tobacco. Thus, while such agencies as the FTC and the Public Health Service have worked for greater regulation of tobacco production and consumption, the Agriculture Department, particularly through its Tobacco Division, has pushed vociferously in precisely the opposite direction.

One can hardly imagine a closer tie between the regulator and the regulated than is found in agriculture, a link enhanced by the actual participation of the latter in governmental decision making. Tobacco producers and their allies are assured of having their way so far as Agriculture Department policy is concerned; and their influence flows up through the bureaucracy and the powerful subcommittees and committees on Capitol Hill. Agricultural constituency interests, department, and committees are joined together in a common bond against any effort to socialize conflict and thereby alter the status quo of distributive politics they have enjoyed for so long.

It has been often noted that the influence of government bureaucracies depends to a great extent upon the types of constituencies they regulate and serve. If an individual department, agency or bureau's constituency interest is large, fairly cohesive, and electorally important, or if it can distribute plenty of projects beneficial to the folks back home (as the Army Corps of Engineers), it can go far in freeing itself from close presidential supervision and coordination. Congress will probably make a special effort to assure its responsiveness to the legislature rather than to the president. On the other hand, if, like the State Department, its constituency is fairly small, then a given department, agency, or bureau will likely enjoy less autonomy and independence.

## The Development of Conflict

The debate over cigarette labeling grew out of the Federal Trade Commission ruling in June 1964 compelling cigarette manufacturers to disclose in their advertising a warning that smoking may cause cancer and other diseases. From the standpoint of the industry the ruling could certainly have been worse, for the FTC did limit the scope of its application to allow manufacturers to determine where the warning would be placed on the packages. In all probability the FTC was surprised by the reaction its ruling received from Congress, for not only had the surgeon general's advisory committee report been praised, but the industry itself had seemed indifferent to the FTC hearings prior to the ruling. But now the industry through Senator Clements and the Tobacco Institute was goaded into action, and it found no lack of support in Congress.

It was obvious almost from the beginning that the FTC was in a weak position on the congressional front. A failure to consult the appropriate committee members of Congress prior to its ruling was treated as an outrage to legislative dignity by some members of the legislature. And Congress surely had the authority to discipline the FTC for its apparent indiscretions. Independent regulatory commissions such as the FTC are created for the purpose of administering policy in restricted areas where Congress either cannot or has no desire to exercise a continual oversight. As a consequence, independent regulatory agencies tend to function as quasi-judicial, quasi-legislative, and quasi-executive bodies.

For the most part Congress has given the independent regulatory commissions a rather wide discretion in administering their particular domains; but if it so desires, Congress can intervene decisively to remove altogether or limit in part the jurisdiction of the commissions. Congress, after all, created these organizations; it can even abolish them if it sees fit. Although the independent regulatory agencies ordinarily can count upon much independence from Congress, they must nevertheless be careful to avoid pushing Congress too far.

The threat to the FTC and its ruling did not derive only from an irate Congress, however. The FTC found little meaningful support from the very groups which might have been expected to cushion it against congressional retaliation. Independent regulatory commissions are often accused of working hand in glove with the very interests they presumably regulate; but in the cigarette labeling and advertising case, the commission found itself devoid of industry support. To make matters worse, prohealth groups as a whole were thoroughly disorganized and quite amateurish in their approach to the battle, unable to decide among themselves just how much and what kind of regulation they wished for the cigarette industry. Their awkward initiatives against the skilled attacks of Senator Clements and the Tobacco Institute made little impression on a Congress whose key elements were already protobacco in orientation. Finally, the prohealth groups were faced with another problem: they could not bring concentrated power to bear simply to proclaim dangers to health which were far from obvious to the average citizen. As suggested previously, these interests which speak in the name of the general consumer are likely to be less successful than are specific groups which stand to lose much from the particular issue under consideration. The average consumer could not be mobilized to pit his resources against smoking, whereas the tobacco industry and its allies, in danger of severe deprivation, were easily organized to defend their interests.

## Congress Resolves the Issue

There was little that could be considered unusual in the manner in which the legislature ultimately passed the Cigarette Labeling and Advertising Act. The bill went through each house, but since the versions were slightly different, a conference committee of the two houses was forced to work out a compromise bill. The latter in turn was quickly passed by voice vote in each chamber.[31]

The House of Representatives was originally more hostile to the FTC and its ruling than was the Senate. Hearings were held, and a bill was even introduced to prohibit entirely the jurisdiction of the commission in the field of cigarette advertising. Such an action was highly unusual, for this was an attempt to eliminate a specific FTC ruling (on tobacco) rather than to limit its jurisdiction or to alter its rule-making procedures in a more general way.

The Senate, on the other hand, was more amenable to moderation than was the House. The Senate Commerce Committee was more divided on the issue of cigarette controls than was the more protobacco House Interstate and Foreign Commerce Committee. In particular, the chairman of the House committee, Congressman Oren Harris of Arkansas, appears to have been much more partisan toward the tobacco interests, not surprisingly given his constituency, than Senator Warren Magnuson of Washington, chairman of the Senate committee. Possibly as a result, the Senate placed less stringent restrictions on the FTC when the committees of each house met in conference to resolve their differences. Moreover, Senator Maurine Neuberger served as a resolute supporter of the antismoking forces in the Senate, whereas no such individual emerged in the House.

The only battle of any consequence took place on June 16, 1965, in the Senate, where the antismoking forces hoped to generate some support. In this first major test of power relationships, the Senate sharply asserted legislative dominance over the Federal Trade Commission in a 72–5 roll-call vote (Republicans 26–0; Democrats 46–5). Indeed, the Senate intended to preempt rule-making power entirely in the health warning area. Among other things, the Senate bill placed a three-year moratorium on antismoking warnings in cigarette commercials, and it applied that moratorium to all federal agencies as well as to state and local governments. In an attempt to reduce the bill's scope, Senator Neuberger took her fight to the floor on behalf of the health groups. First, she sought to have the three-year moratorium reduced to one year, but her amendment was defeated rather handily. In a second amendment, she tried to have the bill applied only to the FTC but not to other national, state, and local agencies. In this instance she also received a setback.

The ballot in the House was far less controversial, as implied in the fact that a voice vote was taken. In addition, some care was taken to avoid controversy, for the bill was brought to the floor on a Tuesday afternoon when few members were present. The major opponent of this piece of legislation, Congressman John Moss, was out of the country, although he had been assured that no vote would be taken prior to his return. This apparent violation of a gentleman's agreement led to some criticism of Mr. Harris, the committee chairman.

The bill, as finally passed, in essence followed Senate recommendations, for it deprived government agencies of any power in the near future to compel the issuance of health warnings in cigarette commercials. Moreover, by prohibiting state and local governments from ruling in this field, it confined any subsequent contest to the chambers of Congress. On the other hand, Congress did require a warning label for cigarette packages, which was no small change in itself.

## Conclusions

Who were the winners in the advertising and labeling debate? At first glance, it might appear that the health interests emerged victorious because a warning label was henceforth required for cigarette packages. Moreover, a by-product of the debate was the subsequent appropriation of $2 million to create a National Clearinghouse for Smoking and Health.

On the other hand, as Professor A. Lee Fritschler has capably pointed out, there can be little doubt that tobacco interests gave up far less than they gained. After all, the surgeon general's report in 1964 as well as the numerous studies suggesting the health hazards of smoking gradually eroded the support of tobacco interests in Congress and therefore brought on an inexorable demand for government action. The tobacco industry as a result could not indefinitely delay anticigarette legislation with promises of more study and safer cigarettes. Its best strategy was to delay, procrastinate, and mitigate the effects of any meaningful legislation. From this standpoint Senator Clements and his friends achieved an undoubted success.

First, while it is true that the 1965 act required a health warning on cigarette packages, it nevertheless failed to stipulate the requirement of a warning so far as commercials were concerned. From the standpoint of the industry, the cigarette package requirement was little more than an irritant.

Second, the prohibition by Congress of state and local action in the advertising and labeling field came at a most opportune time, for such key states as California and New York were moving progressively toward rather stringent controls over advertising. Clearly, many different state laws, including some very harsh ones, would pose innumerable marketing problems for the industry. For example, the types of packages might well have to vary according to individual state laws, and this in itself would involve no small cost to the tobacco manufacturers. In preempting this entire area of rule making, Congress could assure a uniform law for the nation, although it was undoubtedly hoped that little legislation would be enacted in this area.

Third, the Cigarette Labeling and Advertising Act specifically eliminated certain antitobacco pressures. Thus, the Federal Trade Commission as well as other government agencies were ruled out as regulators of the commercial interests of the tobacco industry. Henceforth, not only the FTC, but especially the Federal Communications Commission, would be barred from the interest-group struggle; as a result, future battles could be carried out only in the legislature, where tobacco presumably was assured of a relatively greater number of friends.

The tobacco industry was far from unhappy with the Cigarette Labeling and Advertising Act, as the lopsided 72–5 vote in the Senate demonstrated. The tobacco state senators specifically failed to oppose the bill when it came up for consideration; not a single one of the five opposition votes came from such states. It might be concluded therefore that although the bill was presented as an antismoking one, the tobacco supporters were in fact little disturbed by the outcome of the struggle.

Could strong support from the White House have helped the health interests gain the day? Quite possibly, but it is doubtful. President Lyndon B. Johnson remained above the battle and in the end simply signed the bill into law without comment. On the other hand, he could have opposed the health groups through the Budget Bureau clearing process, but he did not. He seemed content to let the dispute run its normal course.

The case just examined has all the earmarks of a sectorally fragmented policy. The fight took place between interest groups and bureaucrats organized around sectoral concerns. The level of conflict was therefore limited in extent because the health interests could not define the issue in such a manner as to elicit large-scale public participation and concern.

## CONCLUSIONS

The sectorally fragmented type of policy revolves around intra- and intersectoral conflicts. Major participants include sectoral interests and their supporters in the legislature as well as the individual ministers or relatively high-level bureaucrats charged with the administration of the particular sector(s) involved in the issue-dispute. The issue itself is likely to be settled, not in committees, but on the floor of the legislature where there may well be some deviation from the party line. However, these issues usually do not cut widely and deeply enough across a wide array of social and economic groupings to rupture party discipline entirely, so they are consequently unlikely to threaten the lives of particular governments.

The form of government (parliamentary or presidential) and the party system (both in terms of numbers and discipline) give a certain "tone" to the policy process. In Great Britain and Fifth Republic France, which have had parliamentary-type institutions and disciplined majority parties capable of forming governments on their own, individual ministers for the most part hold the initiative in legislation—exactly what would be expected given the disciplined majorities they could depend upon for support. Because the TVA and RPM struggles were sectoral in nature, individual ministers, rather than prime ministers, were most active in the disputes. Nevertheless, despite the disciplined majoritarianism prevalent in each nation, RPM and TVA were characterized by much legislative floor activity, as witnessed both by the numerous amendments offered and, especially in the British case, by the unusually high level of party indiscipline. In fact, of some nine British sectorally fragmented issues considered for possible inclusion in this study, the RPM study displayed the greatest breach of party loyalty. The cause of the backbench rebellion was a piece of legislation forced upon Conservative MPs which threatened one of their older and larger constituent elements, small businessmen. Had a Labour government sought to pass similar legislation, it is likely that backbench reaction would have been far less contentious.

There is an interesting paradox in the British and French case studies on the one hand, and the American cigarette labeling and advertising bill on the other. Despite the more rambunctious reputation of Congress, the level of floor activity was more restrained and less intense in the American case, if the use of voice votes rather than roll calls, and the far smaller number of amendments offered than on RPM or TVA are good indicators of levels of conflict. The reason for the comparative quiescence in the United States in this instance appears for the most part to be that fewer sectors and groups were affected by the pending legislation. After all, antismoking forces never were able to excite particularly large numbers of consumers to action, so the major groups involved were tobacco and tobacco-related interests opposed by health-related ones.

Nonetheless, it may be said in general that the American system offers a better opportunity to observe legislative conflicts than the British and French Fifth Republic systems do because of the United States' separation of powers, checks and balances, and lack of party discipline. As a result, battles in the latter country are more public and usually take place around more institutional checkpoints (bureaucratic and legislative committees and floor debate unencumbered by party discipline). For example, the legislation considered in the case study above was fought over in an independent regulatory commission, in the health and agricultural bureaucracies, within the various congressional committees, and, finally, resolved on the floors of each house of Congress. Therefore, the access of groups to bureaucratic and congressional committees and to individual legislators, uncontrolled by party whips, gives them a relatively greater opportunity to regroup their forces at various points in the process running from introduction to ultimate passage into law. Conversely, in majoritarian parliamentary systems major legislation is worked out in the executive bureaucracy prior to finding its way to the parliament for debate and resolution; hence, the best chance for the interest groups to amend or scuttle a prospective bill lies in gaining access to the bureaucracy while the bill is being formulated, or subsequently, but to a lesser extent, in legislative committee. Otherwise, they must take their cause to the floor where they have to reckon with party discipline, however, not to mention executive dominance over various stages of the legislative process (e.g., agenda, timetable, and debate).

## NOTES

1. See Harry Eckstein, "Introduction: Group Theory and the Comparative Study of Pressure Groups," in David E. Apter and Harry Eckstein, eds., *Comparative Politics: A Reader* (New York: The Free Press of Glencoe, 1963), pp. 389–97. For two of the better statements on the group approach, see Charles B. Hagan, "The Group in Political Science," in Roland Young, ed., *Approaches to the Study of Politics* (Evanston, Ill.: University of Illinois Press, 1958), pp. 38–51; and David B. Truman, *The Governmental Process* (New York: Alfred A. Knopf, 1960).

2. E.g., see Bernard E. Brown, "Alcohol and Politics in France," *American Political Science Review,* December 1957, pp. 976–94; and Samuel Beer, "Pressure Groups and Parties in Britain," *American Political Science Review,* March 1956, pp. 6–9.

3. The next few paragraphs are especially dependent upon Ronald Butt, *The Power of Parliament* (London: Constable, 1967), pp. 251–74; also, see B. S. Yamey, ed., *Resale Price Maintenance* (Chicago: Aldine Publishing Co., 1966), pp. 251–54, 287–98.

4. Since they could be redeemed for cash or prizes, trading stamps had a tendency to reduce the effects of RPM by giving a discount on branded prices. See Butt, *The Power of Parliament,* pp. 260–61.

5. *The Times* (London), February 26, 1964.

6. *Economist,* February 29, 1964, p. 812.

7. Ibid., p. 778.

8. On the role of the Restrictive Practices Court, see R. B. Stevens and B. S. Yamey, *The Restrictive Practices Court* (London: Weidenfeld and Nicolson, 1965).

9. *Economist,* January 18, 1964, pp. 223–24.

10. *The Times* (London), January 24, 1964.

11. *The Manchester Guardian,* February 27, 1964.

12. *The Times* (London), January 16, 1964; *The Manchester Guardian,* February 18, 1964, and March 9, 12, 1964.

13. *The Times* (London), March 11, 1964.

14. Butt, *The Power of Parliament,* p. 267.

15. Ibid., p. 268.

16. *Economist,* January 18, 1964, pp. 179–80.

17. Ibid., February 29, 1964, pp. 811–12.

18. Ibid., p. 815; and Stevens and Yamey, *The Restrictive Practices Court,* pp. 23–50.

19. *The Knoxville News-Sentinel* (Knoxville, Tenn.), February 7, 1971. This article is devoted to Professor John Kenneth Galbraith's opposition to a value-added tax for the United States.

20. Richard E. Slitor, "The Value-Added Tax as an Alternative to the Corporate Income Tax," in Dan Throop Smith et al., *Alternatives to Present Federal Taxes* (Princeton, N.J.: Tax Institute of America, 1964), p. 37. In the same volume, see Maurice E. Peloubet, "European Experience with Value-Added Taxation," pp. 64–75.

21. Philip M. Williams, *The French Parliament: Politics in the Fifth Republic* (New York: Praeger, 1968), p. 93.

22. For an excellent study of the TVA debate, see Jean-Pierre Dussaife, "Les forces en France: le Parlement face à la réforme des taxes sur le chiffre d'affaires," *Revue française de science politique,* June 1966, pp. 521–31; also, Williams, *The French Parliament,* pp. 93–95.

23. Theodore J. Lowi, "American Business, Public Policy, Case-Studies, and Political Theory," *World Politics,* July 1964, pp. 677–715.

24. *Le Monde,* December 23, 1965.

25. *Le Monde,* June 12, 1965; December 24, 1965.

26. In this respect, see the comments of Dussaife, "Les forces en France," pp. 526–28.

27. *Le Monde,* June 23, 26, 1964; December 23, 24, 1965.

28. *Le Monde,* June 23, 1965.

29. Dussaife, "Les forces en France," p. 528.

30. Material for this section is derived mainly from the excellent case study of A. Lee Fritschler, *Smoking and Politics: Policymaking and the Federal Bureaucracy* (New York: Meredith Corp., 1969). Those who would like to consider this problem in greater detail would do well to consult his book. There one may find not only a study of group tactics and activities but a highly informative account of the political relationships existing among the various organs of government.

31. Data on the congressional battle may be obtained from the following issues of *Congressional Quarterly Weekly Report:* No. 22, May 28, 1965, p. 1023; No. 25, June 18, 1965, pp. 1148–49; No. 26, June 26, 1965, pp. 1221–22; No. 28, July 9, 1965, p. 1325.

# 4

# THE POLITICS OF EMOTIVE SYMBOLIZATION

**E** MOTIVE symbolic policies tend to be characterized by high levels of intensity and broad scopes of conflict, for they activate large numbers of citizens who feel deeply about the particular issues in question. Public awareness levels are quite pronounced since the populace understands the debate sufficiently to hold opinions. The frequently stated view that issues have become too complex for the governed does not apply here. People may be misinformed, but they do have strong views regarding the correctness of the issues. It might be suggested that emotive symbolic issues yield opinions characterized by relative stability but that in the course of conflict, latent predispositions simply become more manifest.

Emotive symbolization may perform what Daniel Katz has called a "value-expressive" function in that it enables an individual to meet his emotional needs by giving him the opportunity to express his values in a positive manner. As Katz put it: "The reward to the person in these instances is not so much a matter of gaining social recognition or monetary rewards as of establishing his self-identity and confirming his notion of the sort of person he sees himself to be." [1]

Emotive symbolic policies, then, are types which generate emotional support for deeply held values, but unlike the other types considered in this work, the values sought are essentially noneconomic. [2] Rather, they are "way of life" issues, and as a result they easily arouse the most intense political passions. This is hardly surprising when the conflict takes place over such issues as the death penalty, prayer in the public schools, abortion legislation, laws relating to homosexuality, and segregation in public schools and commercial establishments.

Because they are so intensely felt and are likely to be salient for such large numbers of people, emotive symbolic issues encourage a much wider scope and intensity of conflict than do sectorally fragmented ones. Con-

90

versely, the two types do share certain similarities. For instance, in each one major interest groups and political participants vary according to the particular issue under consideration. The institution which settles issues arising out of emotive symbolization, as in the sectorally fragmented type, is likely to be the legislature—nominally. Nevertheless, there is a profound difference in a qualitative sense in the modes of issue resolution. James B. Christoph has hypothesized that the more emotional an issue, the greater the likelihood that it will be played out in the public.[3] What this portends for legislative bodies is that, while they can meaningfully cope with sectoral issues, they cannot do the same for emotive symbolic ones. The latter produce such profound intensities of feeling among the public that the conflict is pushed downward into the populace for a de facto resolution. An aware populace, closely watching its leaders, will insist on getting its own way.

Another consequence of emotive symbolic conflicts is that feelings of insecurity among government and party leaders may be greatly enhanced. Contrary to much folklore, politicians probably prefer to avoid stressful situations, but this type of policy is likely to place such contradictory demands upon leaders as to prompt them to avoid facing the issue altogether. In other words, because any position they take may alienate significant sections of their parties and electorates, political leaders try to eschew leadership responsibilities by remaining above the battle, or at least neutral in the dispute.

Perhaps if more political commentators understood this fact, they could avoid much useless moralizing about politics. The hesitation on the part of many American state governors over the past few years to become involved in abortion disputes or the wariness of British and Canadian MPs on certain occasions in adopting positions on capital punishment is instructive in this regard. Similarly, even so forceful a Fourth Republic leader as Pierre Mendès-France refused to carve out a position in 1954 with regard to the highly controversial European Defense Community bill. This legislation, which would have integrated French armed forces with those of the Germans, divided party and committee in the National Assembly.

Emotive symbolic policy types create very real problems for individual legislators since parliamentarians are denied—or reject—the support of those in authority. Logic would suggest that issue intensity and issue salience draw constituency and legislator together, with the latter assuming the "delegate" role of faithful recorder of local wishes; or, conversely, that the individual legislator in making his decision may also choose to emphasize the overriding value of his own personal conscience. Either way, it is on these issues, as Christoph has pointed out, that "members of Parliament are most likely to refuse to delegate their power of decision to another level of government." [4] Since parliamentarians are likely to be so closely attuned to their constituencies or their own consciences, it follows that in cases of emotive symbolization party discipline, no matter how rigid, breaks down under pressure, with each man fending for himself.

Particularly in parliamentary regimes such as Great Britain which pride themselves upon the concept of government responsibility before Parliament and party discipline, government leaders will find an excuse to "lift the whips" (i.e., to call for a free vote) and thereby allow each member to vote his constituency or his conscience.

On the other hand, if the distribution of opinion roughly corresponds with party support, the party and its leaders may then play a much more decisive role. In this instance the leadership does not find itself faced with deep divisions in its own ranks, but rather discovers that opinion, while highly intense and aware, nevertheless tends to divide along normal party lines. A congruence of party and opinion on such issues, however, is unlikely to occur with much frequency.

It will be remembered that the emotive symbolic policy type is legislatorially settled; i.e., an attribute of this type of policy seems to be extreme individualism within the legislature. This attribute of extreme individualism likely includes at least four characteristics:

(1) *Government refusal to take a stand on the issue.* Whenever an issue conflict engenders an overt, stated refusal by political leaders to accept responsibility, one may be sure that the issue is highly explosive. In particular, if leaders relinquish the demands of leadership by allowing a free vote, then one may suspect that their fears are quite pronounced; that groups of relatively equal strength within the government orbit are threatening the cohesiveness of the coalition; that the government is almost bound to alienate a significant portion of the public by making its views known; or that constituency pressures are so powerful upon backbenchers as to override leadership or party caucus pressures. The consequence is to give ordinary backbenchers much freedom to maneuver.

(2) *Breakdowns in party discipline.* A refusal by backbenchers to accept the whip obviously implies strong dissension since, after all, followers are pitting themselves against their own government leaders, who can punish transgressions by a denial of patronage, by removal from the legislative caucus, or by thwarting ambitions for higher posts.

(3) *Backbench leadership.* Backbench leadership arises when ordinary legislators become de facto leaders attempting to resolve conflicts. In such instances government ministers or chief executives abdicate their policy-making roles through either design or accident, or simply because nonleaders find the issue to be of special importance.

(4) *Procedural unorthodoxy.* When either government leaders or backbenchers decide that an issue is of such gravity that it requires them to take action which, although quite legal, violates procedural norms, it is probable that the conflict in the legislature is highly inflamed. For example, to entice a large number of congressmen in the House of Representatives to sign a discharge petition bringing a bill out of the Rules Committee is indeed a feat since members who sign the petition risk seeing their own committees placed in a like position in the future or finding their patronage and other desires unmet by angry committee chairmen. Similarly, the

filibuster, while probably not so extreme in the eyes of American leaders, is another instance of procedural revolt as are the guillotine and the Early Day Motion (EDM) in Great Britain and closure in Canada. Even the free vote might be perceived in this manner for, as Professor Christoph has shown in his case study of capital punishment, it can have harmful consequences for governments trying to cope with policy.[5] Because it is somewhat difficult to generalize about procedural unorthodoxy, the respective customs in individual political systems must be considered before making a decision as to when it is taking place.

## CONCLUSIONS

It appears that emotive symbolic policies are the most democratic of the policy types considered in this study, if by democratic one means large-scale participation and involvement as well as a relative lack of leadership controls upon followers. The pronounced degree of democracy is seen in a summary of the following attributes of the type:

(1) They are characterized by a wide scope and intensity of conflict over "way of life" issues.
(2) Not government leaders, but ordinary backbenchers, supported by highly moralistic interest groups, play the major role in the policy process.
(3) Party discipline is likely to be greatly eroded in the disputes.
(4) These policies are legislatorially settled; legislative individualism is likely to be quite pronounced.

## FRANCE

### The European Army Debate

The debate concerning the European Defense Community (EDC) was one of the most divisive issues France faced during the Fourth Republic. With the exception of the Algerian issue, which ultimately returned General de Gaulle to power in May 1958 and brought down the republic itself, the question of a rearmed Germany within a supranational military establishment separated the French political leadership in a way no other issue did.

### Background

Although nationalism has undoubtedly been the more dominant strain, the dream of European unity has long held sway among a small proportion of European intellectuals. With the ending of World War II, a renewed impetus was given to this ancient dream of Charlemagne, and the European proponents could no longer be dismissed so easily as dreamers at best or, at worst, calculating reactionaries bent on restoring the clerical influence of Rome. Europe, decimated by two fratricidal wars within the span of less than a half century, now found itself unable to control events as in the days when its influence had stretched out to other cultures and continents to the east, south, and west. To make matters worse, two huge superpowers, the Soviet Union and the United States, had now come forward to contest for world leadership. In this new world of international struggles, Europe could no longer dominate events; its destiny was controlled by decisions made elsewhere. In order for Europe to play a major role on the international stage, many felt a coalition among older nations such as France, West Germany, and Italy was imperative.

There were other, more immediate, reasons why Western European unity seemed so necessary to its proponents. For one, a basic reason for the historic European discord lay in a perpetual enmity between France and Germany, and their mutual hostility played a large part in the causes of World Wars I and II. A basic aim of European unity was to link these two peoples so closely that never again would either have an interest in the other's defeat or subjugation.

Furthermore, when World War II ended, the Soviet army controlled most of Eastern Europe, including a portion of Germany itself. One expansionist dictator, Hitler, had been defeated only to be succeeded by another, Stalin. In addition, Soviet influence extended into the hearts of major Western nations. Both Italy and France had indigenous Communist movements which could count upon the support of one-fourth or more of these countries' respective electorates. Communist participation in the Resistance had given them a certain legitimacy they had been unable to obtain previously. Spurred on by fears of Soviet domination as well as by the United States' interest in a Western Europe stable enough to contain Communist advances, an increasing number of Western Europeans began to feel that political unity might ultimately be necessary for national survival.

On the other hand, a few Europeans were less concerned about an actual Soviet occupation of their territories than about the more subtle forms of gradual American cultural, social, and economic penetration of European structures. Political and economic unity were thus necessary to ward off both superpowers.

Some Europeans of a more pragmatic bent believed that the path to political unity lay first through the creation of economic unity. Aside from the political question, economic cooperation was a requirement for European prosperity. They emphasized that basic reforms were needed in the relatively short run to encourage the growth and modernization of industry, to eliminate tariffs and quotas, to establish common monetary policies, to develop mass production methods in farming and industry, and, in general, to create a larger market for Europeans. Economic nationalism in the modern world simply made no sense to such hardheaded realists; and it was difficult for them to see how enduring European political institutions could be generated anyway in the absence of economic unification.

Whether out of the desire for a great role in international affairs or out of fear of a potential French-German discord, communism, American hegemony, or economic stagnation, certain Europeans were now ready to bury their old quarrels once and for all in new supranational institutions.

Events alone, however, probably were not sufficient to further the struggle for a united Europe. To carry out their policies the Europeans were fortunate that those in agreement with them occupied key positions in Italy, West Germany, and France in the years immediately following the end of World War II. In Italy and in West Germany, Christian Democratic parties firmly wedded to the European concept took power following World War II, and their respective party leaders, Premier Alcide de Gasperi in Italy and Chancellor Konrad Adenauer in West Germany, were convinced opponents of nationalism. While Christian Democracy in France did not dominate political life to the extent that it did in Italy and West Germany, its spokesman, the MRP, nevertheless contributed to the formation of various governments at crucial times. Significantly, the MRP often controlled the important Foreign Affairs Ministry, and as this minister Robert Schuman became a major exponent of the European ideal. It was de Gasperi, Adenauer, and Schuman who did much following the war to push through their respective parliaments the European Coal and Steel Community for the development of a common market in coal and steel.

Therefore, long-term trends as well as the commitments of strategically placed individuals conjoined to foster the idea of a European union including a combined army. Basically, such an army entailed the creation of a supranational defense community among the Benelux nations, West Germany, France, and Italy consisting of "common institutions, common armed forces, and a common budget" (Article I). The common institutions were drawn up much on the order of the existing European Coal and Steel Community, and therefore were not thought to be especially controversial, but the budget and armed forces were another matter altogether. Critics argued that the common budget could have a disastrous impact upon the various national economies, while the envisioned common forces would lead to a rearmed German *Wehrmacht*. Actually, the proposed German contribution would be twelve divisions, and military unification would not be total by any means, for integration would be realized only at the army corps level and at the very top executive (Commissariat) position.[6]

Ironically, France both initiated and destroyed the EDC ideal. A Third Force government of Popular Republican, Socialist, Radical, and *modéré* persuasion led by a centrist, René Pléven, first proposed a European army in September 1950, but the French National Assembly ultimately rejected that treaty in August 1954. By that time the militantly pro-European MRP had gone into opposition, while the equally militant but nationalist Gaullist RPF (now called Social Republicans) was serving in the government of Pierre Mendès-France, a man with severe doubts about the wisdom of EDC. Moreover, at this time the international stage seemed more peaceful, and the Russian menace not so threatening as in 1950.

### The Emergence of Severe Conflict

The EDC debate was a momentous one in French politics. As an outstanding commentator of the period put it, "From January 1953 to August

1954 took place the greatest ideological and political debate France has known since the Dreyfus affair. . . ."[7] It was therefore no ordinary conflict confined to a few bickering politicians; it was a struggle including major elements within the French political elite and large numbers of ordinary but concerned Frenchmen as well. The impact of the EDC issue upon the masses as well as upon certain elites included the following attributes:

(1) *The state of public opinion.* Although it is difficult to speak with assurance about the intensity of mass feelings with regard to EDC, the evidence of national surveys allows certain statements. Frenchmen in general were favorably disposed toward the ideal of European unification, particularly economic integration. On the other hand, they were usually quite suspicious of German motives and of Germans as a national people; when it was suggested that West Germany would be rearmed through EDC, deep-seated prejudices and fears were quickly aroused. The issue of the European army would soon find its way into the realm of emotive symbolic politics; a poll taken in May 1953 showed that the mere existence of German troops constituted a perceived danger for 57 percent of the French population. Similarly, a sample taken in July 1954, when the EDC struggle was highly salient, found 56 percent of all Frenchmen believing that German rearmament in any form was dangerous. Even those more innocuous suggestions calling for "European" rather than specifically German contributions to a supranational defense were met with much hostility and fear.[8]

European army proponents attempted to play down the fact of German rearmament by emphasizing the much greater threat of communism. They also argued that the German beast could best be tamed by integrating him into the larger European framework. Therefore, they sought to define the issue as one of European armament, not German rearmament. But the EDC advocates were hardly successful in this respect and their opponents presented the European army as a subterfuge through which German rearmament would take place. The national public opinion polls suggest that the anti-EDC forces had much support. For example, in July 1954, only a short time before the National Assembly would vote to destroy the European army, a survey showed that while 36 percent of the French population was willing to sustain EDC, a strong 31 percent was against the project.

A sample of party voters revealed much the same phenomenon. Not surprisingly given an issue of emotive symbolization, with certain exceptions party affiliation bore little relationship to the stand a citizen might take on the treaty itself. Only the Communist and Popular Republican voters were relatively unified in their views. Since the issue cut so deeply across traditional party lines, the argument over the European army found Socialist, Radical, Peasant, and various *modéré* intraparty elites hopelessly at odds with members from their own respective groups. The elites were simply reflecting deep cleavages at the voter levels. The fact that EDC was essentially a question of foreign policy makes this division even more impressive, for usually mass opinion tends to follow government opinion in the area of international politics. As Jean Stoetzel observed, however, in summarizing his study of public attitudes with regard to EDC: "Rightly or wrongly, French opinion could not think of German rearmament without manifesting the most violent fears. There was no majority at any time in favor of German rearmament, and the defeat of EDC (was) inscribed in the collective conscience, still hypersensitive after the three wars." [9]

(2) *The role of the press.* If the general population and party electorates were divided over the possibilities inherent in German rearmament, the press perhaps inadvertently contributed to that division. Much editorial policy was guarded, and many daily newspapers took no stand, or a very moderate one, or contradictory positions. The issue, after all, was a very controversial one, and newspapers did not wish needlessly to alienate subscribers. Nevertheless, the press made sure that the public was kept well aware that EDC would be resolved by the French National Assembly and that, furthermore, the issue was of the utmost importance. Jean José Marchand found that most of the front-page columns of some eighty-one provincial (non-Parisian) daily newspapers were devoted to detailed discussions of EDC for the eight days prior to its defeat in the National Assembly. This concern with a national issue by the provincial press was highly unusual, to say the least. [10]

Moreover, Marchand found that the merits of the proposed bill were seldom debated in either the Parisian or the provincial press and that as the debate proceeded, there was a distinct tendency for much of the press to emphasize a sustained interest only in the problem of German rearmament, not in the purely military or economic aspects of the treaty. Wittingly or not, the concern with German rearmament probably increased tensions within the body politic as a whole, and it most certainly reinforced old prejudices. As a result, the EDC debate was reduced to a question of whether or not Germany should be rearmed; and therefore to support EDC was in fact to advocate a rearmed Germany. Small wonder, then, that the issue so defined became one of emotive symbolization.

(3) *Divisions within the political elite.* The original Pléven Plan was introduced in 1950; the French representative signed the Treaty of Paris on May 25, 1952, thereby creating EDC; but from that point on the forces of resistance set in, and France became the laggard so far as parliamentary ratification of the treaty was concerned.

The benefits of hindsight make it relatively simple to perceive why EDC was doomed almost from the beginning in the National Assembly. A major cause for its defeat certainly was a shifting balance of forces within the French political elite after 1950. The general elections of June 1951 placed in the National Assembly a large number of Gaullists, most of whom were implacably opposed to the European army, and reflected a corresponding decline in support for the MRP and Socialists, each of whom had been favorable in general to EDC. These parliamentary alterations in turn made it increasingly difficult to exclude anti-Europeans from the various cabinet coalitions. For instance, the Pléven government of 1950 included both the

MRP and Socialist party, as well as the redoubtable Robert Schuman in the Foreign Ministry; the Mendès-France government at the time the treaty was defeated was based to a large degree upon Gaullist support.[11]

In a similar manner, after 1950 the more powerful legislative standing committees gradually took on a more anti-EDC coloration. Jules Moch, a Socialist who unceasingly fought EDC, became chairman of the Foreign Affairs Committee during this period, while General Pierre Koenig, a Gaullist and militant nationalist, became chairman of the National Defense Committee.

Although such considerations offer an explanation for the ultimate defeat of EDC, they hardly explain why the conflict was so deeply divisive. Considering that the prospect of German rearmament passionately aroused the public and was emphasized by the nation's press, it is hardly surprising that such concerns would be reflected in even more strident terms in the National Assembly. From what is known of elite attitudes, greater communication, awareness, and concern over EDC would be expected in the Assembly than among the population in general.

The breakdowns in internal party discipline reveal the intensity of the battle within the legislative and executive branches. The vote in the National Assembly on August 30, 1954, which finally killed EDC found most of the parliamentary groups hopelessly split on roll call. With the excep-

Table 2

Index of Party Loyalty on EDC Roll-Call Vote*

(Perfect Cohesion: 100)

| Party | Index |
|-------|-------|
| Communist Party | 100 |
| Radical Socialist Party | 1 |
| Socialist Party | 2 |
| USDR | 54 |
| MRP | 86 |
| Independent Republicans | 50 |
| Peasant Party | 54 |
| ARS (dissident Gaullists) | 7 |
| Social Republicans (Gaullists) | 94 |

*The index of party loyalty, long familiar to political scientists, measures internal party unity by subtracting its minority's vote from that of its majority and then dividing that number by the total party vote:

$$\left( \frac{A - B}{A + B} \times \frac{100}{1} \right).$$

Abstentions were included as being in opposition to established party position if parliamentary party was subject to rigorous discipline.

Source: Daniel Lerner and Raymond Aron, eds., *France Defeats EDC* (New York: Praeger, 1957), p. 162.

tions of the Communists and Social Republicans (Gaullists), who were opposed to EDC for very different reasons, the other parties lacked any meaningful internal unity. In particular, the Socialist, Radical, the various *modéré* groups, dissident Gaullists (*Action républicaine et sociale*), and the USDR (*Union démocratique et socialiste de la Résistance*) tended to divide down the middle over the issue. Even those original supporters of EDC, the MRP, had a few leaders who were in disagreement with provisions in the treaty.[12]

The party battle within the legislative standing committees also exhibited divisive characteristics. Members of prestigious committees in the Fourth Republic National Assembly generally voted closely along traditional party lines, but EDC was a different matter altogether. For instance, both Socialist and Popular Republican members of the Foreign Affairs and Defense Committees opposed their own party policy in committee. As was the case on the floor, behind the scenes EDC cut sharply across existing party lines.[13]

Such breaches of party discipline did not go unnoticed, and possibly because of the highly charged nature of the issue, dissidence was often severely punished. For example, three Socialist leaders (Jules Moch, Daniel Mayer, and Max Lejeune) were actually excluded from the party, although they were later pardoned and allowed to return to the fold. The MRP also discharged two of its deputies and a senator for violating the norm of party discipline. Apparently, some party leaders were in no mood to forgive dissidence over so vital an issue.

The sharp cleavages caused by the conflict over German rearmament were also apparent within the government itself. Premier Mendès-France's behavior was particularly intriguing, for he was surely no ordinary, run-of-the-mill Fourth Republic premier. From his first days as leader, he had broken sharply with parliamentary mores by going over the heads of the various party chieftains to choose his cabinet membership. Moreover, he repeatedly emphasized a contempt for the parliamentary game of politics by articulating a need for responsibility at the top. "To Govern is to Choose" was subsequently the title of one of his books, and he unceasingly spoke of a need to lead, to control, rather than to submit to events. His style as premier was an interesting one, for he enjoyed setting self-imposed deadlines for the resolution of touchy issues, thereby demonstrating forcefully a commitment to personal responsibility for policy making. For example, his settlement of the Indochina crisis in July 1954 at Geneva served to create an impression of dynamic leadership. Certainly no other Fourth Republic premier, with the possible exception of Antoine Pinay, so captured the public imagination.

Yet Mendès-France openly refused to accept responsibility for EDC by staking his government's life on the issue. Rather than risk the implications of a no-confidence vote, he simply presented the proposal to the National Assembly to vote up or down as it saw fit. It has been said in his defense that Mendès-France was being pressured by France's allies as well as by domestic forces to accept a bill with which he personally was most uncomfortable. But this interpretation hardly explains his uncharacteristic position to neither defend or oppose the bill. Perhaps his overt fence-straddling posture is best explained by a realistic observation that a strong stance would simply have cost him too much support—long-run as well as short-run—from too many parties.

Undoubtedly Mendès-France was influenced in his decision not only by the highly rigid views of individual legislators and standing committee members, but also by the cleavages within his own cabinet. Only a few weeks prior to the fateful vote, three Gaullist ministers (Jacques Chaban-Delmas, Maurice Lemaire, and General Koenig) resigned from the government because they resented what they felt were its distasteful compromises with the "Europeans." Then, immediately following the August vote, three other cabinet members (Claudius Petit, Maurice Bourgès-Maunoury, and Emile Hugues) offered their resignations on the grounds that Mendès-France had erred in not supporting EDC. Mendès-France apparently could do nothing to avoid erosions from both his right and his left. To lose six ministers over a single issue suggests that the differences were indeed pronounced.

Ironically, the vote which defeated the European army was not based on the substance of the treaty itself; the roll call was a procedural motion to remove EDC altogether from the parliamentary agenda. Although the pro-European forces had long agitated for a vote on EDC, they were convinced in August 1954 that because of the political climate such a vote might well lead to defeat. They pushed for adjournment, but instead mistakenly allowed a *motion préable* calling for a tabling of the treaty, hardly debated, to come to the floor. Introduced by two militant anti-European backbenchers, Edouard Herriot and General Adolphe Aumeran, the motion passed by 319–264.[14] The Europeans were therefore defeated almost before they knew what had happened. There is, moreover, some evidence that the antitreaty forces were even larger than the vote suggested, and that, if forced, they would have voted against the EDC proponents.

## Conclusion

The European Defense Treaty became an emotive symbolic issue because it was defined largely in terms of the wisdom of rearming the hated Germans, a people with whom the French nation had fought three wars in less than a century. The issue deeply divided Frenchmen, and the public was kept very much aware of EDC by a concerned press. Disagreement on the treaty, which cut sharply across existing political party lines among the voting masses, was strongly reinforced at the topmost parliamentary and cabinet positions. The parliamentary parties and the standing committees were hopelessly divided. Similarly, intraparty divisions were quite severe. The cabinet cleavages were also so deep that Premier Mendès-France could not prevent resignations by both his pro- and anti-European ministers.

This is without doubt a major emotive symbolic type of policy. The issue was certainly not resolved by the more formal leaders in standing committees and cabinet, but was fought out on the floor of the National Assembly. This was bound to occur given the intracabinet and intraparty leadership dissension, not to mention the independent attitudes of ordinary backbenchers. Mendès-France's decision to remain neutral democratized the policy resolution process still further, since there was no stable government leadership against which to react.

A recent roll-call analysis of EDC asserts that the issue's ideological aspects ("issue-specificity") suggest strongly that French politics as a whole has been much more ideological than some writers have recently assumed.[15] Specifically, the study is critical of what it calls the "game of politics" thesis of Nathan Leites, which purportedly gives excessive importance to the personal ambitions and concerns of deputies in explaining their legislative behavior. Actually, EDC demonstrates little in this respect since it was so atypical a debate. Certainly it does not begin to refute Leites' argument, which in its largest sense is a study of French authority relationships and therefore must be criticized on a different level. While it is clear that EDC was a highly ideologically charged battle, one must question its representativeness. In fact, it was an emotive symbolic issue, and such policies simply do not occur with much frequency.

# THE UNITED STATES

### The Controversy Over Civil Rights

Black Americans' demands for equal social and political rights, particularly in recent years, and the resistance of many whites to those demands have led to much tension between the races. Deep-seated fears and prejudices have on various occasions cut asunder those ties which are intended to bind Americans together under a common political system. So long as most blacks remained in the southern part of the nation, tied to a caste type of social system, most of white America was not forced to face the incompatibility of the southern social system with its own proclaimed ideals of political and social equality. The South therefore developed in its own special way; and, in return for a total sectional loyalty to the national Democratic party, it was largely left to its own devices in resolving racial problems. Whenever black rights came into conflict with entrenched southern mores, the latter usually triumphed, and the powerful position of the South within the Democratic party and the halls of Congress choked off appeals for alterations in existing arrangements.

### Background

The exigencies of war, international politics, and industrialization become great social and political levelers. Following World War II, perceptible changes began to occur within the United States. The war was contested in the name of democracy against fascism, and this fact was not lost on returning black soldiers who could not attend the school of their choice, drink from certain fountains, or eat at preferred restaurants. In their first contact with foreign nations, many of these black soldiers had experienced the absence of social barriers they had encountered back in the States; their return home only heightened their awareness of the inherent contradictions between the ideals and the realities of American life.

The needs of foreign policy after the war also helped to facilitate domestic social change. When that great encounter was resolved in favor of democracies at the expense of fascism, a new threat quickly emerged in the form of Soviet communism. This postwar struggle between the Western nations and the Communist powers was to a large extent a contest for the loyalty of the newly emerging ex-colonial nations of the Third World. Since most of the former colonies were nonwhite and therefore highly sensitive to any sign of racism on the part of the ex-colonial powers or their friends, they forced American foreign policy elites to reckon with the costs of a segregated domestic order to American foreign interests. Because domestic and foreign policy could no longer be so neatly separated as in the past, national aims might well be thwarted unless segregation could be ended.

Nonetheless, war and the realities of foreign policy were probably not the major factors contributing to demands for major alterations in black-white relationships. Industrialization and economic boom in the postwar period were very important in creating a growing black awareness of social, political, and legal deprivation. Industrialization unsettled the old rural caste system by encouraging migrations of rural people to the urban centers. Uprooted rural people were exposed to new patterns of living; they saw new choices open to them as never before. Individuals in urban areas, less encumbered by older ways and in closer proximity, were now more open to social mobilization. Older systems of values and authority came into conflict with newly received ones. Radio and television fostered group cohesion and dissatisfaction with the status quo by driving home the point that many Americans were living much richer lives than urban black dwellers. And improvements in communication were bound to erode in time the received systems of truth, even in the predominantly rural regions of the South.

Moreover, growing demands for labor gave many blacks a new economic independence. Such increases in income and social mobility make deprived groups even more aware of and discontented with their relative position, according to social analysts. If one also considers the rising educational level among blacks following the war, one can understand why new demands came to be made upon the political system.

Many politicians quickly noted the blacks' new militancy, and the black migration into the huge urban centers of the North provided new political power. The peculiarities of the American presidential electoral college system give the largest and most urban states a disproportionate power to swing elections, and such states are the very ones where many blacks settled. With such a swing vote, the previously disenfranchised blacks suddenly found an increasing number of champions for their cause in the executive and legislative branches of government. And part of championing their cause was a requirement that politicians do something to aid the urban blacks' friends and relatives in the South.

This rising political power of blacks was bound to result in specific government action to right ancient wrongs. As early as the postwar administration of President Harry S Truman, advocates of broadened civil rights legislation found a supporter for their cause. Employing his immense executive powers, Truman issued orders eliminating segregation in the armed services, prohibited discrimination in the hiring of federal employees, and tried to end discrimination in work carried out by private employers under federal contract.

The president also followed the legislative route in his efforts to end racism in American society. He sought legislation to prohibit the poll tax; he called for an end to segregation in transportation; and he requested a Fair Employment Practices Commission. In this struggle, however, Truman was singularly unsuccessful, and his proposals quickly died in Congress, mostly at the hands of a Senate which had very strong southern representation.

The president's activism was not appreciated by southern politicians. As far as they were concerned, Truman had gone much too far in his legislative programs; when he decided to stand for election in 1948, many southern Democrats walked out of that year's nominating convention. They proceeded to form the Dixiecrat party and nominated Strom Thurmond of South Carolina as their presidential candidate. This act by many white politicians from the South, severing their loyalty to the national party, demonstrated only too well the emerging frenetic and emotional qualities of the racial issue in modern America.

This was only the beginning, however, in the struggles for racial equality. The Eisenhower administration continued along the lines laid down by Truman, and in 1957 and 1960 it pushed through with the aid of key Democrats the first civil rights legislation of the century. The 1957 act empowered the attorney general to seek court injunctions whenever voting rights were infringed upon; it founded a Commission on Civil Rights; and it created a Civil Rights Division in the Justice Department. The major provision of the 1960 bill enabled judges to aid blacks in registering and voting. Finally, during President Eisenhower's tenure of office, federal troops were sent South to enforce public school desegregation for the first time during the Little Rock, Arkansas, episode.

The momentous events of the administration of President John F. Kennedy led directly to the Civil Rights Act of 1964. Kennedy was elected in 1960 by the narrowest of margins, and he very much needed southern support to carry through his program. He therefore delayed proposing formal civil rights legislation during his first two years, although through presidential executive orders he did end discrimination in such areas as federally supported housing.

Although his initial legislative requests in the civil rights field were relatively noncontroversial, events taking place in the South finally led President Kennedy to request a strong program from Congress in June 1963. Beginning in early spring and extending into the summer of 1963, a plethora of sit-ins, boycotts, demonstrations, and well-publicized beatings and even murders of blacks and white sympathizers forced President Kennedy to move much faster than he might have preferred to quell racial hostilities. In introducing his new legislation, he called for a much larger federal effort in the civil rights field. For example, his new program would have allowed the government to file suits to end discrimination in public accommodations as well as to cut off federal funds to areas and programs which discriminated between the races. However, Kennedy's assassination in November 1963 prevented his carrying his proposals to completion, although much of them ultimately found their way into law in 1964 through the efforts of his successor, President Lyndon B. Johnson.

However, the roles of the postwar presidents in the civil rights area should not be exaggerated. In fact, it was the Supreme Court, in a few landmark decisions, which played the major part in the drive for racial equality. In particular, the Court ruled in 1954 in *Brown* v. *Board of Education* that segregation of public schools was unconstitutional. This decision, upsetting a practice long established in the South and reversing an 1896 ruling (*Plessy* v. *Ferguson*), thrust the judiciary into a policy realm where Congress itself had feared to move.

While the outlawing of segregation in the public schools has been the most salient aspect of judicial litigation, the Court has also achieved a remarkable impact in other civil rights spheres as well. For example, the Court prohibited segregation in transportation facilities involved in interstate commerce. It also doomed restrictive covenants which had previously given legal standing to private agreements restraining the sale of property to blacks. Following a series of sit-ins and demonstrations which began in 1960, the Court on various grounds decided in favor of those who had been denied access to restaurants and other places of public accommodation. In expanding civil rights opportunities, the Supreme Court went much further than did the politically elected authorities in Congress or the presidency.

### The Growth of Emotive Symbolization

Growing black awareness of prior deprivations combined with greater optimism about the possibilities for meaningful change would in themselves likely have increased black-white tensions in the South, at least in the short run. But another source of tension lay in the tactic of massive resistance to laws deemed unjust, as enunciated by the Reverend Martin Luther King, Jr., and those who followed him, which invited strong retaliation from hostile whites. The newer tendency to rely upon mass pressures for immediate alterations in the status quo, rather than the slower pace of court decisions, led to increasing mobilization of southern whites and blacks in defense of their perceived interests.

From 1960 on, all of the ingredients of emotive symbolization were present. Civil rights leaders sought the goodwill of the great majority in the rest of the country in an effort to strike down Jim Crow statutes, appealing to a higher law than those laws existing in the South. Their opponents argued that it is always evil to break existing laws, and that any change must come through proper legal or legislative recourse. Seeing reality, and hence legitimacy, through such differing lenses made compromise in civil rights situations exceedingly difficult. The conflict was perceived as one of zero-sum, not mutual adjustment of interests.

Racial conflicts in the 1960s were much more likely to revolve around face-to-face confrontations than in the two previous decades. When the initiative for racial equality was taken by a distant executive and judicial establishment, disgruntled whites did not find it easy to vent their grievances directly. As the civil rights movement turned increasingly to more direct and localized boycotts, demonstrations, and sit-ins, however, it was certainly more difficult to contain the scope and intensity of conflict; that is, to avoid antagonizing the usually more passive, less sophisticated, but more volatile elements in the population. Incompatible versions of what was just law, combined with an increasing number of face-to-face conflicts (as well as brutalities), brought deep-seated racial cleavages into the open with greater force than at any other time in memory.

Discord between the races accelerated rapidly in the years immediately preceding the passage of the Civil Rights Act of 1964. The first sit-in occurred in Greensboro, North Carolina, in February 1960, when college students at North Carolina Agricultural and Technical College protested against racial discrimination at a local dime store counter. The technique quickly spread to other cities and towns, and the sit-in became a major weapon in the racial struggle. Another technique was used the following year when buses carrying "Freedom Riders" drove through the South to test segregation in bus terminals. The rides were marred by some violence and much racial tension along the route.

Civil rights advocates increased their actions in defiance of local laws and customs; when many of their opponents refused to yield and instead turned to violence, protests often ended in bloodshed and arrests. Major demonstrations occurred in the spring of 1963 in such cities as Birmingham, Alabama; Jackson, Mississippi; and Baltimore, Maryland. Even cities in the North were not immune to protests. School boycotts unsettled Chicago and New York City, and quite often demonstrations ended in violence as well. Throughout this period murder inflamed passions on the American scene still more: Medgar Evers, head of the Mississippi branch of the National Association for the Advancement of Colored People (NAACP), was shot in Jackson, Mississippi; a white postman protesting racial discrimination was killed in northeast Alabama; and four children were brutally slain in Birmingham, Alabama.

The civil rights bill of 1964 was therefore contested in a climate of aggravated tension within the American polity. Indeed, in the year preceding its enactment into law, some 800 cities and towns were struck by demonstrations.[16] The year was climaxed by the massive August "March on Washington" by some 200,000 American citizens to pressure Congress into enacting new legislation.

If numerous demonstrations, boycotts, and sit-ins and violence were not enough to inform the public that a major issue was confronting the nation, then surely the assassination of President Kennedy in November 1963 achieved such an impact. This tragedy confirmed what a growing number of concerned citizens had come to believe: that a prior failure to punish violators of the law had created a climate conducive to violence and anarchy. Many blacks, however, saw Kennedy's death in a far different light. Because of his ringing declarations for racial justice, he represented a symbol of justice in the United States.

Ironically, the ultimate passage of a strong civil rights bill may have been due in large measure to Lyndon B. Johnson's elevation to the presidency. As a southerner and so-called moderate on the issue of racial equality, he could hardly employ the tactical options available to his predecessor, a northerner with a stronger record in the civil rights field. Because the new president was not completely trusted by many spokesmen within the liberal constituency of his Democratic party, he had to come forth immediately as a strong proponent of racial equality. Moreover, Johnson was a more skillful negotiator with Congress than was the man he succeeded. Finally, Kennedy's tragic death may have led some congressmen out of sympathy to support a bill they previously would have opposed.

The provisions of the bill as presented by Johnson were contentious enough to bring forth a momentous debate over civil rights. For instance, it facilitated voting by blacks by making a sixth-grade education sufficient for literacy purposes; it enabled the attorney general to file suits to force school integration; it denied federal funds to states, schools, or other organizations which continued to practice segregation; through an Equal Employment Opportunity section, it outlawed discrimination in much of the business and labor world; it guaranteed access regardless of race to such owner-operated facilities as lunchrooms, restaurants, counters, theaters, hotels, stadiums, and large rooming houses; and, to enforce this access to public accommodations, it empowered the attorney general to bring suit when such rights were violated.

Resistance to such a bill was bound to be massive, for its contents struck harshly at the basic values of many Americans. For instance, private property has an aura of sanctity in the United States, and the right of owners to exercise practically unlimited control over their property has been extolled repeatedly. Lawyers and other learned men could argue whether the

1964 bill, in applying the commerce clause of the Constitution to so much of business, had not hopelessly blurred the distinction between private and public; but for many small businessmen and their apologists, a basic right had been removed with one stroke of the legislative pen. Although most of them knew little of constitutional clauses, they felt deeply that a man's right to use his property in the manner he saw fit had been severely compromised by Congress. From their point of view, it was an individual's prerogative if he wished to discriminate between the races so far as his place of business was concerned. Similarly, the provision of the new legislation for monitoring federally supported programs and funds to foster desegregation was bound to antagonize local politicians and bring charges of oppression by a grasping, centralized, omnipresent federal government. The bill was aimed at two forces which commanded a relatively high degree of political influence: small business and the South. In the case of business it conflicted with a value system. In the case of the South it did that and more: it portended the beginning of new social patterns and a changing balance of political power. In such situations men do not tamely give up that which they have hitherto enjoyed.

Yet, as the 1964 act wound its way through Congress, it never did begin to resemble a redistributive issue. This might seem strange given the low status and poverty-ridden situation of large numbers of blacks, especially in the South. However, the demands of the Civil Rights Act of 1964 were addressed essentially to middle-class needs. There was no demand to alter the economic status quo; rather, the right to service in restaurants and motels or to attend better schools, for example, would primarily benefit in the short run relatively well-off blacks seeking middle-class advantages. Business and labor were not ranged in economic battle against one another over this issue; in fact large business interests offered no visible aid and comfort to their small business brethren. Therefore, business and labor did not view the situation in antagonistic terms, and without the aid of large corporate interests, the artisan and shopkeeper were left to their own devices.

The churches also played a large role in reducing the possibility of class conflict. Much of the civil rights leadership in 1964, both black and white, derived from the clergy, who gave moral strength to the demand for racial equality. In fact, church groups were quite important in mobilizing sentiment among Republican legislators who were somewhat uncommitted or neutral on the issue.

Finally, the civil rights struggle of 1964 was primarily one of sectional division, and on the final vote in Congress the southern delegation overwhelmingly opposed the act's provisions. The battle united various classes in other regions against classes in the South. National business and labor organizations were not arrayed in opposition to one another, nor did poor black or white proletarians demand in unison a larger slice of the economic pie at the expense of upper- and middle-class interests. Contrary to an assumption which sometimes appears to underlie Schattschneider's work, the wide socialization of conflict often requires little economic or class conflict; conflict on an emotive symbolic issue is quite sufficient to generate national debate.

## The Struggle in Congress

The civil rights bill of 1964, despite its deeply conflictual quality, passed as easily as it did because leading Democrats and Republicans alike found it possible to work in harmony to assure its passage.[17] This display of bipartisanship at the top was somewhat unusual, for in many instances a conservative coalition of southern Democrats and Republicans had previously throttled more liberal congressional and presidential leadership. By 1964, however, many conservative Republicans had concluded that only federal action in the civil rights field would keep violence to a minimum. The momentum gathered by the civil rights revolution seemed to be propelling it toward even more racial confrontations, and many legislators felt that help from Washington would reduce tensions and give comfort to the more moderate black leaders. Certain younger blacks by this time had begun to argue that meaningful change was impossible within the existing political system.

The chief obstacle to civil rights legislation in the past had come from the Senate, but in 1964 Senate Minority Leader Everett M. Dirksen led many of his Republican troops out of the conservative coalition and joined with northern Democrats to beat back a southern Democratic challenge. The northern Democrat-Republican coalition was equally successful in the House of Representatives. There, Democrat Emanuel Celler, whose House Judiciary Committee had control of the 1964 bill, collaborated closely with his Republican colleague, William M. McCulloch, to forge a similar relationship. Consulting closely with Justice Department officials, these two men and their committee wrote an extremely strong bill which remained largely intact as it wound its way first through the House and then through the Senate. Nonetheless, this new-found bipartisanship did not eliminate the intensity of feeling over civil rights. Senators and representatives from the South were determined to utilize every conceivable legislative device to thwart their opponents on the issue of race.

Southern senators have been unwilling to allow normal procedures to operate within the Senate as far as racial matters are concerned. A main line of defense has been the filibuster. Euphemistically designated "extended debate," the filibuster in reality denotes the refusal to close debate and allow a vote. As a result all legislative business is brought to a standstill. A minority may therefore work its will simply by holding the floor until a majority reluctantly concludes that the costs of further delay outweigh any possible benefits. Of course, such delays in legislative business cause much irritation, and southerners have often been accused by their colleagues of being antidemocratic for refusing to allow votes on the racial issue. For many senators, however, a profound moral dilemma is involved. They may well support the cause of civil rights, but they are exceedingly hesitant to shut off debate in an assembly where the individual's right to have his full say is valued so highly. This stance, of course, plays into the hands of the civil rights opponents.

Because it could not be killed in committee, the civil rights bill of 1964 brought forth a Southern filibuster on the floor. Senator James Eastland's Judiciary Committee ordinarily considered civil rights legislation, but the senator from Mississippi was strongly opposed to black demands for racial equality. To thwart Eastland and his supporters, the leadership decided on a tactic to delay developing a Senate bill and instead to accept a previously passed House version. Senate rules required that legislation initiated in the Senate first be routed through the standing committees; House-sponsored legislation, on the other hand, upon reception from the lower house could be placed immediately on the calendar for consideration on the floor. But contrary to the hopes of Senate Majority Leader Mike Mansfield that the House bill be voted upon in the "morning hour," the southern forces, led by Senator Richard Russell of Georgia, forced a delay in consideration. This tactic forced Mansfield next to ask for a full-scale debate. At that point the southerners began debate as to whether the Senate should take up the bill for consideration. They lost by 67–17. Following the vote on this procedural question, the senators began debate on the substance of the House bill. Finally, on June 8, 1964, more than three months after having first received the House bill, the Senate at last ended the Southern filibuster by invoking cloture by 71–29. A few days later the legislation was voted into law.

The use of the filibuster and cloture in the Senate debate each indicate that an intense battle involving high stakes took place on the floor of the Senate, and that one interest felt it necessary to force its views upon another interest. Similarly, the bypassing of a committee may be regarded as a demonstration of deep disagreement and a willingness to accept the future consequences of procedural deviation. Such issue confrontations suggest a severe breakdown of normal legislative procedures involving peaceful negotiation and compromise. These alterations in normal operating styles are not likely to occur unless politicians become agitated enough to run roughshod over their opposition.

The Senate filibuster is known to the general public as a method by which a determined minority may overrule a majority, but the discharge petition in the House of Representatives has failed to achieve so much notoriety. It may, however, be of equal, if not more, importance in denoting intense conflict within the legislative process. Since both filibuster (as well as cloture) and discharge petition were utilized as legislative weapons during the civil rights debate of 1964, it clearly can be considered a most controversial policy type.

The discharge petition is a method by which a bill can be pried out of a committee in the House of Representatives. Any member may initiate such a procedure by placing a petition on the House Speaker's desk requesting that an individual piece of legislation be discharged from a particular committee so that it might be considered by the entire House. The petition is then left on the Speaker's desk to be signed by individual members of the House of Representatives. If more than half the membership does sign, and if subsequently a majority vote to bring the bill to the House floor, then, and only then, can the bill itself actually be put to a vote.

At a superficial glance nothing could appear less fraught with conflict or unpleasant consequences, but in reality the invoking of a discharge petition implies great consequences for the individual member of the House. In the first instance, it is a departure from normal procedures, intruding into the sacred domain of the congressional committee. The individual congressman who signs such a petition is, in the words of Daniel Berman, made to feel that he is committing an act of heresy. Moreover, to sign such a document is to displease the powerful committee chairmen who can be most helpful to individual backbench members in meeting their personal and constituency needs. In addition, seizing a bill from one committee today can more easily justify a piece of legislation being removed from one's own committee in the future. No, most congressmen reason, far better to let well enough alone and confine oneself to one's own area of interest, else events lead Congress as a whole in directions it would rather not go.[18] With such practical and moral obstacles in the way, it is readily perceived why a majority of signatures is almost impossible to achieve. The successful use of the discharge petition as a weapon against the powerful House Rules Committee in 1964 is testimony to the excitement, emotionalism, and commitment that the racial issue could generate.

When the civil rights bill of 1964 was introduced in the House of Representatives, rather than in the Senate, it was first referred to the House Judiciary Committee, where Celler and McCulloch developed a strong bill. From that point it went to the Rules Committee for consideration, since the latter can determine with few exceptions (e.g., the House Ways and Means Committee may bypass it) what legislation reaches the House floor, the time spent in debate, whether amendments may be considered, who offers them, and how many may be offered.

Under the wily leadership of Chairman Howard Smith, the Rules Committee had long hindered civil rights legislation from reaching the floor for a vote. Smith's main technique was delay, which he achieved simply by refusing to hold hearings on the legislation under consideration. Because his committee had such a stranglehold over all legislation, it is understandable that individual members of the House were reluctant to incur Smith's wrath by signing a discharge petition.

But this was no ordinary bill, and no committee could possibly retain it very long, not even the powerful Rules Committee. As would later occur in the Senate, control over its passage through the House of Representatives passed beyond the confines of the standing committees to the floor of the legislature itself. When the signatures to the discharge petition initiated by Celler and McCulloch mounted in number and finally came dangerously close to the magic majority, Smith, to avoid further humiliation, released the bill and allowed it to go to the House floor. Thus, ordinary backbenchers triumphed for once over one of the most powerful committees on Capitol Hill.

It might possibly be argued that Celler and McCulloch retained control of the bill and that this leadership thereby demonstrates the orthodox rather than the backbench type; but in Celler's decision to pry the bill loose from the Rules Committee, he gave an entirely new dimension to the conflict. He brought eager backbenchers into the decision-making process by helping to mobilize them against the established leadership of the House Rules Committee. Therefore, a part of the House power elite had appealed against another part; backbenchers became the decisive weapon in the decision-making process.

Only a part of the established leadership controlled events, and in appealing to the ordinary members to sign a discharge petition, Celler and his committee lost effective domination of events. From this point on, a new group seized the initiative, primarily under the leadership of a group of backbench House liberals called the Democratic Study Group (DSG). In the case of the 1964 bill, the DSG functioned as a whip organization, a duty ordinarily reserved for the established House leaders such as the Speaker, the majority leader, and especially the authorized whip himself. This is not surprising, however, given the nature of the issue.

In its leadership functions, the DSG sought to mobilize all representatives publicly committed to civil rights by seeking assurances from individual legislators that they would be on the floor during debates over important amendments and, furthermore, that these representatives would not waver when the time came to vote. In these attempts to round up congressmen and to assure their continuing devotion to the cause, the DSG was given immeasurable aid by a coordinating committee of the various civil rights organizations called the Leadership Conference on Civil Rights. Leadership Conference members kept watch over small groups of representatives by carefully recording votes on the floor and, when necessary, sending word to legislators through messengers to hurry to the floor for a crucial ballot. The system was a resounding success since it prevented crippling southern amendments on the floor and therefore kept the bill for the most part in its original committee form.

In addition to congressional activities on behalf of the bill, President Johnson was a particularly influential force in his own right. Throughout the course of the debate he gave moral and political leadership to the civil rights forces. Because of the strong positions southerners occupied within the congressional committee system, previous presidents had been hesitant to risk antagonizing them over racial matters. But from the outset of his own administration Johnson took a strong position on the race issue. His funeral address to a joint session of Congress following Kennedy's assassination was a moving plea for racial justice and swift enactment of the Kennedy legislative program. In his subsequent State of the Union message to Congress, the president gave his personal priority to civil rights legislation. Finally, during the legislative struggle he used his considerable powers of persuasion and the prestige of his office to pressure wavering senators and representatives. His telephone calls to hesitant members proved especially useful to the DSG when signatures were needed in the House of Representatives for the discharge petition.

In sum, once civil rights legislation found its way from behind committee doors, new forces took up leadership. Ordinary House members who signed the discharge petition, the DSG, and the Leadership Conference all joined forces to bring the powerful House Rules Committee to heel.

### Conclusions

Filibuster and cloture, the use of a discharge petition, and backbench leadership all testify to the immensely controversial aspects of civil rights within the Senate and House of Representatives during the 1964 debate. The final votes divided the legislatures along strictly sectional lines; and the racial issue, as usual, splintered the always fragile unity of the Democratic majority. Only strong Republican and presidential support for the bill made passage of the legislation seem more absolute than in fact it was. Nevertheless, one should not forget the atmosphere within which this legislation took place. Strikes, demonstrations, and riots had marred the social peace in the months preceding enactment, and many congressmen, especially Republicans who had grave doubts concerning particular parts of the bill, believed that something had to be done to preserve a peaceful society. In some instances the civil rights forces were able to overcome the resistance of congressmen who came from areas having few black voters or who were deeply worried about the constitutionality of various parts of the bill by using clergymen as lobbyists (in itself suggesting an issue of emotive symbolization).

It is indeed intriguing that such an issue could take place in the United States. Even the great upheavals of 1936 and 1968 in France hardly rivaled this issue in the scope of conflict generated. That old stereotype of the Anglo-American political culture as less emotional and ideological, but more prone toward bargaining, openness, and consensus than the French one, for example, did not manifest itself in the civil rights debate of 1964 and in the events surrounding it.

# CANADA

### The Great Flag Debate

Although many Americans are well acquainted with Canada as a vacationland, few have much knowledge of its political and social institutions. Many Canadians, however, are surely aware of the American presence on the continent. The sheer economic and cultural dominance of an industrial giant of some 200 million people has long been a source of concern for members of the Canadian elite who fear that their nation of some 20 million may be rapidly evolving into a sociocultural extension of the United States. One result has been an identity crisis of the first order.

To avoid becoming an extension of the American personality would be enough of a problem in itself, but the arousal of nationalist tendencies in Quebec in recent years has exacerbated the difficulty of identification and has divided the nation. In the struggle of Anglo-Saxon against Frenchman for the soul of Canada, the immediate threat to the south pales in significance. Nationalism among the French-speaking citizens of Quebec has led its spokesmen increasingly to insist upon a preferred economic role for Quebec within the confederation, to demand a greater place for its culture and language, and, in a few instances, to opt for its independence from Canada. Thus, the major question for Canada has become whether an increasingly assertive Quebec can be peacefully accommodated without disrupting the fabric of the political system. Many doubt that it can.

The response to these pressures from the United States and Quebec has been varied. Anglophiles would reinforce Canadian ties with Great Britain and the British roots as protection against the economic and cultural onslaught of the American giant. The difficulty with this attitude is that, aside from the economic consequences, it has little relevance for a French Quebec long humiliated by Anglo-Saxons and their symbols. While Quebec nationalists may well be anti-American, they are also anti-British; their sympathies lie with reinforcing links with France. Still other Canadians would forge new symbols based on the Canadian experience alone, thereby hoping to reduce English-speaking and French-speaking antagonism. Whether such attempts can placate Quebec is uncertain, for ever since Wolfe defeated Montcalm in 1759, the dominant ethnic groups have derived from the British isles, and a recognition of French sensitivities would require some reorientation of thought. Indeed, the most salient tendency has been strong resistance by ordinary English-speaking Canadians to French demands, a feeling that is particularly pronounced in the Maritimes and in the Prairie provinces. However, most anti-Quebec attitudes derive from ethnic hostilities and not from a self-conscious concern about the quality of Canadian existence; the latter remains principally a matter for intellectuals and politicians. These different views about what kind of nation Canada should aspire to be go far in explaining the so-called great flag debate.

### Background

The flag debate of 1964 symbolized in a most dramatic manner the problem of Canadian identity.[19] Between July 17, 1964, and December 15, 1964, Canadians witnessed one of the most turbulent parliamentary sessions seen in many years. Tempers flared, some 308 speeches were delivered on the merits of particular positions, and legislative attention to other basic needs for the society was brought to a virtual standstill before the disagreement was ultimately resolved.

This dispute arose because throughout its history Canada had never been able to agree upon an official flag which could truly represent all Canadians. Various governments had quietly shelved the issue out of an understandable fear that merely to raise it meant dividing the nation over a piece of cloth. The reluctance of various governments to engage the country over the question betokens a profound fear of the possible conse-quences. A flag would symbolize that which Canada aspired to be, and too many Canadians were divided in their aspirations.

Quite a few early Canadians believed strongly that, as part of the British Empire, this vast land should fly the British Union Jack over its territory. Obviously, such people were often royalists. Nevertheless, over the years there gradually developed a distinct inclination to adopt the Red Ensign as the national flag. The Canadian Red Ensign, based on the flag of the British merchant marine, displayed the Canadian coat of arms in the lower right corner and in its upper right corner the British Union Jack. The advantage of the Red Ensign over the Union Jack was obvious enough: it avoided confusion about which buildings, residences, ships, and other properties were British and which were Canadian. A major reason the Red Ensign has been flown at sea was to assure the vessel's recognition as distinctly Canadian. Moreover, the Red Ensign in time developed a legiti-macy within its own right, since it was displayed as the flag of Canadian troops during the two major wars of this century.

The various governments also seemed to give their tacit blessings to the Red Ensign over the years. True, the British colonial secretary said in 1912 that the Union Jack was the proper flag for Canadians to fly, but the British Admiralty as early as 1892 had authorized that the Red Ensign be flown on all Canadian ships. Similarly, various Canadian governments simply operated as if the Red Ensign were indeed the proper flag for Canada. An order-in-council in 1924 permitted its use at diplomatic offices abroad, and a similar order-in-council as late as 1945 permitted its use as the Canadian flag until Parliament saw fit to designate a purely Canadian banner. Thus, through custom, legality, and especially pragmatism, the Red Ensign rather than the Union Jack acquired respectability as the official flag.

Yet ordinary Canadians themselves were far from agreement on what kind of flag should represent them as a nation. Public opinion polls taken periodically over the years conclusively attested to a profound lack of national unanimity on the issue.[20] Despite official support, the Red Ensign did not achieve nearly the popular support which might be logically ex-pected; more Canadians seemed to prefer a distinctly national flag.

Table 3
Choice of Flag for Canada by Canadians

| Type | 1952 | 1953 | 1962 | 1963 |
|------|------|------|------|------|
| A New National Flag | 46 | 39 | 46 | 45 |
| The Union Jack | 30 | 35 | 26 | 25 |
| The Red Ensign | 14 | 15 | 18 | 16 |

Source: Mildred A. Schwartz, *Public Opinion and Canadian Identity* (Berkeley, Calif.: University of California Press, 1967), p. 107.

Moreover, with the passage of time the Union Jack declined in popularity to a greater extent than did the other two choices, whose support remained relatively stable. There is also some evidence that Red Ensign supporters preferred a distinctly new type of flag for their second choice. For instance, 79 percent of the respondents polled in August 1958 opted for an entirely new flag for Canada, distinct from any found elsewhere.[21]

As Table 4 suggests, there were large regional variations in attitudes toward an entirely new national flag, and such support, as in so many issue areas of conflict, tended to pit Quebec against English-speaking Canada. Small wonder, then, that the flag debate became charged with intense partisanship. To a large extent, the Liberal party was based in Quebec, whereas the Progressive Conservatives were much stronger elsewhere. The flag issue ultimately became one more dispute between the major ethnic forces of Canada; and because the PCs rallied to a flag based upon North America's British heritage, they discovered to their chagrin Quebec Conservatives breaking ranks to join the Liberals.

Perhaps the flag issue would have remained confined to the world of the pollsters had Prime Minister Lester B. Pearson been content to allow it to do so. He felt strongly that the flag disagreement ought to be resolved one way or another and, furthermore, that the flag ultimately selected should be acceptable to all Canadians—English, French, or whatever. He was therefore determined to do the one thing his predecessors had scrupulously avoided, to take the risk of irreparable ethnic division by bringing the issue into Parliament for debate and resolution by vote. Thus, at his instigation the Liberal party in its 1961 platform solemnly pledged to establish a Canadian flag within two years of taking office. Pearson made his pledge official on May 14, 1964, at a meeting of the Royal Canadian Legion.

Both practical and moral considerations may have influenced Pearson in his grave decision to raise the flag issue. His government's commitment to a distinct Canadian flag would be welcomed in a Quebec forever suspicious of British symbolic trappings. As champions of a strictly Canadian pennant without Empire symbols, the Liberal party might hope to reinforce credit in its traditional bastions of electoral strength. In addition, the prime minister was a liberal with a small "l." He optimistically faced a Canadian

Table 4

Percent Favorable by Region to a New National Flag

| Year | Quebec | Ontario | Maritimes | West |
|------|--------|---------|-----------|------|
| 1962 | 69 | 40 | 19 | 38* |
| 1963 | 74 | 35 | 23 | 35 |

*Average of Prairies (41 percent) and British Columbia (35 percent)

Source: Schwartz, *Public Opinion and Canadian Identity*, p. 108.

future shorn of its past all too often scarred with ethnic cleavages. As a small "l" liberal he was also oriented essentially toward the individual, not as a member of a traditional grouping so much as a person qua person. In his opinion a neutral flag would not so easily arouse the more parochial ethnic loyalties, and it might even contribute to the elimination of ethnic disagreements among Canadians. Out of a genuine concern to avoid antagonizing either of the "two nations" of Canada, Pearson introduced into the House of Commons what came to be derisively referred to as "the Pearson pennant," a flag with three maple leaves meeting in a single stem, against a white background with lines of blue on the upper and lower parts.

At first glance the hostility with which the prime minister's resolution was greeted is surprising, for the bland quality of his flag should have precluded its offensiveness to any groups. But Conservative party leader John Diefenbaker was hardly the man to allow the new banner to go uncontested. Like his opponent, he had both practical and ideological reasons for adopting his own particular stance on the issue. The Progressive Conservatives found their greatest support in those areas settled by British immigrants; they needed little more practical encouragement to fight for the retention of British symbols. Moreover, Diefenbaker was an Anglophile; he had long spoken out for the British fact. Also, because he was a tory in the deepest sense, he could see little utility in flags which denied the Canadian heritage; to him Pearson's flag was no flag at all. Diefenbaker was certainly not anti-French, but he was a strong nationalist, firmly arrayed against the centrifugal forces which threatened Canadian society. He therefore tended to perceive French-Canadians as merely another ethnic group, surely not entitled to special treatment; so any loose talk about "two nations" appeared to him as perfidious prattle.

Despite their closeness in age, therefore, no two men could have been more different than were Pearson and Diefenbaker. Diefenbaker never tired of recalling the past while Pearson continually spoke of future possibilities. Their differences in this context would probably have mattered little had they not been spokesmen for such different forces in the flag dispute. In this instance, so-called "cross-cutting" cleavages were hardly operative since each major party was so anchored in particular sectional and ethnic loyalties. Therefore, the party battle reflected a far deeper conflict within the Canadian community, i.e., one which pitted French culture against the English heritage. The Maple Leaf and the Red Ensign became the symbols of that division.

## The Growth of Conflict

The great flag debate was unusually contentious for Canada. From the moment Prime Minister Pearson decided to make it an issue, he must have looked to the future with foreboding. His public announcement of May 17, 1964, before the Royal Canadian Legion was greeted with catcalls, derision, and demonstrations; and worse still, the spectacle was subsequently shown on television throughout Canada. From that day forward the public was increasingly aroused, and when Mr. Pearson introduced his flag proposal in Parliament in mid-June, the turmoil and dissension were so pronounced that all other legislation up for consideration had to be put aside. For some six months the flag dispute dominated all else in political life.

The extent to which the public involved itself in the dispute was shown in many instances. For example, immense demonstrations were held on the grounds of Parliament in Ottawa. At a large gathering in Toronto Maple Leaf and Red Ensign supporters were prevented from coming to violent blows only through the timely intervention of the Royal Canadian Mounted Police (RCMP). Even meetings of political professionals became less gentlemanly. At an early June gathering of the Confederation of Mayors and Municipalities, the sessions were repeatedly disrupted by demonstrations. Only preventive measures by the RCMP kept violence to a minimum.[22]

Many more Canadians, of course, preferred to display their feelings about their particular flag preferences through more conventional means. Thousands of students and other groups signed petitions and forwarded them to the prime minister and to Parliament. MPs reported during the course of the debate that the volume of mail received from their ridings (constituencies) was the heaviest in memory. In British Columbia 18,000 names signed to a single petition were sent to Ottawa pleading for retention of the Red Ensign. The barrage of mail which found its way to the office of the prime minister was so great that the government was forced to increase sharply its secretarial service. In little more than two weeks following his May 17 speech, Pearson received more than 8,000 letters devoted to the flag problem.[23]

## Protracted Debate within the House

The battle within the House of Commons could hardly have been more intense, and disagreement over whether the flag design should include the Maple Leaf or the Red Ensign led some MPs to behave in totally uncharacteristic ways, according to experienced observers of the Canadian political scene. The violation of procedural rules and norms and, in general, the vituperativeness of the debates seemed rather strange since there was a wide range of forces arrayed in favor of a distinct Canadian flag. Indeed, there was little expectation from the very beginning that Prime Minister Pearson would suffer a defeat, given the sympathy for an independent flag expressed by the New Democratic party (NDP) and the *Créditistes* (Quebec branch of Social Credit) of Réal Caouette. But by the time the Diefenbaker-led Conservatives had completed their onslaught, Parliament could think of little else but flags. Observers would not soon forget this momentous struggle between the forces for a new Canada and those who wished to recapture the illustrious past of Empire—or to be more realistic, the bitter fight over symbols favorable to English-speaking Canadians and symbols deemed inoffensive to French-speaking Canadians.

The rising tension within the Canadian polity following Pearson's announcement of May 17 made many parliamentarians quite nervous about the possible consequences of the struggle. The major political groupings therefore tried to avoid responsibility for any results which might ensue. The behavior of the prime minister is quite instructive in this instance. Possibly because the great majority in his own party seemed to be in favor of a distinctly Canadian flag, Pearson at first decided to make the issue a test of confidence in his government, although he conceded at the same time that the issue was fundamentally one for the individual MP to decide according to the dictates of his own conscience. This position was not particularly welcome to certain Liberal followers who quite rightly felt they were being placed in a most ambivalent position. On the one hand, they were being requested to consult their own consciences as to what was right and proper, while on the other hand, they were being warned that the government regarded their vote as one of confidence in its ability to continue in office. Therefore, such a vote was not really free in the least, since the government might feel the necessity to resign in the face of an adverse decision, thereby propelling the party into an unwanted election campaign.

Perhaps Pearson might be excused for taking such an ambivalent position since he was undoubtedly aware of the potential explosiveness of the issue, which might well fracture unity within his own party. For instance, a small group of Liberals from the more rural and English-speaking parts of Canada and quite often from the Maritimes were uneasy with the Pearson pennant. These men derived from a party tradition "emotionally and intellectually wedded to the French Canada,"[24] but they also were subject to constituency pressures opposed to the Maple Leaf. Party tradition and normal pressures to conform to government leadership were ultimately sufficient to neutralize their desire to break away from the majority of their peers, but they must have given their leaders some anxious moments behind the scenes.[25]

In the days immediately following his May speech, Pearson appeared content to ride out the criticism, but the grass-roots outcry later caused his confidence to waver. In August he did an about-face by designating the flag issue as a free vote after all. The parliamentary vote as a result would not endanger his government, at least in the short run. Since he could not easily dominate events in the normal ways of parliamentary government, he tempered his intention to lead by withdrawing his prior decision to engage his government's responsibility. Quite simply, the issue was, in Diefenbaker's own words as quoted in the Toronto *Globe and Mail* (August 17, 1964), "too hot to handle." Significantly, the prime minister's stance immediately reduced tensions, and Pearson was widely praised in Parliament for his action.[26]

The Conservatives also produced their own version of a free vote, proposing a national plebiscite to resolve the flag dispute. Such a suggestion is highly unusual. It distorts the parliamentary form of government because it erodes the concept of the cabinet's responsibility to the legislature. Moreover, to call for a national referendum in Canada was to summon up painful memories of its past. In particular, it made many Canadians recall the plebiscite of 1942 on conscription for overseas service. In that year Canada was severely split when an isolationist-prone Quebec reacted strongly against being forced by an English-speaking majority into what Quebec considered an unjust war. History might be repeated if a new plebiscite resulted in English-speaking Canada forcing a flag with British symbols upon a Quebec increasingly restive in its subordinate position. Many observers were convinced that the reaction to the results of such a vote would be extreme indeed.[27]

Since the Liberals had much to lose and little to gain from a plebiscite, they naturally resisted the Conservative solution. From a practical standpoint, the Liberals, with the NDP and *Créditiste* legislators, could hope for victory in the House of Commons. Nonetheless, the Conservative proposal placed them in an awkward dilemma. To respond negatively was to risk being called antidemocratic on an issue of basic importance to all Canadians; to support a plebiscite meant antagonizing Quebec, the source of so much Liberal parliamentary support. To draw out the debate in the usual manner, however, might exacerbate tensions within the House to the point of impairing future working relationships between the two major parties.

At this point, in early September, the Pearson cabinet turned the flag problem over to an all-party parliamentary committee for resolution. The government pledged itself to abide by the committee's ultimate decision. The committee of fifteen, which included seven Liberals, five Conservatives, and a single representative from each of the other parties, was an attempt to avoid responsibility for what was by then a highly charged issue. The committee device is often resorted to by leaders when they calculate that they can only lose in assuming leadership functions. The Pearson government had decided that it had nothing to gain in prolonging the debate, so it was now prepared to let others resolve the issue, which might be expected given the type of policy involved.

The Conservatives were not about to let Pearson and his colleagues off so easily, for they were unwilling to allow a redefinition of the issue and resisted its transfer to another arena for resolution. Diefenbaker's response was to accept the committee decision only if it approached unanimity, and, as he put it, "a high degree of unanimity" implied at least thirteen committee members in agreement. Thus, when the all-party parliamentary committee subsequently reported in favor of a single maple leaf design by a vote of ten to four (Pearson's design called for three leaves), the government immediately accepted the decision. Diefenbaker, however, resumed his offensive by calling once again for a plebiscite.

There was clearly a tendency on the part of Liberal and Conservative leadership alike to avoid responsibility in a constitutional order which makes the concept of responsibility one of its formal and normative capstones. But the nature of the issue under consideration precludes ordinary types of political behavior. Free votes, special committees, and plebiscites are all directed toward the avoidance of political and organizational responsibility and blame for whatever consequences may ensue. In parliamentary systems such devices are looked upon with more trepidation and wariness than in presidential systems such as the United States, mainly because they violate widely acknowledged procedural norms. This is especially true of plebiscites, somewhat less true of free votes which may be justified on grounds of conscience, but even less true of special committees (e.g., Royal Commissions and other appointive groups which often function to gain time and/or to push issues into the background away from greater public scrutiny).

These were, however, not the only indications that the politics of an emotive symbolization issue were taking place. For instance, it became obvious early in the flag debate that the Conservatives were deliberately resorting to filibustering tactics in order to prevent a vote on the "Pearson pennant." It is rather unlikely that their long-winded speeches were contrived as part of an effort to force the government into calling an early election.[28] An immediate election was hardly in the Conservative interest, for the party's financial condition was quite precarious then, and many Tories were deeply vexed over perceived weaknesses in Diefenbaker's leadership qualities. Therefore, a more likely explanation for Diefenbaker's tactic lay in his long-time fervent Empire loyalties as well as his belief that he was taking a position acceptable to the greatest number of Canadians. Whatever the reason for the ill-disguised filibuster, Conservative orators delivered some 210 speeches in the course of the debate and refused almost totally to cooperate with the government on its legislative timetable. For example, at the end of June, with a summer recess approaching, the government sought a temporary delay in the flag debate in order to pass an interim supply bill of three months. Pearson also hoped to enact six other pieces of legislation before resuming consideration of the flag, but the Conservatives steadfastly refused to cooperate. Claiming that he only wished to gain all the facts, Diefenbaker deliberately delayed a vote on the supply bill in order to prevent any consideration of the flag design before the recess. Such obstructionist tactics were quite typical throughout the entire period of the debate.[29]

Conservative obstructionism reached its high point in September when party spokesmen refused to support the all-party parliamentary committee, even though some of its own committee representatives had voted with the Liberal members in support of the single maple leaf pennant. This amusing coincidence of opinion occurred when, contrary to Tory expectations, the Liberal committee members voted for the single maple leaf flag rather than the one favored personally by Pearson. Such embarrassment, however, did not prevent Diefenbaker and his colleagues from renewing the struggle with gusto.

Diefenbaker's endeavor to continue the Conservative filibuster even after the all-party committee had reported, however, led many members of Parliament to turn against him and demand an end to the debate. He now found it increasingly difficult to maintain discipline among his own troops. A growing number of MPs began to talk freely about doing the one thing almost universally abhorred, to invoke closure. In Canada closure is an unusually sure sign of deep stress, and is regarded as even more distasteful by Canadian legislators than by their British counterparts. Until 1964, closure had been used only eight times in the history of the Canadian House of Commons.[30] The last time it had been invoked was in 1956, when a Liberal government had restricted debate on a pipeline bill. An all-Canadian pipeline had been proposed to carry natural gas from the fields of Alberta to the eastern industrial markets. Numerous smaller communities would have been aided along the way. The traumatic impact of that battle was well remembered even in 1964. As Blair Fraser put it so well with regard to the flag debate:

> Since the pipeline debate in 1956 an almost superstitious horror had grown up against using the ultimate weapon of closure to choke off debate. Both major parties, or large sections of them, really believed the Liberals had been turned out of office in punishment for using this sinful device, and to use it in so emotional an issue as the flag seemed to be, was considered doubly dangerous.[31]

Despite profound fears of the consequences of closure, a parliamentary majority was eventually mustered in support of it for several reasons. The protracted struggle for their own version of a flag finally eroded the resistance of many Conservatives, but also stiffened the staying powers of those in favor of a neutral design. Between mid-May and mid-December the House heard little but flag speeches, and all other legislative business was brought to a halt. Emotions were spent, and by December many MPs had become bored with the whole enterprise. Demands were increasingly heard for resolving the debate one way or another, by any means. At first such behavior seems somewhat strange for men who had recently invested so much emotional capital defending their own version of a pennant; but on reflection, however, it is not so strange. Weariness itself sometimes forces a consensus, as anyone well acquainted with committee meetings can attest. Furthermore, after the all-party committee had reported, increasing public demands that the issue be settled may have led many legislators to conclude that continued legislative stagnation might well redound against their interests outside the halls of Parliament.

Diefenbaker's determination to obstruct the business of the House and, if possible, to prevent a vote on the flag issue gradually began to anger a growing number of parliamentarians. In particular, after the committee had reported, it appeared to some of Diefenbaker's followers that to struggle any longer for the Red Ensign was fruitless and unreasonable. The Tory leader began to appear as a selfish obstructionist, determined to get his own way whatever the costs.

All these pressures had an effect upon Conservative morale, but it was a small band of Quebec Conservatives, particularly disenchanted with the Tory leadership, who openly revolted and hence eroded the united front against the Liberals. These Quebec members of Parliament were especially fearful that Diefenbaker's tactics would destroy their reelection chances, so they could see little sense in making the sacrifice, especially for a flag with British symbols. Led by Léon Balcer, they defied party discipline on several key votes, and Balcer publicly invited Pearson to invoke closure. Actually, the Balcer faction had been understandably unsympathetic throughout the debate to the Conservative position. Nine members of the Quebec delegation were French-speaking and a tenth had many constituents of French ancestry. On key votes the Quebec delegation backed the Pearson government rather than its own party majority. On closure, Quebec MPs voted 4–3 against the motion; they balloted 8–0 for Pearson's single maple leaf design; and they voted 8–0 against the Conservative attempt to recommit the bill to committee.[32]

With such defections from Conservative ranks, Pearson had little trouble in gaining his majority for a distinctly Canadian flag; in addition to his own Liberals (minus one), he received strong support from the other parties. As Professor W. E. Lyons has said:

> In the House of Commons the voting was almost exclusively along French-English lines. The twelve *Créditistes,* all from Quebec, supported the maple leaf flag *en masse.* The performance of the regular Social Credit caucus featured Quebec MPs casting ballots against MPs from western Canada. The PC split along French-English lines, with the ten Quebec PCs casting votes against Diefenbaker's red ensign supporters.[33]

For an issue which burst upon the Canadian political scene with such ferocity and created such deep cleavages in Parliament, the great flag debate ended with little fanfare. Canadians were so thoroughly weary of all the commotion about alternative flag designs that once closure was voted upon and the conflict finally terminated in the early morning hours of December 15, 1964, the press took almost no notice of the event. In retrospect, it appears that the all-party committee report served a cathartic function by thoroughly demobilizing opposition to the maple leaf. The remainder of the debate was simply going through the motions to a predetermined end.

## Conclusion: The Politics of "Ideological Reaffirmation"?

The flag debate in general is a typical study in the politics of emotive symbolization. There was certainly nothing unexpected in the manner in which the debate upset so many of the usual political conventions. The attempt to democratize the issue by introducing a plebiscite, the public concern shown by demonstrations and correspondence to political leaders, the procedural unorthodoxy in the House of Commons, the large number of speeches, amendments, and delays on the House floor, and a free vote situation in which the government refused to accept responsibility all delineate quite well the politics of value expressiveness.

This case study, however, does provide an interesting nuance when compared with other cases. It might be useful to designate the case as the "politics of ideological reaffirmation," a possible species of the genus emotive symbolization, for although the flag debate did produce some deviation by Quebec MPs within the Progressive Conservative party, the governing Liberals tended to remain cohesive. This degree of party discipline appears rather surprising until one realizes that the cleavage brought about by the flag conflict coincided so neatly with the Canadian party divisions generally. In all probability such a coincidence does not occur often, but whenever it does, it has interesting consequences. Orthodox party and government leaders are given a decisive role to play denied them in other instances of emotive symbolization. This reinforcement of leadership takes place simply because leaders can express more easily the demands made upon them by their backbench followers.

## CONCLUSIONS

The emotive symbolic type of policy and cases considered in this chapter are highly conflictual, cutting for the most part across various kinds of sociopolitical and economic groupings. Because these issues excite such large-scale, intense involvement, it is normal for ordinary legislators to look for guidance to their individual consciences but even more to their constituents, thereby refusing to accept the leadership of their nominal political superiors. The usual result is a breakdown of party discipline and the development of legislative individualism. Because of the broad and deep cleavages wrought by these issues, leaders as a rule find it expedient to avoid staking out positions except upon those relatively rare occasions when the cleavage over the issue corresponds roughly to normal partisan political divisions.

There are certain dissimilarities which should be mentioned with regard to the specific American, Canadian, and French Fourth Republic cases presented above. The EDC debate split almost every French political party down the middle, wreaking havoc among the more centrist and governing parties. The civil rights controversy in the United States caused much conflict within the governing Democratic party, in whose ranks the great majority of southerners resided and through which some southerners occupied key positions in the legislative hierarchy. On this issue the Republicans were arrayed against the political power of the South. The consequence was to pit the South as a region against other regions. Unlike Premier Mendès-France, President Johnson could more readily become involved in the dispute, for he could count upon the minority party as well as a major portion of his own party. Finally, the Canadian flag dispute provides an excellent illustration of a wide and deep conflict which coincided rather neatly with political and party divisions. Unlike the American and French case studies, it involved little deviation in party voting on the issue. Although Prime Minister Pearson found it expedient to lift the whips and call for a free vote, he nonetheless could play a more informal leadership role since most of his followers came from areas of Canada relatively favorable to his particular version of a flag.

In general, one might speculate that certain kinds of political systems are especially vulnerable to outbreaks of emotive symbolic issue conflicts. It can be hypothesized that the fewer the institutional barriers placed between the legislator and his constituency, the greater the likelihood that such policies will arise. To be more specific, it may be that the British parliamentary system with its fusion of executive and legislature, its party discipline, and its majoritarianism better serves to insulate legislators from sudden and massive demands than does either the American system with its separation of powers, checks and balances, and lack of party discipline, or the French Fourth Republic with its coalition governments composed of several parties.

The reasoning behind this view is as follows: large-scale outbursts of emotive symbolization are less likely to become a reality if ordinary legislators are subject to party discipline and penalties for party dissidence and are keenly aware that disloyalty may threaten the political life of their government. In this respect parliamentary procedural devices such as the free vote may function as a safety valve for coping with highly discordant issues such as capital punishment or homosexuality. At least this seems to be true of Great Britain, where in four cases involving capital punishment and homosexuality, the whips were indeed lifted (see Appendix). The typicality of this phenomenon is, of course, open to question, however, since there are so few cases.

On the other hand, there are fewer reasons to conform to leadership demands in nations like the United States and Fourth Republic France. In these countries the benefits deriving from disloyalty to party may far outweigh the costs. Discipline is unenforceable in the United States, while a major characteristic of the Fourth Republic was government by party coalitions in which the existing leadership was fragile, ephemeral, and tenuous, unable to control more than a handful of deputies at any one time. This was especially characteristic of those parties which actually governed or were potential governors of the country.

## NOTES

1. Daniel Katz, "The Functional Approach to the Study of Attitudes," *Public Opinion Quarterly*, Summer 1960, pp. 163–204; also, see the study of Silvan Tomkins, "Left and Right: A Basic Dimension of Ideology and Personality," in Robert W. White, ed., *The Study of Lives* (New York: Atherton Press, 1963), pp. 389–411.

2. Katz, "The Functional Approach," p. 173.

3. James B. Christoph, *Capital Punishment and British Politics* (Chicago: University of Chicago Press, 1962), p. 173.

4. Ibid., p. 174.

5. Ibid., pp. 175–80.

6. See Raymond Aron, "Historical Sketch of the Great Debate," in Daniel Lerner and Raymond Aron, eds., *France Defeats EDC* (New York: Praeger, 1957), p. 5. This volume of essays remains one of the best so far as the domestic aspects of EDC are concerned.

7. Ibid., p. 10.

8. A thorough study of public opinion at this juncture may be found in Jean Stoetzel, "The Evolution of French Opinion," in *France Defeats EDC*, pp. 72–101.

9. Ibid., p. 89

10. See Jean José Marchand, "A Tableau of the French Press," in *France Defeats EDC*, pp. 102–25.

11. E.g., see Jacques Fauvet, "Birth and Death of a Treaty," in *France Defeats EDC*, pp. 128–30.

12. Duncan MacRae, Jr., *Parliament, Parties, and Society in France: 1946–1958* (New York: St. Martin's Press, 1967), pp. 125–29.

13. See Philip M. Williams, *Crisis and Compromise: Politics in the Fourth Republic* (Garden City, N.Y.: Anchor Books, 1966), pp. 263–64.

14. See Fauvet, "Birth and Death of a Treaty," p. 162; and MacRae, *Parliament, Parties, and Society in France,* p. 127. For a breakdown of the vote on August 30, 1954, see Fauvet, ibid.

15. See Arnold Kanter, "The European Defense Community in the French National Assembly: A Roll Call Analysis," *Comparative Politics,* January 1970, pp. 203–28. In addition to Leites, such writers as Stanley Hoffman, Harry Eckstein, and especially Michel Crozier might be mentioned as utilizing in varying ways the authority relationships concept.

16. At least according to *Revolution in Civil Rights* (Washington, D.C.: Congressional Quarterly Service, 1965), p. 39.

17. Detailed studies of the 1964 Civil Rights Act to be considered here may be found in no better place than Daniel M. Berman, *A Bill Becomes Law: Congress Enacts Civil Rights Legislation* (New York: The Macmillan Co., 1966), 2nd ed.; and Congressional Quarterly Service, *Revolution in Civil Rights.* These two works were consulted heavily in preparing this section.

18. The problems involved in gaining the release of a bill from the Rules Committee are explored in detail in Berman, *A Bill Becomes Law,* pp. 88–97.

19. From a political scientist's standpoint, probably the best study of the flag debate is Henry S. Albinski, "Politics and Biculturalism in Canada: The Flag Debate," *The Australian Journal of Politics and History,* August 1967, pp. 169–88. Other general studies one might consult are the following: J. D. Heasman, "The Politics of Canadian Nationhood," *Parliamentary Affairs,* Spring 1966, pp. 144–61; "The Great Flag Debate: Maple Leaf Rampant," in Blair Fraser, *The Search for Identity: Canada, 1945–1967* (Toronto: Doubleday Canada Ltd., 1967), chap. 23; and "The Great Flag Debate," in Peter C. Newman, *A Nation Divided: Canada and the Coming of Pierre Trudeau* (New York: Alfred A. Knopf, 1969), chap. 18.

20. Mildred A. Schwartz, *Public Opinion and Canadian Identity* (Berkeley, Calif.: University of California Press, 1967), pp. 106–10.

21. Ibid., pp. 106–7.

22. See the following issues of the *Globe and Mail* (Toronto) for discussions of such conflicts: May 27, 1964; June 2, 1964; June 3, 1964; July 3, 1964. Also, see Albinski, "Politics and Biculturalism in Canada," p. 185.

23. See, for example, the *Globe and Mail* (Toronto), May 23, 1964; June 3, 1964; July 3, 1964.

24. W. E. Lyons, "The New Democratic Party in the Canadian Political System," (Ph.D. diss., The Pennsylvania State University, 1965), p. 393.

25. These points were brought to the author's attention in the course of a conversation with Professor W. E. Lyons of the University of Kentucky.

26. The *Globe and Mail* (Toronto), August 22, 1964.

27. Albinski, "Politics and Biculturalism in Canada," pp. 182–83.

28. This is the contention of Newman. See his *A Nation Divided*, p. 259. Nevertheless, this interpretation does not appear to be generally accepted as the major explanation for Diefenbaker's behavior. See, for example, Albinski, "Politics and Biculturalism in Canada," p. 184; also, the *Globe and Mail* (Toronto), November 4, 1964.

29. The *Globe and Mail* (Toronto), July 1, 4, 1964; also, see issues of August 1, 4, 6, 14, 1964.

30. The *Globe and Mail* (Toronto), December 12, 1964.

31. See Fraser, *The Search for Identity*, p. 245.

32. Albinski, "Politics and Biculturalism in Canada," pp. 184–85.

33. See Lyons, "The New Democratic Party," p. 393.

# 5

# THE POLITICS OF REDISTRIBUTION

**T**HE redistributive type of policy is not nearly so prevalent in modern Western democracies as are the other three types considered in this book. The intense antagonisms redistributive issues evoke between socio-economic classes are so striking that it is difficult to see how any political system could withstand the strain of numerous redistributive demands. However, they may be more infrequent today because modern industrial systems have reduced the size of the traditional proletariat and bourgeoisie, increased the variation and divisions within a growing middle- and white-collar class, and homogenized life-styles and values in general through mass media and the effects on consumption patterns. Hence, it is hardly surprising that issues capable of exciting class cleavages in a Marxian sense occur with less frequency in Western systems.

Redistributive issues tend to be defined by the participants in the conflict in such a way as to offer severe prospects to the losers in the struggle, including deprivations in their incomes, jobs, and economic security. It is for this reason that the short-run stakes in the battle are likely to be perceived as even more important than those in the great majority of emotive symbolic struggles. After all, the daily lives of most people are largely unaffected by changes in flag styles, abolition of the death penalty, or the elimination of prayer in the public schools.

Unlike sectorally fragmented struggles, which are limited to sectors, but like emotive symbolic ones, redistributive cases are characterized by a great intensity and wide scope of conflict.[1] Roughly speaking, because a redistributive struggle impinges upon class relationships, the structure of the conflict is much more predictable than in sectorally fragmented disputes, where varying issues give rise to varying sectoral participants, or in emotive symbolic instances, where there is a strong tendency for issues to cut across numerous social and economic groupings.

Since redistributive conflicts are limited in a general way to class relationships, it is not surprising that a more or less continuing body of leaders will represent the major classes; i.e., a more stable conflict structure in turn generates a more stable leadership structure. For this reason, large peak associations of management and labor assume leadership positions in the redistributive area to an extent never possible in emotive symbolic or sectorally fragmented issues. Since peak organizations bring so many diverse interests under their umbrellas, they might well find their own membership taking different stands on sectoral types of issues, but on redistributive ones they can take positive positions without running the risk of antagonizing some part of their membership. When an issue impinging upon class relationships occurs, such mammoths as the Confederation of British Industries (CBI), the National Council of French Employers (CNPF), and the National Association of Manufacturers (NAM) and their trade union equivalents become quite agitated. Activation will probably take the form of emotionally charged ideological debates and pronouncements, with each side loudly proclaiming the virtues and legitimacy of free enterprise or the rights of the working man. The conflict takes on a strong ideological dimension.[2] More ominously, the struggle will be marked by riots, demonstrations, industrial strikes, sit-ins, or lock-ins.

Furthermore, peak associations negotiate with their opposite numbers in the political elite, such as presidents and prime ministers. Despite the large involvement by the public, in cases of wide class conflict orthodox spokesmen for major class interests assume positions of leadership. This flow of influence to the top makes it extremely difficult for legislatures to contain such struggles within their halls. As Gustave Le Bon observed long ago about the individualistic French National Assembly of the last century, the threatened imposition of new taxes gave leaders a control over their own factions never possible in ordinary circumstances. He noted that on "local grants" (distribution) opinions were very stable, with each deputy going his own respective way; but if a tax issue arose, the deputies became quite agitated and coalesced around particular leaders.[3] A consequence of such issues, especially in two-party systems, may be to reinforce legislative party discipline—in itself favorable to prime ministerial and presidential decision making—with a cutting adrift of the more recalcitrant minority elements.

In multiparty systems such as France or Italy, however, it is the center parties and their leaders who are likely to suffer most in redistributive cases, although they can most easily deal with sectorally related and distributive issues. In a polarized social environment, however, the leaders are apt to be forced into retirement by more coherent, homogeneous, and ideologically pure coalitions.[4] While the same economic elites are always likely to be activated in redistributive politics, the political elites with whom they negotiate may undergo some changes toward the extremes in terms of doctrinal purity. To use French politics as an example, it is the popular front, not the radical center, which emerges as the political bargaining agent.

It is not surprising that the redistributive case studies have been drawn from nations having long traditions of class conflict, France and Germany. Nonetheless, it ought not to be concluded that even an ideologically middle-class and non-Marxist society such as the United States has been totally immune from such conflicts. For instance, the labor disputes in Michigan in 1936–37 might offer some insight into the nature of redistributive politics.[5] The autoworkers sought to organize within the factories, but were faced with unbridled hostility from a corporate hierarchy with practically unlimited control over hiring, firing, and conditions of work. Many Americans believed that to challenge this system of industrial organization was to question the concept of private property and capitalism itself. However, it was precisely this authoritarianism within the plant that the workers sought to destroy.

The method the unions chose for realizing their aim was the sit-down strike. But this tactic was immediately declared illegal by a local court and subsequently upheld by the United States Supreme Court. The autoworkers' decision to organize and to engage in strikes was bound to excite widespread debate, for not only did they oppose the capitalist-worker authority system, but they used essentially illegal means to get their way. The third case study below deals with a similar conflict over authority among unions and businessmen in West Germany at the time of the debate over codetermination.

As the strikes spread from factory to factory, Governor Murphy of Michigan, who had refused to abide by the court injunction against the strikers, finally intervened by bringing the corporate and union leadership together to resolve their differences. In this case, as in the others considered here, there is a pattern peculiar to the politics of redistribution. Compared with previous cases, it is the apparent paradox of broad, often rather violent confrontations involving large numbers of citizens which nonetheless are decided by leaders occupying the most formal posts at the top decision-making levels of polity and economy.

## CONCLUSIONS

Redistributive policies display large-scale conflict in which the major divisions more or less follow traditional class lines. Like emotive symbolic issues, this type also involves large numbers of people, but the conflict is more structured and its limits more predictable, less scattered across various socioeconomic strata. Therefore the redistributive type of policy is characterized by the following attributes:

(1) The struggle takes place between middle- and working-class interests (bourgeoisie and proletariat), between forces on the ideological right and left. The social peace is likely to be marred by such occurrences as riots, demonstrations, strikes, sit-ins, or lock-ins.

(2) Major participants are the top political executives on the one hand, and leaders of peak associations representing labor and management on the other.

(3) Party discipline is relatively high, especially in two-party systems, but deep divisions may occur among center parties in multiparty regimes. In general, however, there is a reinforcement of party discipline.

(4) Decisions are concluded by presidents and prime ministers in the course of negotiations with representatives of peak associations. The legislature is relatively quiescent.

# FRANCE: THE THIRD REPUBLIC

*The Matignon Agreement*

## Background

In hindsight the eruption of a great class conflict in 1936 does not appear especially surprising, for the economic and social ingredients were surely present. At the time France was experiencing overwhelming social and economic difficulties. Since it was relatively less advanced industrially than the United States, Great Britain, or Germany, France felt the impact of the great depression somewhat later than other nations in the West. Unemployment levels in 1936 were very high and incomes were down sharply. For example, although farmers represented 35 percent of the population, they received only 18 percent of the national income. Similarly, when the depression struck France most severely, in 1935, unemployment levels hovered around 425,000. Although greater numbers of workers, peasants, and marginal businessmen were thrown into the ranks of the unemployed than ever before, the state seemed unable or unwilling to meet its responsibilities.

In such periods of industrial and social turmoil, political extremism becomes more fashionable and acceptable. In France the Communist party began to speak for a growing number of people, in particular the members of the working classes. Of more importance, however, was the growth of the so-called "leagues" on the right. Their threat to the republic lay mainly in the disorder they could provoke through riots, demonstrations, and fights with police and leftists. They therefore threatened to polarize still further an already deeply divided society. Some of the leagues, which were often composed of ex-servicemen, became quasi-military orders armed with enough firearms to be considered a threat to the existing regime. Probably the most famous group on the far right was the *Action Française* of Charles Maurras, but surely the most politically prominent was the *Croix de Feu* of Colonel de la Rocque. Although the colonel himself was no extremist, many of his followers were; and the threat of his group combined with the threat of several other extremist groups in existence at the time appeared far from negligible.

The favor given extreme right-wing groups in Europe by political trends may have heightened the impetus for local movements in France. This was a period when Mussolini dominated Italy and when Hitler had only re-

cently assumed command in Germany. Moreover, Hitler's decision to occupy the Rhineland in 1936, only a short time prior to the French general
election of that year, excited French nationalist sentiment, but it also lent
support to fascism. It contributed to the belief that fascism was in tune
with the times and as such should be supported. It also added to a growing
contempt for a republic unable to work its will against an ancient enemy.
This demoralization caused from abroad could only help strengthen far
right groups in their struggles against the existing order.

The far right surely had much evidence of decadency and corruption to
buttress its case against the existing republic. The rightist indictment of the
government's failures became especially pertinent in late 1933, when the
Stavisky scandal shook the Radical Socialist ministry of Edouard Daladier.
Serge Alexandre Stavisky, who had been involved in several questionable
transactions but had apparently escaped prosecution because of well-
placed political connections, was found dead from what was designated
officially as suicide. Certain indications that he had been slain by the police
to prevent disclosures of his protectors' names led to right-wing rioting in
the streets. Daladier's reaction was to dismiss his police chief for failing to
suppress the demonstrations. The various rightist groups, given such information to utilize against the moderate, center-left regime, called for a
monumental protest on February 9, 1934. When the demonstration took
place, it did not take the crowd long to become unruly; and when the
throng surged toward the Palais Bourbon, where the Chamber of Deputies
held its meetings, a confrontation between police and demonstrators en-
sued. Fifteen people were killed and over one hundred were wounded.

In hopes of avoiding still further trouble, Daladier chose to submit his
resignation. His successor, Gaston Doumergue, a right-of-center politician,
was designated to form a "government of national union," but he too soon
fell from power, as did the two following governments of Pierre Flandin
and Pierre Laval. Forced to introduce unpopular deflationary measures,
these more conservative cabinets were unable to stem a growing conflict
between right and left.

Almost by default the left became the staunch defender of the republic.
In doing so it unwittingly contributed to the deepening crisis in French
politics. Many Frenchmen were hostile to the corrupt and weak republic,
but they were nevertheless democratic in inclination. Now they were
increasingly being forced to make a clear choice between rather stark and
distasteful alternatives: a weak republic or a dictatorship from the right.
Following the famous February 1934 riots and three short-lived governments which it considered hopelessly authoritarian, the left began to assume a more militant stance in defense of the republic. On Bastille Day
in 1935, it held a gigantic rally to demonstrate support for the existing
regime, a gesture hardly likely to win consensus among the populace at
large. A few months later, Socialists, Radicals, and Communists joined
together to form a Popular Front election pact. As a result the political gulf
was widened still further, since in less tense periods the democratic left

would hardly have sought the embrace of the Communist party. But these were not ordinary times, and there was a genuine belief that democratic government might be overthrown by a rightist coup.

## The Growth of Class Polarization

There was an increasing tendency beginning in the 1930s for French society to become polarized along fairly distinct class lines. It was particularly significant that these class divisions were catapulted so easily into the political arena for debate. The massive demonstration of February 6, 1934, which erupted in violence was perceived as a rightist attempt to bring down the government of the day. Led by the various leagues, the effort to descend upon the Palais Bourbon was a clear endeavor to impose government from the streets upon the republican state.

This right-wing power play encouraged the left to respond in kind. As early as February 6, the Communists called for protest demonstrations against the right-wing demonstrations. Three days later, the two major trade unions, the *Confédération Générale du Travail* (CGT) and the *Confédération Générale du Travail Unitaire* (CGTU), which hitherto had struggled militantly against one another for the loyalty of the working class, suddenly joined together in calling for a twenty-four-hour general strike against the "fascist menace." However, the most impressive show of leftist political power came more than a year later at the famous Bastille Day rally of July 14, 1935. Shouting slogans in defense of republican legality, the procession of 300,000 took peacefully to the streets. Radicals and Socialists, who previously had kept the Communists at a distance, joined arms and walked the streets as one powerful force. Ominously, on that very day on the other side of Paris, the *Croix de Feu* was holding a large rally of its own. Fortunately, the two crowds did not cross paths.

Because of the growing fear of the right, the gradual coalescing of Communist, Socialist, and Radical interests steadily gained momentum. As Denis Brogan put it, "By the time of the great manifestation of July 14, 1935, the parliamentary situation had become too paradoxical to be tolerable; it would have to be ended one way or the other, by a sweeping victory of the Left or of the Right."[6] Out of these fears and the new spirit of unity on the left rose the Popular Front. Huge rallies in Paris could undoubtedly affect public opinion, but the decision to form a Popular Front coalition had a much larger political significance.

There had been previous leftist coalitions; the Socialists and Radicals had agreed to a "United Front" in July 1934. In the 1932 general elections, when these two parties had established a common electoral pact, the accord had proved so successful that the Radicals had gained forty-eight seats and the Socialists seventeen. There was nevertheless a fundamental difference between that coalition and the Popular Front established in 1936. After all, both the Socialists and Radicals were open, democratic, somewhat reformist in inclination (at least the Socialists were), wedded to the political symbols of 1789, and especially supportive of the democratic republic; there was no fundamental reason they could not align for electoral purposes. But the Communist party was another matter: it was totalitarian, revolutionary, and thoroughly committed to the creation of an entirely new form of society.

It was not easy to develop a common platform of principles among three such divergent groups. Nonetheless, the parties did agree to a program vague enough in content to avoid a rupture prior to the upcoming legislative elections of May 1936. The compromises in the document were rather obvious to anyone who understood the revolutionary nature of the Communist party on the one hand and the basic social conservatism of the Radicals on the other. The major points of agreement were: a call for the dissolution of the fascist leagues; a foreign policy guided by support for the League of Nations; collective security; disarmament; a systematic attack on unemployment; the nationalization of the Bank of France; the creation of old-age pensions; the formation of a War Pension Fund; and the development of a more steeply graded income tax.

The decision to pool their electoral resources was no small accomplishment for the three left-wing groups. The Third Republic electoral system involved the single-member constituency with two ballots. If no candidate captured an absolute majority in the first round in his own constituency, then a run-off ballot was required. Therefore, it was agreed prior to the 1936 elections that in the second round two of the three Popular Front parties would step aside for the one which had received the most ballots in the first round. As a result of this agreement, it was possible for the left to unite around a single candidate during the second-round balloting. Such an arrangement was particularly beneficial to the Communist party, which in the past had often been pitted against the other left-wing groups. Indeed, it had not been uncommon for Radicals and Socialists to prefer more centrist candidates to the Communists. The integration of the extreme left into the designs of the other two left-wing parties meant that it was no longer at the mercy of an electoral system which encouraged more moderate groups to come together during the crucial negotiating period between the two ballots. With a strong core of support from the proletariat, the Communist party could now hope to be the second-round candidate for the left in many constituencies.

At the same time that political groups were joining forces within the left-wing movement, there was a historic merger of the labor movement at Toulouse in March 1936. This coming together of two heretofore hostile unions signified a further unification of the left and a growing polarization in French society. The CGT and CGTU had been at odds since 1920–21. At that time the schism had been brought on largely by the pressures arising out of World War I. Many labor leaders had joined the patriotic struggle against imperial Germany, but a significant minority of the CGT had remained attached to revolutionary internationalism.[7]

Following the war the leadership of the CGT sought to lead the trade union movement in a more moderate direction; but a Communist, syndicalist, and anarchist minority broke away from the socialist-oriented parent group to form the CGTU. This new group was heavily influenced by the Russian revolution and the establishment of communism in a major nation, desirous of ties with the Russian-led international trade union movement, and charged by revolutionary optimism following the victory over Germany. Believing that the old CGT leadership had subordinated itself to the bourgeoisie, the newly formed CGTU initially claimed some 500,000 union-affiliated members, thus reducing the CGT to a mere 250,-000 men and women. From the moment of its inception the CGTU remained the revolutionary vanguard within the labor movement, ready at a moment's notice to strike against the hated capitalist system. By 1924 this militant organization was securely under the influence of the Communists, and as a result many anarchist and syndicalist workers resigned from its ranks. Subsequently, it was subordinated totally to the tactical and strategic needs of the Communist party; there was a close overlapping in the top positions of each organization since the CGTU leaders were also mainly Communist party members. At the same time, the CGT became ever more supportive of the reformist-minded Socialist party.

Just as the Communists never ceased deriding the Socialists as tools of capitalism, the CGTU continually castigated the CGT as mere servants of management; however, the threat from the rightist leagues in the middle thirties led the CGTU to reconsider its hostile position and to seek readmission into the CGT. Its step toward moderation was apparently based upon several considerations: Russian foreign interests dictated that France remain in the anti-Germany camp, and internal squabbles on the left could only weaken the anti-fascist forces within France. Because the French right might be more pro-German, it was imperative from the Russian standpoint to keep it at bay.

Moreover, the drive for unity within the trade union movement gained momentum as a result of increasingly friendly ties between the Communist and Socialist parties. The "United Front" accord between the two party groups on July 27, 1934, was particularly significant in this respect. Since the links between the parties and the unions were so close, any growth of amity on the political horizon was likely to be felt within the union movement as well. Despite the fact the CGTU leaders had originally walked out of the CGT, they now practically begged to be allowed to return to the fold. In fact, by 1935 they were willing to accede to most of the conditions stipulated by the CGT. They even agreed to conditions which assured that their influence would be neutralized in the new organization. For example, the CGTU was forced to agree to begin unification at the local levels; the CGT, with more members at the base of the union hierarchy, could be assured of success whenever elections were held within local unions to choose delegates to the higher offices. The CGT would probably have placed strict conditions upon CGTU readmission in any event; various schisms within the latter since its founding had gradually made it a smaller organization anyway.

The reunification of the CGT and CGTU took place only two months prior to the 1936 legislative elections. From a sociological standpoint, the event signified something more than mere unity between two feuding peak associations; it suggested also that apparently cross-cutting cleavages had become increasingly inoperative in French society. Forces united loosely around bourgeoisie and proletariat were becoming ever more apparent. Thus, on one side of a symbolic barricade stood workers, the unions, the political left, supporters of the republic, proponents of parliamentary sovereignty, and the anti-Germans. On the other side of the barricade were the middle and upper classes, the political right extending from moderates to fascists, the proponents of constitutional changes in the direction of a strong executive, and fewer outright anti-Germans. There were, of course, many nuances, but political life in general was polarized as at no time in recent memory. As David Thomson has suggested, "Between 1934 and 1936 all the circumstances favourable to a Fascist revolution co-existed in France. They are the supreme crisis-years of the Third Republic—even more critical, probably, than the days of the Dreyfus affair."[8]

Nevertheless, the left won the day, as the May 3, 1936, elections to the Chamber of Deputies clearly demonstrated; indeed, the right wing proved to be much weaker than many commentators had assumed. For example, note in Table 5 (below) the party breakdown of the new chamber.

Table 5

Political Parties in Chamber of Deputies (1936)*

| Popular Front | | Opposition | |
|---|---|---|---|
| Communists | 72 | Democratic Left and Inde- | |
| Socialists | 149 | pendent Radicals | 39 |
| Social and Republican Union | | Popular Democrats | 13 |
| (Dissidents) | 29 | Left Republicans | 44 |
| Radical Socialists | 109 | Social Action and Agrarians | 39 |
| Independent Left | 28 | Popular Action | 16 |
| | | Republican Federation | 59 |
| | | Independent Republicans | 12 |
| Total | 387 | Total | 222 |

*9 deputies not listed were unaffiliated.

Source: Walter R. Sharp, "The Popular Front in France: Prelude or Interlude?" *American Political Science Review*, October 1936, p. 868.

The election of 387 Popular Front candidates against 222 opposition members, a lopsided majority of 165, demonstrated very well the weakness of the right or, more basically, the effects of class polarization on French political life. The left had been thoroughly frightened for its political existence; it had responded in a unified manner to that threat; and over the months it successfully unified its disparate forces against a possible right-wing takeover. In such polarized situations it is not surprising that the center becomes a major casualty in the political warfare because the climate of elite and public opinion precludes its functioning as a bargaining agent among various factions. Ordinarily, its role as a bargaining, moderating power tends to make it indispensable to the formation of governments and places it in an advantageous position in second-round run-offs during election campaigns.* But the influences which initiate polarization exclude centrism as a significant alternative. This effect became clearly apparent in May 1936. In 1932 the center groups could claim some 156 deputies; in 1936 they could muster only 116, a loss of 40 seats. Rightist parties, on the other hand, increased their share of seats from 81 to 122.[9]

In some respects, however, the most interesting alterations occurred within the Popular Front coalition itself. The most centrist of the coalition parties, the Radicals, actually slipped in electoral strength despite their entry into the Popular Front and were driven from their dominant position on the left. They lost 44 seats, dropping from 160 deputies in 1932 to 116 in 1936. Conversely, the most extreme party of the left, the Communist party, grew from a mere ten seats in 1932 to seventy-two in 1936. The other group committed to significant alterations in the social system, albeit by democratic means, were the Socialists. With 149 members in the new chamber, they could now become the dominant party in the new legislature. Also significant was the arrival of many inexperienced and young deputies; some 277 of them had no previous parliamentary experience. More than ever before, political life seemed polarized and precarious, and under such circumstances the center was naturally denied its traditional role of governing.

As expected, the new government was of the left, not the center or moderate right as had been typical in the past. The newly designated premier, Léon Blum, a Socialist, set out to form a Popular Front cabinet. He was disappointed almost from the start, however, for the Communists refused to join his ministry on the grounds that to do so might unduly frighten the bourgeoisie. Nevertheless, they did agree to support Blum and his program on key votes. Neither could Blum persuade Léon Jouhaux, the CGT leader, to accept a ministerial portfolio. Despite Blum's failure to lure all Popular Front factions into his government, he ultimately did form a cabinet consisting of twenty-one ministers and fourteen under secretaries, which included sixteen Socialists, thirteen Radicals, three Independent

---

*Under *scrutin d' arrondissement à deux tours* center groups presumably have more opportunities to receive endorsements in various constituencies from other parties during the negotiating periods between the two election rounds. Logically a party of either the left or right would rather throw its support to a center party than to one on the other end of the political spectrum.

Socialists, and three non-affiliated members. Although the Communists and CGT remained outside the government, Blum's cabinet was still clearly oriented toward the left. Morever, twenty-five of the thirty-five cabinet officials were without previous ministerial experience. All things considered, France seemed to be experiencing profound social and political changes—in the short run, at any rate.

## The Paradox of Class Conflict: Popular Participation and Elite Resolution

The events leading up to the Matignon agreement of June 7, 1936, must have seemed democratic politics at its best to the French syndicalists. This was not a struggle which required the worker to find his spokesman in bourgeois Socialist or totalitarian Communist parties or in intermediaries such as the trade unions; rather, the proletarian rose and asserted his rights outside the established institutions by taking over directly the means of production. As Professor Henry W. Ehrmann points out in referring to this democratic quality of the strikes: "There is no doubt that these strikes were a spontaneous mass movement; they certainly were not initiated by the CGT or any political party."[10]

The wave of sit-ins began five days after the May election and spread quickly throughout the nation. The spontaneity of the strikes may be seen by contrasting the militance of the workers during April with proletarian agitation during June. In April only thirty-two strikes took place throughout France, but by June nearly one-fourth of all wage-earners in industry and commerce were refusing to work. The fact that three-fourths of all the strikes in June were of the sit-in variety is significant because the labor organizations themselves had never advocated this method for resolving industrial disputes.[11] Although the strikes were clearly illegal, they were nevertheless overwhelmingly nonviolent; in fact, an almost holiday mood prevailed within the factories.

What ignited these massive and illegal strikes is not clear, but what does seem to be abundantly evident from many commentaries of this period is that both unions and Communist party were genuinely taken by surprise. Many writers are inclined to believe that the astounding electoral triumph of the Popular Front and the creation of the Blum cabinet gave the ordinary workers so much optimism that their needs would be quickly met in the new order that they spontaneously began the sit-ins in the belief that their passive resistance would strengthen the government's hand.

This argument suggests that the proletariat had been disappointed so often in the past that it was fearful that, in the absence of pressures, the status quo within French society would reassert itself. Indeed there is some evidence that Blum, his close personal adviser, Jouhaux, and even the Communist party wished to move somewhat more warily than the ultimate accords implied. The Communists apparently made many efforts to contain the strikes, fearing that the strikers would arouse enmity in the bourgeoisie at a moment when the party felt that national unity against

Hitlerian Germany was imperative. Similarly, the CGT was initially content to make a rather orthodox demand for a simple public works program. It was quite willing to set aside for the moment its other priorities and subordinate the trade union movement to economic policies geared to creating an upswing in the business cycle.

But events surpassed the institutionalized leadership of party and union. When Blum announced the formation of his cabinet on June 4, 500,000 Parisian workers were at the moment occupying factories; it became obvious that more dynamic gestures toward reform were needed if social peace was to be restored. Standing before the Chamber of Deputies on June 5, Blum declared that while he agreed the strikes were clearly illegal, a Popular Front government could hardly take action against the strikers. On that same day, he made a dramatic radio appeal to the workers. While pleading for "calm, dignity, and discipline," he promised to enact by the end of the summer three basic reforms: paid vacations, the forty-hour week, and collective wage contracts.

By this time powerful pressures had built up. The premier now called for action to restore social peace, for the workers still showed no inclination to abandon the factories. In fact, according to much testimony, they were more than ever convinced that their activities would push the government farther toward the establishment of labor-management relations on an entirely new basis. Although their revolt so far had gained promises from the government, the workers wanted to cement their already strong bargaining position so long as they held the initiative.

Seeing no way out of his difficulties and believing that promises were no longer sufficient to quiet the proletariat, Blum decided to move immediately toward the gratification of worker demands. On June 6, only a day after his dramatic radio appeal, he appeared before Parliament and quickly received a strong vote of confidence (384–210) for his government and its program. Significantly, the normally rambunctious and assertive Chamber of Deputies, ever ready to bring any upstart government to its knees, was amazingly quiet and restrained.[12] Perhaps the chamber's quiescence was due to demoralization on the right-wing benches, but there is an additional explanation. The chamber, or any other intermediate body, except a primarily class-oriented one, could not be expected to play the major role in a momentous class debate. Legislatures (as distinct from their standing committees) function best in bargaining situations in which the various participants represent relatively manageable sectoral demands. In a pronounced class conflict, however, they find themselves bypassed by greater and more coherent forces.

Demonstrating the ineffectuality of the intermediate bodies, Blum summoned the major peak associations of labor and business, the CGT and the *Confédération Générale de la Production Française* (CGPF), to the Hotel Matignon to negotiate an accord on the day following his vote of confidence. At this meeting which included government, CGT, and CGPF officials, the business world found itself in a very weak bargaining position. Since its origin the CGPF had been perceived by much of small business principally as a spokesman for big business; as a result, merchants and proprietors on the whole had been unwilling to ally themselves with the CGPF. Consequently, the latter could hardly claim to speak for the entire business community. In addition, the peasants, who in the past could be counted upon to tame the red fervor of Parisian radicalism, were themselves alienated, sullen, and unwilling to join actively with business to bring pressure against the political left and the workers.

The CGPF position was weakened still more in other ways. When the sit-ins first began, a number of patrons had quickly reached agreements with their workers; thus, if any sign of CGPF intransigence occurred, the argument could be used that it was simply being obstinate and uncompromising when many of its followers had already shown statesmanship. Perhaps most significant of all was the election victory of the Popular Front and the subsequent creation of the Blum government. This had placed in power politicians with a distinct prolabor bias, unlikely to sympathize very much with business demands. To prove its antibusiness proclivities in this period of social turmoil, the government was apparently prepared to requisition certain industrial and commercial establishments, to order laborers back to work, and to pay them with public funds. Once such a train of events began, it could easily end in large-scale nationalizations, something the CGPF surely wanted to avoid. The growing pressures of over 2 million workers occupying factories and a prolabor government in office probably were sufficient to create the CGPF representatives' belief that delay was hardly in their interest in this particular dispute.[13]

Not surprisingly, when the accord was reached, it was clearly contrary to business interests. Indeed, it represented a major readjustment in labor-management power relationships. René Duchemin, the president of the CGPF, trying to justify the humiliation he had received that night in the Hotel Matignon from a predominantly Socialist government and a CGT delegation including two Communists, lamely suggested that he had given away so much to labor because until that moment he had not understood just how low wages were in certain industries.[14] Actually, it would be more accurate to say that big business had been overwhelmed by superior force, as a reading of the final document starkly suggests. The CGPF agreed to recognize the right of workers to organize; it acceded to immediate wage increases of from 7 percent to 15 percent; and, finally, it guaranteed that French workers would have paid vacations. Although these demands had previously been met in most other industrial nations of the West, they represented nothing short of a new basis for class relationships in a France which would not soon forget the night of the Matignon agreement.

*Conclusions*

While it is possible to explain the sheer magnitude of this issue of redistribution in terms of a centralized society's greater propensity to push disagreement more quickly to the very top of the political system for resolution, in the case described here, the two peak associations, the CGT and CGPF, could hardly claim to represent in any official capacity overwhelming majorities of their respective clienteles. Indeed, for some time many workers and businessmen had remained outside the official umbrella of CGT and CGPF activities. The CGPF in particular had quite limited authority to mobilize business support for collective class action. Yet the fact that these two groups were called upon to resolve the conflict suggests that redistribution issues are inevitably pushed to the "command posts" for settlement, even when the commanders themselves can neither speak officially for large numbers in their class nor meaningfully guide the terms of the debate. Indeed, it is almost as if broadly representative top leadership must be created to resolve these policies, even when little prior institutionalized authority has existed. This instance is reminiscent of the famous revolutionary leader who, when learning that his people had taken to the streets, exclaimed that he must hurry and catch up with them in order that he might lead them to victory.

## FRANCE: THE FIFTH REPUBLIC

### The May Revolution

#### The Rise of Student Dissent

At the beginning of 1968 few commentators suspected that France would soon be torn by a conflict serious enough to shake the foundations of the regime itself.[15] It was certainly the most convulsive issue in many years. Riots, demonstrations, nationwide strikes, union-employer disputes, intense prime ministerial and presidential activity, and cabinet resignations were all part of the social scene in this momentous year. When 1968 opened, students were demonstrating sporadically in Paris and elsewhere, protesting such diverse issues as the American role in Vietnam and conditions within the *lycées* (high schools) and universities. In January large groups of high school students battled policemen in the streets because one of their colleagues had been disciplined in a manner they thought unfair. Throughout February rallies were held demonstrating support for the Vietcong in their war against the United States. Sometimes such gatherings ended in skirmishes with the police. These protests against the war in Vietnam took a more ominous turn in March, when several American banks and other businesses were bombed. Politicization of students was clearly apparent in this period, but hardly unusual in a nation long accustomed to youthful political excesses.

Students played a very significant part in the May revolution of 1968, particularly the student revolutionaries from the University of Nanterre; for they initiated the political warfare which ultimately included both the working class and the political leadership of the nation.

Because there were more than 30,000 liberal arts students at the Sorbonne who were crowded into a small portion of Paris, often inhabiting living quarters hardly conducive to rigorous study, the opening of a *Faculté des Lettres et Sciences Humaines* in the fall of 1964 at Nanterre seemed an excellent method to alleviate many of the university problems. The erection of new dormitories meant that Nanterre students could depend upon cleaner, less cramped quarters for living and study. Their new buildings were more spacious and better equipped, heated, and lighted than were those in Paris. Not only were physical conditions superior, but an effort was made to increase the number of faculty in order to create smaller classes for discussion and, in general, to facilitate better interpersonal relationships between faculty and students. A major criticism of the Sorbonne was that students seldom had any personal contact with faculty; indeed, they found it almost impossible to gain physical access to large lecture halls. The usual practice was for professors to pass around copies of their lectures to students, who were required for all practical purposes to memorize by rote the content of the notes. No system was more contrived to keep faculty and students sharply isolated from one another.

Yet the new campus at Nanterre undoubtedly had its disadvantages as well. For one thing, although the new facility was originally intended to house only 10,000 students, it already contained 12,000 young men and women by 1967–68. This remarkable increase was caused to a great extent by a neighborhood school concept which gave youngsters from certain sections of Paris the alternative of going either to Nanterre or to no university at all—unless, of course, they chose a religious school.[16] In addition, the esthetic qualities left much to be desired. The campus was surrounded by railway yards, factories, and working-class houses and establishments. Students were continually subjected to the roar of construction equipment, and the first rain turned the area into a muddy morass. Because the university library had not been built, students were forced to make the twenty-three-mile trip to Paris to find appropriate library facilities. To make matters worse, the problems of transportation would not be eased until 1971 at the earliest. Finally, students had no place to study between classes.

Housing was a particularly grating problem for the noncommuting student, since there were few attractive rooms in the slums surrounding the campus. Those who lived in the dormitories, on the other hand, were subject to restrictions, many of which the students perceived as childish and degrading. The sexual segregation seems to have been particularly resented by the students, especially in the girls' dormitories, where it was severely enforced. Conversely, in the men's residences restrictions were enforced hardly at all. These rules became useful for uniting students in the ensuing debates because they were not only contrary to student desires, but the overwhelming number of parents, when asked, favored permitting their children to entertain members of the opposite sex in their rooms. Hence, authorities were enforcing a policy increasingly at odds with student and parent desires.[17]

In all probability the argument about dormitory visitation rights more than anything else set off the explosion at Nanterre, for this was an issue especially calculated to activate young people more than mere abstract ideological discussions about political systems. Immediately prior to the Easter holidays in the spring of 1967, male students invaded the women's dormitories and were forced out only by the intervention of firemen and policemen. On February 14, 1968, similar activities quickly spread throughout France, this time encouraged by the major student organization, the *Union Nationale des Etudiants de France* (UNEF). Meanwhile, Nanterre radicals, calling themselves the *enragées,* had become increasingly fretful about not gaining their ends in university reform. At the instigation of sociology faculty and students, they formed a joint committee of students and faculty to submit reform proposals to Paris.

It is not surprising that sociologists would dominate the debate. Because of their disciplinary concerns, such students were more likely to be interested in social problems and also better equipped to offer ideological solutions to those problems. Moreover, it is possible that they and their professors felt a certain status deprivation relative to other academic disciplines. The study of sociology did not generate the levels of prestige associated with older and more entrenched disciplines. Finally, the occupational prospects of many sociology students were not especially propitious, for many of them did not have the skills demanded by an increasingly technologized society and economy. Historically, graduation from the university practically guaranteed a good job; now, however, the supply of graduates was outrunning demand, at least in the areas of relatively higher occupational prestige. It was only natural for students in such circumstances to give vent to their frustrations.

It was apparent that the joint faculty-student committee was not going to achieve its ends and this failure set the stage for a profound radicalization of the student body. On March 18, small explosives were detonated in the Paris offices of the Chase Manhattan Bank, the Bank of America, and Trans-World Airlines. Two days later the American Express office was bombed. Policemen responded immediately by arresting five youngsters, all members of extremist organizations. On March 22, a meeting at Nanterre was called to protest the arrests. The youthful insurgents occupied lecture halls and offices. Throughout the night the students argued political questions, a right denied to them under existing university regulations. They finally approved by 142–2 a motion calling for the right to organize politically on campus. Calling themselves the Movement of March 22, these students would soon help ignite a revolt powerful enough to constitute a threat to the state itself.

On May 3, called by Professor Bernard E. Brown "the most important single day of the whole crisis," [18] the rector of the University of Paris called in the police to clear the grounds of some 400 demonstrators, mostly Nanterre students whose own university had been closed the previous day because of protracted demonstrations. Since Prime Minister Georges Pompidou was out of the country and the working day-to-day leadership of the government was therefore essentially headless, the students found this an opportune time to revolt without effective opposition. When the patience of the police was finally exhausted, they rounded up some 400 students for questioning, only to release their prisoners the next day (May 4). The students promptly returned to their street demonstrations, and forty-eight hours later they repulsed a police attempt to control their activities. To their delight policemen were forced to retreat in disorder and disarray. By this time pitched battles between the forces of law and order and the demonstrators were quite commonplace, and in some cases the police were using rather brutal methods to quell the rioters.

As a consequence of police brutality, public opinion in this period was sharply in favor of the students. For instance, on May 8, a French Institute of Public Opinion Poll published in *Le Monde* showed that four-fifths of the Parisians were sympathetic to the student position. Significantly, so long as the proletariat was uninvolved, the students did not risk unsettling respectable bourgeois opinion, for many middle-class and upper-class sons were manning the barricades.

The next two weeks witnessed a pronounced elevation in the level of violence. In fact, Patrick Seale and Maureen McConville go so far as to conclude that between May 6 and May 13, "the students' revolt changed fundamentally in character: from pranks and street brawls it became a mass insurrection."[19] Clubbings of mere bystanders as well as students, injuries to policemen, tear gas, barricades in the streets, and overturned and burned automobiles became familiar sights to Parisians as well as to citizens in those cities where provincial universities were located. For example, on May 10, about 20,000 demonstrators took to the streets in Paris, and by May 11, it seemed as if the city were in revolt. The fact that 367 people were injured facilitated the belief that these were perilous times indeed.

On May 11, Prime Minister Pompidou returned to Paris from his trip abroad and immediately proceeded to make concessions to the students by granting amnesty, withdrawing policemen from the Sorbonne, and reopening the university doors. Since this was a time of pronounced student-police conflict, the immediate result of his actions was to lower police morale and increase disgruntlement. However, the concessions had little effect on the students' behavior, for by now trade union and teacher demonstrators had joined the fray. On May 13, a huge rally of students, teachers, and unions was held. Student extremists, unable to foment violence at the rally, proceeded to occupy the unguarded Sorbonne and create so-called student soviets. Even with this provocation the Pompidou government refused to take the revolt seriously, as General de Gaulle's departure on May 14 for a state visit to Rumania attests.

### The Proletariat Enters the Fray

Until this time the revolt had been a student-dominated affair; and so far, middle-class, traditional France had shown little but sympathy for the demonstrators. Even during the great outpouring of people into the streets on May 13 the left-wing, union, and Communist elites and politicians played a relatively small role. Nonetheless, although the students continued to demonstrate and riot as before, the revolt now entered a new phase. Whether because of a holiday mood or because of aggressive tendencies encouraged by government capitulation to the students, workers suddenly began to lay down their tools, take over factories, and expel their managers from the premises (or, in some cases, lock them in rooms). On May 14, only 200 men were on strike; but by May 22, almost 10,000 proletarians refused to work. In the Marxist sense the proletariat had indeed taken over the means of production, although it did not know exactly what to do with its newly won dominance. As was true in 1936, the revolt of 1968 was largely spontaneous. In fact, most observers are in agreement that the Communist party and its union ally, the CGT, did not issue strike orders from Paris.[20] Students and workers were not alone in striking, for by this time other occupational groups such as engineers, doctors, actors, journalists, technicians, and even athletes had leveled their own grievances against the system. France gave every impression of a society in the throes of anarchy.

As the proletarian demonstrations began to grow rapidly in intensity and scope, they placed the Communist party and the CGT in an increasingly difficult position. For one thing, the Communists had to contend with a threat from their left of radical influences upon the working-class movement. Their immediate response in the face of youthful disorders and revolutionary activity had been to make light of the students as mere youngsters having a final fling prior to entry into comfortable middle-class occupations and organizations. But the *Parti Communiste Français* (PCF) had an additional reason for discrediting the young revolutionaries: these young men and women had repeatedly expressed nothing but contempt for the PCF bureaucracy and its leadership; the Communist leadership was particularly concerned that young workers not be influenced by the students' hostile propaganda.

After May 14 it was apparent that if the PCF did not move quickly to recapture its moral leadership of the thousands of workers engaged in strikes, sit-ins, and lock-ins, the vacuum might well be filled by assorted groups of anarchists, Trotskyites, Maoists, and the militantly left-wing *Parti Socialiste Unifié* (PSU), as well as by the major rival of the CGT, the *Confédération Française Démocratique du Travail* (CFDT). All these groups made no secret of their belief that the Communist party had become a conservative force exploiting the masses in tacit alliance with the bourgeois Gaullist regime. On the other hand, if the PCF were to compete dynamically with left-wing radicals for proletarian support by threatening revolutionary activity, it would risk being outlawed by the bourgeois state. To the PCF, revolution was legitimate, of course, but in its opinion the time was hardly ripe for open insurrection.

Moreover, as is the case with Communist parties in most nations, the French Communists favor only those revolutions in which they are the

leading participant; otherwise they denounce the insurrections as premature. In general, their reluctance to join a movement initiated by others and
their fear of being outlawed are quite understandable. Because of such
fears the last thing the PCF desired in 1968 was a classic redistributive
issue. These considerations explain the party's tendency throughout the
revolt to define working-class needs in terms of wage and salary adjust-
ments alone. Caught in a dilemma not of its own choosing, the party
sought to classify the radical revolt as adventurism of the worst sort, while
at the same time, in order to reassert its dominance over the working-class
movement, it called for general strikes of a relatively short duration. During the week of the student revolt, the PCF announced a general strike for
May 13, simultaneously condemning Daniel Cohn-Bendit and his student
friends from the Sorbonne and Nanterre as adventurers. When the spontaneous wave of strikes took place on May 14, the CGT immediately demanded concessions by the government to the working class. Such tactics
were sufficient to antagonize many ordinary citizens.

At no point did the PCF call for riot or revolution; indeed, at a strategic
and highly dangerous moment, it agreed to reduce the tension by accepting
a Gaullist challenge to hold an election at a time hardly favorable to
Communist prospects. As the subsequent Gaullist landslide victory in June
suggested, the government easily controlled the situation. It was able to
persuade the public that the PCF wanted revolution, largely because the
Communists, in their desperate attempts to retain their dominance of the
proletariat, had issued strike orders in key areas affecting major sectors of
the economy. In this sense, the PCF and CGT contributed to the economic
breakdown. Two weeks after the initial worker revolts, the party launched
a "popular government" slogan and demanded a share in power in a future
anti-Gaullist government. Again, given the social tensions of the time, this
sloganeering kindled fears of a PCF takeover.[21] Neither revolutionary under the circumstances nor conservative enough to gain the confidence of
the great French middle groups, the party was crushed between its enemies
on the right and the left.

## The Growing Polarization in French Politics

With the rapid growth of worker sit-ins and lock-ins throughout France
and the accelerating activity of the PCF and CGT in response to proletarian
discontent, the nature of the conflict began to change. Students, artists,
technicians, and others continued their strikes and demonstrations, of
course, but two major forces increasingly confronted each other across the
mythical barricade: Gaullism versus communism. Students and other
groups were still quite capable of gaining attention, but Gaullism and
communism were the suns around which other bodies revolved. Increasingly, then, the terms of the debate were defined as a bourgeois-proletarian
confrontation.

It is easy to perceive why bourgeois France approved of demonstrations
and strikes when they were carried out only by students but disapproved

when they were led by unions and Communists. At the height of student influence, only a few people were out of work; but by May 22, 10,000 were on strike. By the time General de Gaulle had returned from Rumania on May 18, the insurrection had turned into a far more sinister revolt. As a CGT communiqué bluntly put it: "The situation has changed. . . . It is now a conflict between the forces of labor on the one hand and, on the other, the regime faced with the bankruptcy of its policies."[22]

With the growth of proletarian power, an altered state of opinion was particularly apparent at the elite levels of the French polity. At first, on May 8, the reaction in the National Assembly to the university turmoil was remarkably restrained; only a handful of deputies even bothered to attend the session. Six days later, when Pompidou announced his concessions to the students, he spoke pessimistically of the university crisis as a deeper crisis of civilization, and condemned the student radicals. Nonetheless, he gave in to their demands by granting amnesty and agreeing to reforms in university governance. On this occasion criticism came from most benches in the chamber for the manner in which the government had allowed a crisis to develop, and a motion of censure was introduced and defeated. The government, however, would not allow the vote to be taken before May 22, a decision it would not regret.

All things considered, the parliamentary situation was not particularly unusual; a government was in difficulty, and its opposition had attempted to reap the benefits. National Assembly sessions during the period of student ascendancy and leadership were characterized by strong criticism from all benches, including the Gaullist one, for a government which had allowed an explosive situation to endure in the universities for so long. The Pompidou government, by agreeing to concessions, had in effect admitted its own guilt under the circumstances. Indeed, had a censure vote been taken it is likely that the government would have fallen, for it had been placed on the defensive by its friends and foes alike.[23]

By May 22, however, the circumstances had greatly changed and much more than university reform was clearly at stake. Deputies within the Gaullist party as well as those in the ranks of its coalition partner, the Independent Republican party, were now under much greater pressure to cooperate. Anger over the state of the French university system had originally led several of them to contemplate opposition, but with the social order itself increasingly under threat, Gaullists and Independent Republicans instinctively closed ranks behind their government. With the issue defined as one of government mismanagement of the universities, they had had some reason to threaten the government coalition—or at least to assert a degree of independence. However, when class relationships came to the fore, these fundamentally conservative deputies immediately rallied behind the leadership of the prime minister.

The behavior of Independent Republican leader Valéry Giscard d'Estaing in this regard is instructive. At the time of the censure vote he was critical of Pompidou for allowing the situation, as he put it, "to rot," but he refused to vote against the government so long as "disorder" and "adventurism" were clearly present. In his speech he made it clear that he was particularly disillusioned with the democratic left, the *Fédération de la Gauche Démocratique et Socialiste* (FGDS), for flirting with the Communists in such perilous times.

Although only a few days before massive defections from the Independent Republican ranks and losses to the government of certain Gaullist deputies would not have been surprising, both groups now united as one against their enemies on the left. The major left-wing groups (PCF and FGDS) just as predictably joined forces against the right and voted overwhelmingly for censure. The centrists *(Progrès et Démocratie Moderne),* on the other hand, were split sharply over the issue. As expected, therefore, the progressive development of a redistributive case led to a sharp polarization of two warring camps in the National Assembly. Had the censure vote taken place a week earlier and had the issue been defined in a different manner, it is entirely possible that the Pompidou government might have been brought down. As it was, on May 22, the prime minister suffered only two defections from his own party's ranks (René Capitant and Edgard Pisani).[24]

## *The Grenelle Agreement*

During the censure debate Pompidou offered to negotiate with the unions, who quickly agreed to his offer. Over the weekend of May 25–27 marathon negotiations were held in the Ministry of Social Affairs on the Rue de Grenelle. Participating on the union side were the CGT, the CFDT the Socialist-oriented *Force Ouvrière* (FO), the *Confédération Française des Travailleurs Chrétiens* (CFTC), the *Confédération Générale des Cadres* (CGC), and the *Fédération de l'Education Nationale* (FEN). Representing the employers were the CNPF and the PME. It quickly became clear that the spokesmen differed profoundly in importance. For example, it was the CGT which spoke mainly for the workers. In fact, Georges Pompidou and CGT leaders Benoît Frachon and Georges Séguy dominated the negotiations. When Pompidou and Séguy in particular faced one another across the table, they represented in a very real but also symbolic way the two major forces in French society: the Communist party and the bourgeois state. The CFDT, which previously lent its ardent support to the students, now found itself playing a purely secondary role. Apparently, it was content to defer to the CGT spokesmen.

The representatives of the *patron,* as in 1936, were once more placed on the defensive, seemingly demoralized by recent events.[25] Socialist Jules Moch at the time contrasted the Matignon and Grenelle accords in an interesting way. Because the Blum government, he argued, was already favorably disposed toward the workers, in 1936 they had made their demands upon the *patronat* directly; but in 1968 they forced their will upon the employer's spokesman, the French state. Seen from this perspective, it is not surprising that the CNPF officials played a relatively small role in the talks. After all, they had a spokesman in Pompidou, an ex-banker himself.[26] The *patronat* may not have been particularly pleased with the prime minister's large concessions to the unions, but they could hardly object to one who came from their own ranks. The merger of state and *patron* interests in the Fifth Republic meant that the CNPF need exercise little initiative. Also, because the state was the largest employer in France, any spokesman for it—in this case, Pompidou—was bound to exercise much influence on the outcome of the talks. From this perspective it is hardly surprising that he was exceedingly active in the talks.

From the beginning of the talks, the prime minister sought to disarm his opponents by offering to them staggering wage increases. The minimum wage rate was raised by about 35 percent. In agriculture, the rates were increased by 56 percent. Even in some industries not covered by minimum wage rates, large concessions were quickly granted. Major changes were also announced in other areas of the economy as well. Promises were made to study the feasibility of lowering the retirement age of men from sixty-five to sixty and of women from sixty-five to fifty-five. Also promised was a gradual reduction of the workweek from forty-seven hours to forty hours. The unions were granted much greater freedom in establishing the closed shop and other controls on the factory floor. All things considered, the Grenelle accord was a major victory for the forces representing the left, surely their most significant victory since 1936.[27]

Why had Pompidou so suddenly acquiesced to union demands? Perhaps he had a genuine fear of revolution and consequently believed that concessions were the only way to calm passions. Or perhaps he had a tacit agreement with the Communists to "economize" the debate, to keep it within the boundaries of a trade union dispute. After all, the PCF had made it clear since the outbreak of hostilities that it opposed the revolutionary antics of the radicals to its left; the prime minister may have been attempting to facilitate the recovery of PCF leadership on the left. At any rate, at this juncture certain aims of the Communists and the government did objectively coincide.

Pompidou's large concessions to the unions may have been motivated by another and possibly decisive consideration: his survival as a prime minister and heir to de Gaulle. It was no secret that he had replaced de Gaulle as the major government official charged with resolving the crisis. When the general had returned from his Eastern European trip, he had immediately called for a national referendum to support his projects for reform. This time, however, his call for action was derided by an opposition determined to bring him to his knees. When it became immediately apparent that the general's strategy would not calm hostilities, Pompidou stepped into the breach and persuaded de Gaulle to dissolve Parliament. It was subsequently widely reported that the president and his prime minister quarrelled and that, for once, events forced the general to acquiesce to the leadership of one of his underlings. From that moment it was said that the president was determined to replace his prime minister whenever the opportunity presented itself. It is understandable why Pompidou was so intent upon having the talks regarded a success, for he had staked his political reputation on concessions to the students and workers as a necessary prerequisite for social peace.

## The Aftermath: Resurgence on the Right

The government may have appeared weak during the early part of the student revolt as well as during the negotiations with the unions and employers, but unfolding events soon placed it securely in a commanding position of leadership. By appearing conciliatory while simultaneously allowing the political situation to deteriorate to such an extent that the social order seemed threatened, the government finally awakened those deep forces of conservatism in French society—precisely what the PCF had feared.

When Georges Séguy and Benoît Frachon triumphantly returned from the Grenelle meeting to the Renault factory at suburban Boulogne-Billancourt with their proposals, they were greeted with catcalls and derision. The workers seemed to be particularly angry because the negotiators had failed to repeal the social security law of the previous year. That piece of legislation had increased worker contributions to the fund while lowering their benefits. In addition, the workers were unhappy because an immediate reduction in the workweek was not being initiated. As a consequence, rank-and-file employees, in the Renault factory and elsewhere, loudly repudiated the accords.

At no time in recent years had the average French worker disobeyed his superiors within the unions and the Communist party. To the government's chagrin, comments were increasingly heard on the need for an anti-Gaullist "government of the people" or "popular front." Finally, at this moment of renewed agitation from the proletariat, the student movement began to awaken once again. In violation of a government injunction against demonstrations, the UNEF called for a mass rally on the night of May 27. At this giant rally, which included much of the leadership on the non-Communist left, speakers called repeatedly for a new government. Even the PCF, which had advised its followers to stay away from the gathering, now began to insist upon a new anti-Gaullist government; and to make its demand a realistic one, it actively began to seek an arrangement with the FGDS. Apparently, these steps toward establishing a popular front alliance finally aroused the de Gaulle regime to action.

On May 30, after consulting with the military, the government seized the initiative. President de Gaulle addressed the nation by television and focused on threats to the state by the leftist revolutionary forces. Referring darkly to a "totalitarian enterprise" said to be under preparation, he emphasized forcefully that law and order would be maintained by all the necessary means at his disposal. Then, throwing out a challenge to his opposition, he announced that he intended to dissolve Parliament immediately and call for new elections to the National Assembly.

With the conclusion of his fiery speech, de Gaulle seemed to dissipate left-wing opposition almost at once. In this respect it is tempting to agree with Raymond Aron's characterization of the revolution as possibly a "psychodrama."[28] Nonetheless, one should also never underestimate the profoundly conservative and counterrevolutionary aspects of French society. No sooner had General de Gaulle finished his television address than the streets of Paris were suddenly flooded with massive crowds demonstrating their support for the government. This was no outpouring of unkempt students and poorly dressed workers; no, this was a well-dressed, white-collar, and bourgeois France in revolt against a breakdown of authority, against Communists, and against anarchists who threatened its material and social interests.

Now that the government had gained momentum, it quickly mobilized reservists to maintain essential public services. As if to give a pointed reminder that it meant business, it moved military troops to the outskirts of Paris to thwart any possible insurrection which might occur. Numerous Committees of Civic Action to maintain order were initiated overnight throughout the country. As if realizing that the time for direct action was past, workers began to sit down with employers and negotiate their differences; and many union members returned to work almost immediately. Finally, the Communist party itself helped to defuse the potential for a widespread conflict by quickly agreeing with General de Gaulle that a new election was the best means for resolving the dispute. But in agreeing to an election on Gaullist terms, the party was also preparing itself for electoral disaster in the immediate future. The revolution had ended; conflict would now be diverted into legal channels.

When the election was held on June 23 and June 30, the Gaullist party and its allies captured a huge majority of over 300 seats in the new National Assembly. Not surprisingly, both de Gaulle and Pompidou conducted the campaign on a "red scare" theme by blaming the Communist party for the recent ills of France. As in many previous elections fought under social and economic stress, rural and small-town France and the Parisian bourgeoisie voted against radicalism in the capital. Georges Pompidou was therefore returned to Parliament with a majority of unparalleled size. Conversely, the supporters of the left were weaker than at any other time in memory. Economic victory through the Grenelle accord was thus followed by an electoral disaster.

# WEST GERMANY*

*The Struggle for Codetermination*
Whether due to the growth of an affluent, middle-class society or the consolidation of certain economic and political power arrangements, redistributive issues have been rare in the Federal Republic since its founding

---

* Prepared by Margot Nyitray.

in 1949. This relative peacefulness contrasts sharply with the frequent turbulent ideological clashes during that other brief German experiment with democracy, the Weimar Republic. While the policy process for code-termination followed closely the redistributive pattern that characterized the French cases, the socioeconomic and political conditions surrounding this issue differed considerably from those in France in 1936 and 1968.

## Background

Sharp class conflict has been a major factor in German history. Socialism and a strong labor movement have deep roots in German tradition, while the conditions of German development and industrialization fostered the growth of business and management interests that were dependent on the state and whose attitudes and relationships with their workers were characterized by authoritarianism mixed with paternalism (the tradition of "Herr im Haus"). Thus, while Germany was the first Western country to introduce welfare legislation, the benefits for labor were not accomplished through political pressures from a working-class movement upon a democratic government, but were instituted from above by Bismarck. Looking back to the first shaky years of the new democratic experiment in West Germany, prior to the stabilization of socioeconomic and political arrangements under Adenauer's leadership, the conflict over codetermination, or worker participation in management, stands out not only as an important clash between classes, but as perhaps the last great redistributive battle which the German labor movement has fought.

The idea of worker participation in decision making within the plant actually goes back to the nineteenth century. By the turn of the century many German factories had worker committees which were consulted by management on questions of worker benefits and company welfare plans. During the revolutionary situation after World War I, union demands for a voice in economic decision making resulted in an article in the Weimar constitution that recognized the right of labor to participation in decision making at every level of the economy. It authorized the creation of factory, regional, and national worker councils to participate in industrial decision making. It also authorized the establishment of economic committees at the district and national levels composed of an equal number of business and labor representatives to advise government on economic and social legislation and to administer economic regulations. As succeeding governments turned more to the right and the unions lost strength, most of these constitutional provisions were never put into practice. However, a Works Council Law passed in 1920 required all plants to establish worker-elected Works Councils, which were to participate with management in making social and some personnel decisions and to select labor representatives to serve on the corporation Board of Directors (*Aufsichtsrat*).[29]

None of these practices, of course, survived the Nazi takeover. However, in the initial period of shock over the destruction and occupation at the end of World War II, the question of "economic democracy" and relations between business and labor—indeed, the question of the rights of private property—received the attention of many groups.[30] For the labor movement, struggling to reorganize, the codetermination principle represented a general program for restructuring political and economic relationships and for strengthening the new democracy by applying democratic principles to economic life. While codetermination initially received some support from other quarters, it was to become a symbol of conflict between labor and management—a conflict which challenged not just industrial relations procedures but the nature of economic relationships in the new Federal Republic.

Between 1945 and 1948, before management and labor organized into peak associations, the concept of codetermination was widely discussed in various publications and assemblies. Some Catholic circles revived the Catholic corporatist social theory, which stressed the need for partnership between various economic groups in society. Early SPD and CDU party programs in the different Allied occupation zones supported the idea in principle. In individual union-management negotiations in some firms, a few business managers conceded certain codetermination rights. Yet even then the party most closely associated with business interests, the FDP, opposed any codetermination which went beyond consultation within individual firms regarding social and personnel policy. But the earliest zonal meeting of union representatives in 1946 and 1947 passed resolutions which urged enactment of a new Works Council Law and the establishment of procedures and bodies for worker participation in all economic decision making.

The limited management support for codetermination prior to 1948 was due to business weakness resulting from the war and occupation, the need for union cooperation to renew production, and, in a few cases, responsiveness to Catholic social teachings. Works Councils reappeared in most factories as soon as the Allied occupation forces took control, and these arrangements were eventually sanctioned by the individual countries (France, Britain, U.S.) within their respective occupation zones. The unions, however, were unable through collective bargaining to get management agreement to extend codetermination within plants to economic decisions. Several of the newly created states (*Laender*) had clauses in their constitutions which provided for a right of codetermination as well as public ownership of production. However, efforts to pass implementing legislation were unsuccessful since the occupation authorities were unwilling to approve such legislation prior to the formation of a new national government. These factors, plus a certain German legalism which tends to see formal, legal governmental authorization as necessary for arrangements which might be established through private bargaining agreements in other countries (such as the U.S.), served to propel the issue onto the national policy-making agenda.

During this period, the most extensive codetermination arrangements existed in the iron and steel industries. In order to deconcentrate these

basic industries, American and British authorities set up a trustee association to provide management for iron and steel until they could be restored
to individual German companies. The German managers appointed to the
association board worked out an arrangement with the unions which provided for equal representation for unions within the trustee association, on
the boards of directors of the companies, and on the management boards
appointed by the directors. Although reports on the operation of these
industries seemed to indicate that management was satisfied with these
arrangements,[31] by the end of 1948 and early 1949 the reorganized employers were clearly rejecting any challenges to their traditional prerogatives. This set the stage for a gradual growth of conflict and polarization
over the codetermination issue.

## The Growth of Conflict

The major business interest groups were organized in 1949. The peak
association of employers with regard to labor policy, the *Bundesvereinigung
der Deutschen Arbeitgeberverbaende* (BDA), emerged as the chief spokesman
for opposition to union demands on codetermination. It was joined by the
other major peak association, the *Bundesverband der Deutschen Industrie*
(BDI), which links together industrial employer groups to influence economic policy. This association eventually developed close ties with the
Federal Republic's first chancellor, Konrad Adenauer.

Following the election of 1949, in which Adenauer's party won the most
seats in the *Bundestag,* the newly organized union peak association, the
*Deutscher Gewerkschaftsbund* (DGB), held its first national convention. At
this convention the DGB expressed its view that the government parties
should keep their campaign promises to labor by adopting a codetermination plan which would ensure the redistribution of economic and political
power. The labor leadership, having analyzed Weimar's collapse, was convinced of the need to prevent any future collaboration between business
and reactionary political forces. The DGB's proposal for reorganization of
the German economy called for the establishment of codetermination in
all areas of policy both within enterprises and at the supraenterprise level.
Codetermination at the enterprise level was to be achieved through equal
union representation on the *Aufsichtsrat.* At the supraenterprise level, the
various local economic chambers, which performed quasi-governmental
and administrative functions, were to be reorganized to include union
representatives, and economic councils were to be formed at the state and
national levels to initiate and discuss governmental economic policy proposals.

At the same time, leaders of the BDA and BDI were making clear in
numerous public statements that they believed codetermination to be a
step on the road to socialism and a threat to the rights of private property,
and as such incompatible with the new economic philosophy embodied in
the notion of the "social-market economy." This neoliberal doctrine was
most closely associated with the first economics minister, Ludwig Erhard,

whose economic decisions in 1948 were widely believed to have produced the rapid German economic recovery (frequently referred to as an "economic miracle"). This doctrine was rapidly adopted in principle, if not always in practice, by German business. Neoliberalism stresses the importance of individual initiative in a free competitive market. The state's only role is to insure competition and correct gross injustices (the social component) through taxation, but not to interfere with basic property relations or market mechanisms, which business perceived as threatened by union proposals, particularly those favoring enterprise codetermination.[32]

What, then, eventually led to the creation of a redistributive type of policy? Unlike the French cases, the increased level of conflict was not due to fairly spontaneous public outbursts. Indeed, the first actions appeared designed to avoid conflict on what was feared to be a highly explosive issue, for despite DGB pressure for action, the Adenauer government seemed in no hurry to initiate legislation. In early 1950, hoping to achieve immediate compromise and thus avert the escalation of conflict, Adenauer arranged for a series of meetings between business and labor peak association representatives. The first meetings took place at Hattenheim in March and April of 1950.

From these sessions the specific points of disagreement between both sides emerged more clearly. The employers did not really object to the establishment of economic councils with advisory functions at the state and national levels, although, perhaps justifiably, they did refuse to call this codetermination (a term which does imply participation in decisions, not just consultation). They also preferred the establishment of separate economic councils at the district level, rather than the union plan to reorganize existing economic chambers (at the time composed solely of employer groups) to include union representation. The employers completely rejected the DGB's proposals for enterprise codetermination, particularly in the area of economic decision making. It was here that they felt their power and control over property most directly threatened. The DGB had proposed that the Works Council with union approval select one-half of the board of directors in any firm of over 1,000 employees, that these labor directors then appoint a labor representative to the management board, and that codetermination be extended to all economic decisions as well as to social and personnel policy within the firm. The employers, on the other hand, were unwilling to go beyond minority representation for labor on the board of directors. They rejected the appointment of a labor manager and were unwilling to extend limited labor participation beyond social and personnel policy, which had existed under the Weimar Works Council Act.[33]

The conflict was not further escalated until the fall of 1950, when the special codetermination arrangements in the Allied-controlled iron and steel industries appeared to be threatened. In mid-November, the occupation authorities announced that the iron, coal, and steel industries would soon be returned to German ownership. The unions also learned that the

Economics Ministry was drafting legislation under which these industries would be organized according to existing corporate law, i.e., without providing for codetermination beyond the limited procedures in the 1920 Works Council Law. In addition, the DGB interpreted public remarks of Economics Minister Erhard as indications that he opposed the continuation of equal union representation on the board of directors and the appointment of labor managers. Labor spokesmen had already become increasingly concerned about the close links between the new government and business interests, and they now saw a real threat in the possibility that complete codetermination rights might be eliminated from the only industries where they were already in operation. From this point on, the DGB directed all its attention to protecting the practices in these industries, with Hans Boeckler, the DGB chairman, as the key labor spokesman. The issue was considered not only a matter of concern to the workers in the basic industries, but also a threat to the whole movement favoring democratization of economic power. It was particularly important since these Ruhr concerns were believed to have played a key role in the downfall of Weimar.

After getting no satisfaction from conversations with Erhard, Boeckler wrote Chancellor Adenauer and warned him of impending strike votes if no government action were taken. He informed the chancellor that, at the request of the DGB executive committee, the workers in the iron, steel and coal industries were to be asked to vote on their willingness to strike over the codetermination issue. The next letters exchanged between Adenauer and Boeckler did nothing further to resolve the conflict, although they did make clear the labor and government positions. Adenauer charged that strikes would be dangerous to the democratic order and constitute illegal pressure on the government, while Boeckler defended DGB actions as favorable to the extension and strengthening of democracy. In the meantime, both the mine workers and metal workers held their conventions. They voted overwhelmingly to strike unless the issue was resolved by February 1, 1951, with legislation continuing codetermination in iron and steel and extending the existing arrangements to the third basic industry, coal mining. It was apparent that the workers supported their peak association leadership.

It was also clear by this time that the employers were responding to union actions with pressures of their own. Both the BDA and BDI issued statements denouncing union activities. At a mass rally held by the BDI in November, codetermination was denounced as both a threat to traditional managerial prerogatives and a tool for the dangerous growth of union economic control. Seventy employers in the iron industry, not represented by the BDI, sent a telegram to the government supporting the peak association position and denouncing union threats.[34] Leaflets comparing the DGB strike votes to Hitler referenda were anonymously distributed in industrial areas. Since the unions regarded practices in the iron and steel industries as a model for all corporations, it is not surprising that business circles united behind their peak association leaders to attack codetermination in these industries as a threat to free enterprise and the "natural" economic order.

Polarization on the issue was also taking place within other groups and in the general public. The Catholic church hierarchy, which had previously made statements moderately supportive of codetermination, now spoke out against the DGB proposals and suggested delaying their introduction. Working-class support for the DGB position was clear, but the rest of the public appeared to favor management's position because of concern over the economic consequences of a strike in the basic industries. At a time of continued economic insecurity, the union strike threat was somewhat counterproductive.

## The First Round: The Special Codetermination Issue

With the strike deadline fast approaching and fearing the consequences of disruption to an economy then in the midst of recovery, Chancellor Adenauer moved to resolve the conflict. On January 11, 1951, he held a private meeting with Hans Boeckler. While there is no public record of their discussion, it was likely at this point that Adenauer made a commitment to continuing the special codetermination arrangements in the basic industries. Whether he became convinced of the justice of union demands, or more pragmatically hoped to forestall increased pressure for codetermination to be extended to all industries, Adenauer intervened directly after his session with Boeckler to settle the issue in the unions' favor. The chancellor immediately announced the preparation of a government bill to deal with the problem and proposed a conference between labor and business leaders.

Adenauer himself presided at the meetings which opened on January 19. Business efforts to block any agreement continued apace. Fritz Berg, president of the BDI, telegrammed Adenauer to warn of the dangers of setting a precedent to which business was unalterably opposed. At one point it appeared that these sessions would collapse; consequently, the DGB announced that it was going ahead with the strikes. However, Adenauer conferred separately with each side; and after a final joint meeting on January 25, an agreement was announced. The strikes were called off, and principles were agreed to which essentially continued existing arrangements with only minor changes. These formed the basis of the bill which the government submitted to the *Bundesrat* and *Bundestag* in February.

The *Bundestag* in this case was not the arena for conflict resolution as it often is in issues of sectoral fragmentation. Although sharp and acrimonious, the legislative debate was not lengthy: the legislature was simply given a choice to ratify an agreement reached previously outside its domain. The SPD was the principal spokesman for the DGB in the parliamentary debate, but CDU/CSU legislators rallied strongly behind Adenauer, even though some of them were under considerable pressure to support the business position. Although the smaller rightist parties in the government coalition sharply attacked the legislation, it passed the *Bundestag* unchanged on April 10, 1951, and the *Bundesrat* on April 19, 1951.

In a clear-cut working-class victory, the Special Codetermination Act confirmed the establishment of extensive codetermination arrangements in the iron, steel and coal industries. It is clear that Adenauer's support and intervention determined this success, but as events in 1952 would show, this redistributive issue did not result in a permanent polarization favorable to the left.

## The Second Round: The Extension of Codetermination

After the passage of the Special Codetermination Act in April 1951, attention returned to the general codetermination proposals discussed prior to the dispute over the basic industries. The DGB reiterated its demands that the special codetermination arrangements be extended to all other industries and the public service and that supraenterprise codetermination be established. The first reading debate in the *Bundestag,* in which the parties divided along class lines, had already taken place in the summer of 1950. By this time there were three bills under consideration by the *Bundestag* Labor and Economic Committees. The SPD draft was in fact the text of the DGB proposals, whereas the government and CDU/CSU parliamentary bills favored business positions and provided for no more than minor changes from the 1920 Works Council Law. These bills made no mention of supraenterprise codetermination, which was incompatible with the government's position of freeing the economy from governmental restraints. The question of worker representation in public corporations and administration was to be dealt with in separate legislation.

Hans Boeckler's death in February was a great loss to the labor movement, for he was the only figure with sufficient public stature to deal directly on nearly equal terms with Adenauer. The new DGB chairman was Christian Fette. In the summer of 1951, the DGB executive committee decided to increase its pressure in hopes of forcing the executive toward another favorable resolution of the issue. Its first action was to announce its intention to stop participating in the newly created economic committees within the Ministries of Labor and Economics. Such DGB statements apparently aroused some governmental concern about a new escalation of conflict.

Interestingly, the chancellor now appeared to harden his position. In a series of unproductive meetings with DGB representatives, he refused to compromise on the most important points dealing with economic codetermination within the plant and unified legislation for private industry and public corporations. In September, the DGB issued another statement that accused the government of yielding to business pressures and attacked some rightist party ministers for statements hostile to labor. In December, the DGB actually pulled out of the government committees. This final action in 1951 formed the prelude to the serious socialization of conflict which took place in 1952.

The DGB at first appeared to be attempting to resolve the issue through pressure on the legislative committees, but in April 1952, the *Bundestag* committees reported out a bill which left the government draft virtually unchanged. Despite divisions within the committees, Adenauer and Labor Minister Anton Storch had been able to pressure the more prolabor CDU Labor Committee chairman to withdraw the parliamentary party draft.[35] Parliamentary debate continued from this time through the second and third readings in July. But as pressures intensified, the major activity—hardly surprising given the nature of the issue—shifted away from the parliamentary arena. In May the DGB published a detailed critique of the government bill and began preparations for a strike vote. Fette wrote Adenauer stating the labor position and threatened strikes if changes were not made in the bill. Adenauer's response contrasted sharply with the amicable statements of the previous year and clearly indicated a polarization toward the right within the government. He defended the government's proposal as satisfying the need for legislation which would not fundamentally alter the economic order. But an alteration was precisely what the DGB wished. The chancellor also again raised the specter of unconstitutional pressures and suggested that the unions wait until the election campaign to pressure the government. In addition, he made an implied comparison between union activities and the staged demonstrations in the Soviet zone of Germany against the proposed treaty with the Western Allies to restore German sovereignty.

From mid-May through June, the DGB conducted a propaganda campaign urging working-class support in the fight for economic democracy and held a series of protest rallies, demonstrations and work stoppages. Beginning with protest rallies in four cities in which over 350,000 workers participated, demonstrations and work stoppages spread throughout the Federal Republic and led to a significant production decline.[36] In addition, DGB statements about further actions were interpreted as a threat of a general strike. Antilabor attitudes were undoubtedly solidified when the Printers and Paper Workers' Union called a two-day protest strike which virtually shut down the press.

In the meantime, the employers rallied in support of the government bill. The BDA directed an enormous antiunion propaganda campaign. The business peak associations placed particular emphasis on the dangers to a free economy of increased union power, without, of course, mentioning their own economic power. They also revived the somewhat feeble charges of communist influences within the unions. There were even some unsuccessful efforts to get court orders against union activities. However, unlike its position in 1951, the government now took the side of business. The renewed conflict over codetermination had thus polarized the political spectrum to a greater extent and moved the CDU/CSU somewhat further to the right.[37]

In early June, Adenauer again offered to meet with DGB representatives if the unions would discontinue their protest activities. Since union efforts had only succeeded in hardening the lines of conflict and making compromise more difficult, Fette agreed to this condition. CDU state Minister-President Karl Arnold arranged a meeting between Adenauer and other governmental representatives and DGB leaders. These participants agreed to establish a commission to try to resolve the differences between the "social partners." The commission failed, however, meeting only once before the DGB decided to withdraw. With this failure Adenauer moved to ensure passage of the government bill. No doubt his awareness that union actions had antagonized public opinion strengthened his support for the business position.

The level of activity in the legislature was what might be expected. Party discipline in the *Bundestag* was strong, and even the CDU/CSU legislators favorable to labor voted against all SDP efforts to amend the bill in the direction of union demands. As in 1951, the government bill passed virtually unchanged. Once again the *Bundestag* had little choice but to ratify a decision made elsewhere. There were only seven abstentions on the government side (presumably labor supporters). Not surprisingly, the SPD voted overwhelmingly against the government.

The general codetermination legislation of 1952 thus represented a clear victory for a bourgeoisie defeated only one year before. The BDA declared the act a victory for employers and the free enterprise system; the DGB called it an affront to labor and a threat to democracy, vowing to continue the fight in the upcoming national legislative elections of 1953.

### Aftermath: Strengthening the Status Quo

Though the unions won in 1951 and lost in 1952, the conflict over codetermination in each year was resolved by executive intervention on the side of the status quo. In 1951 the DGB defended existing arrangements, while the employers argued for greater management control. In 1952, on the other hand, it was the aggressive unions who pressed for a redistribution of economic power between the capitalist and the worker. Adenauer's support was crucial to the different outcomes.

By 1952 political opinion was moving to the right, and this trend was strengthened in the 1953 elections. The DGB had based its campaign on continued demands for union participation in economic decisions in enterprises and for the establishment of district, state and national bodies for supraenterprise codetermination. The SPD campaign echoed union demands, but the electoral result of 1953 was a shift to the right and a clear victory for the government parties. The CDU/CSU, which campaigned in support of the status quo, attained a majority of seats in the legislature. In a sense this election ended the issue as a source of major class conflict in the Federal Republic. Related questions concerning the application of special codetermination to the holding companies in the basic industries and worker representation in public corporations and the bureaucracy were reduced to the sectorally fragmented type of debates, not raised to redistributive claims between business and labor.

By 1953, the economic structure in the Federal Republic was stabilized, and business interests were represented by the CDU/CSU governments, which remained in power through 1966. Neoliberalism became the prevailing ideology, and even the SPD dropped its demands for socialism in favor of a New Deal type of economic philosophy. These conditions prevented the consideration of issues which raised fundamental questions about basic economic relationships. The unions turned from political action to more traditional concerns in industrial bargaining such as wage increases —issues on which the member unions were more active than the DGB.

As for the effects of the legislation itself, assessments continue to depend on the perspective, or bias, of the observer.[38] It is difficult to compare special and general codetermination industries since the once basic industries have had a variety of problems due to other economic factors. While codetermination's effect on the ordinary worker is unclear, it has undoubtedly provided union leadership with valuable managerial experience. It is also difficult to determine whether it has promoted greater business and labor understanding for each other's point of view and thus contributed to the low level of industrial conflict in West Germany, since other factors, including the reconstruction experiences, no doubt were also important. However, a recent government commission report issued in 1970 did emphasize better understanding between the "social partners" as a positive benefit of the codetermination procedures in operation.[39]

## CONCLUSIONS

In redistributive policies one finds large-scale class conflicts involving presidents and prime ministers negotiating with peak associations of managers and workers. In brief, the formal command posts of polity and economy are activated for decision making.

The German case, however, does differ in certain respects from the two French ones. The substance of the codetermination dispute revolved less around a direct redistribution of income than around a redefinition of authority relationships among capitalists and workers. It was not so much who was to use income and property as who was to control it, and to what extent. This profound desire for changes in authority relationships was also apparent among many workers in France in 1968, especially the younger ones. Unlike the peak associations participating in the Matignon accord, the West German peak associations had already achieved unity, although no doubt the issue did serve to solidify support, as it did in the Fifth Republic in 1968.

In addition, although rather large-scale strikes and demonstrations did take place throughout the country, the German conflict was more channeled and organized from beginning to end by the various institutional leaders of government, management, and labor. As a result, it was more civil, less threatening to the public order. In France the class battles of 1936 and 1968 burst upon the scene with such suddenness and ferocity that political leaders were enveloped very quickly. Perhaps the cause lay in a propensity for direct revolutionary action or the apparent hostility for authority which seemingly characterizes the French social and economic patterns; or perhaps it was the greater fragility and, at the same time, centralized nature of France's institutions. It may be that greater strength of pluralism and autonomy in West German political structures serve to choke off a certain spontaneity from below while simultaneously enabling leaders to achieve relatively more autonomy, deference, and hence freedom of action. In this respect, the DGB was much better organized and more radical in 1951–52 than the French PCF in 1968. Whereas German labor leaders were able to control and use the workers to pressure the government, the French leaders essentially reacted to the unexpected outbursts from below.

On the other hand, it was executive intervention by the state which determined the decisional outcomes in all three struggles. In the Third Republic of France, a Popular Front government in effect sided with the workers, and thirty-two years later in the Fifth Republic, a conservative government also acceded to major working-class demands. In West Germany, however, a center-right government came to the aid of management. In this connection, none of the chief political executives had much trouble with their legislatures, although Socialist Léon Blum clearly lacked a majority in 1936. In fact, there was a tendency among governing parties in each of the nations to close ranks behind their leaders. As a consequence, relatively little legislative activity was apparent.

# NOTES

1. This is in effect the burden of Schattschneider's argument over the years so far as the United States is concerned. The nationalization of politics means a greater emphasis will be placed upon broad economic interests rather than localized racial, ethnic, religious, or regional interests. See E. E. Schattschneider, *The Semisovereign People* (New York: Holt, Rinehart and Winston, 1960), pp. 78–96.

2. It should not be concluded, of course, that peak associations operate only in the redistributive arena. In fact, they often take part in distributive politics. The success with which the National Confederation of French Employers has received favors for its membership from parliamentary and administrative committees has been noted by many observers.

3. Gustave Le Bon, *The Crowd: A Study of the Popular Mind* (New York: The Viking Press, 1960), pp. 188–89, 200–201.

4. To quote Le Bon, *The Crowd,* p. 199: "Assemblies only constitute crowds at certain moments." He goes on to suggest that it is when individual deputies are working in committee that expertise and ability can be utilized. At such times, he says, "technical laws" can be passed (i.e., distributive politics can take place).

5. For example, see Michael Walzer, *Obligations: Essays on Disobedience, War, and Citizenship* (Cambridge: Harvard University Press, 1970), pp. 36–43.

6. See D. W. Brogan, *France Under the Republic: The Development of Modern France (1870–1939)* (New York: Harper & Brothers Publishers, 1940), p. 673. For a general study in English of this period, one might consult, in addition to Brogan's work, that of David Thomson, *Democracy in France since 1870,* 4th ed. (New York: Oxford University Press, 1964).

7. The relationship of the CGT to the CGTU as well as a discussion of trends on the left in general have been thoroughly considered by Henry W. Ehrmann, *French Labor: From Popular Front to Liberation* (New York: Oxford University Press, 1947), especially pp. 20–59.

8. Thomson, *Democracy in France,* p. 196.

9. These points have been discussed in Walter Sharp, "The Popular Front: Prelude or Interlude?" *The American Political Science Review,* October 1936, pp. 857–83.

10. See Ehrmann, *French Labor,* p. 387; also, Sharp, "The Popular Front," p. 874.

11. Ehrmann, *French Labor,* p. 387.

12. See, e.g., *New York Times,* June 7, 1936.

13. Sharp, "The Popular Front," p. 875.

14. Ehrmann, *French Labor,* p. 290.

15. There have been many studies of the 1968 revolution. The American reader might begin with the interpretations of Raymond Aron and Alain Touraine, two of France's leading sociologists. See Raymond Aron, *The Elusive Revolution: Anatomy of a Student Revolt* (New York: Praeger, 1969); and Alain Touraine, *The May Movement: Revolt and Reform* (New York: Random House, 1971).

16. Epistémon, *Ces Idées qui ont ébranlé la France* (Paris: A. Fayard, 1969), p. 15.

17. See Patrick Seale and Maureen McConville, *Red Flag/Black Flag: French Revolution 1968* (New York: G. P. Putnam's Sons, 1968), pp. 24–26.

18. Bernard E. Brown, *The French Revolt: May 1968* (New York: The McCaleb-Seiler Publishing Co., 1970), p. 3. A good bibliography may be found on page 22 of this work.

19. Seale and McConville, *Red Flag/Black Flag,* p. 68.

20. Ibid., p. 153.

21. Aron, *The Elusive Revolution,* pp. 87–89.

22. *Newsweek,* May 27, 1968, p. 47.

23. See the following issues of *Le Monde* for accounts of parliamentary activities: May 9, 10, 16, 1968.

24. Examples relating to the deep divisions between left and right on May 22 may be found by consulting *Le Monde,* May 22, 23, 1968; also, see Christian Charrière, *Le Printemps des enragés* (Paris: A. Fayard, 1968), pp. 256–57.

25. For a good discussion of the negotiations and the participants involved in the Grenelle meetings, see Jean Ferniot in *Le Journal du Dimanche,* (Paris), May 26, 1968.

26. *Le Monde,* May 28, 1968.

27. E.g., see Seale and McConville, *Red Flag/Black Flag,* pp. 175–77.

28. For a discussion of this point, see Aron, *The Elusive Revolution,* pp. 9–37.

29. Social decisions refer to insurance, retirement, and welfare plans administered by the firms. German corporate law provides for three governing bodies: (1) a board of directors that determines general policy, and appoints (2) a management board *(Vorstand)* that directs day-to-day operations, and (3) the general assembly, equivalent to U.S. annual stockholders' meetings.

30. For a detailed history of codetermination and its origins in Germany, see Abraham Shuchman, *Codetermination: Labor's Middle Way in Germany* (Washington, D.C.: Public Affairs Press, 1957), pp. 11–25, 59–91. The best available study of the codetermination battle in the Federal Republic in the early 1950s, from which much of the following account is taken, can be found in Wolfgang Hirsch-Weber, *Gewerkschaften in der Politick* (Cologne: Westdeutscher Verlag, 1959). For two slightly different views on the issue by U.S. observers, compare Shuchman's work and Herbert Spiro, *The Politics of German Codetermination* (Cambridge: Harvard University Press, 1958).

31. Hirsch-Weber, *Gewerkschaften in der Politik*, p. 88.

32. For a description of BDA views on codetermination and its counterproposals, see Ronald Bunn, "Codetermination and the Federation of German Employers," *Midwest Journal of Political Science*, August 1958, pp. 278–97.

33. For the text of the DGB proposals, see Shuchman, *Codetermination*, pp. 127–31.

34. See Bunn, "Codetermination"; and for BDI activities, Gerard Braunthal, *The Federation of German Industry in Politics* (Ithaca, N.Y.; Cornell University Press, 1961), pp. 271–73.

35. Braunthal, *The Federation of German Industry in Politics*, p. 43.

36. Hirsch-Weber, *Gewerkschaften in der Politik*, p. 104–5.

37. Ibid., p. 107.

38. See, for example, the difference between Shuchman and Spiro's books.

39. The grand coalition government established a commission in 1968 to study the operation of codetermination and recommend reforms. The report recommended some minor changes in favor of greater worker access to information, but did not meet DGB demands. See *Bericht der Sachverstandigenkommission zur Auswertung der bisherigen Erfahrungen bei der Mitbestimmung* (Stuttgart: W. Kohlhammer GMBH, 1970).

# CONCLUDING
# REMARKS

THE study of policy has recently become a major interest for political scientists, especially students of the American political system. Undoubtedly the demand for relevance in the 1960s and the general desire to make the discipline useful to policy makers accelerated this trend. As a result of these catalysts, studies of policy are often descriptive and empirical but essentially nontheoretical, as shown in the recent tendency to conceptualize policy in terms of specific, substantive areas like welfare policy, environmental policy, or educational policy.[1] This emphasis on substantive areas probably grows out of many political scientists' understandable desire to get on with the job of advising decision makers in government and making the discipline more useful to problem solving. There is therefore a greater emphasis upon policy *analysis* than upon the policy *process.*

Perhaps, however, the attention given to policy analysis is premature, for studies oriented around substantive areas tend to favor relatively narrow empiricism and description over theoretically significant problems. Consequently, political scientists expend ever-increasing energy upon problems which do not let them focus meaningfully upon the policy process as a whole. For example, a student may learn much about the welfare system and its politics but little of the policy process in general, unless, of course, he develops a theory of the policy process in welfare which can explain activity in other substantive areas as well.

Recent efforts to explore the nature of policy in a more consistently theoretical manner have been influenced by the preoccupations of scholars in American politics. But in the United States a behavioral or micropolitical orientation has dominated policy studies. Whether based upon decision making, incremental, or economic rationality models, such research is addressed to psychological and individualistic phenomena and is therefore limited largely to the characteristics, attitudes, and situations of individual decision makers in face-to-face encounters. However, as this typology of the comparative policy process suggests, concentrating upon individual choices offers only a partial explanation of the policy process, since such activity takes place within committees in the legislative, executive, and judicial branches of government (i.e., as distributive politics).

If scholars in American government have theorized about policy in too microscopic a manner, scholars in the comparative field have done little conscious theorizing at all. Nevertheless, although not readily apparent and seldom explicitly stated, there is an implicit theoretical attitude toward a conceptual framework for the policy process to which many comparativists adhere—the interest group approach. This fact contains a certain irony, for unlike their American government counterparts, relatively few forthright adherents of group theory are also comparativists.[2] But there is a tendency for interest group assumptions to intrude silently and unobtrusively into the work of comparative specialists when they face policy-related problems. Thus comparativists implicitly view public policy as a result of the interplay of groups, as a struggle over the authoritative allocation of values. Even when these political scientists use the so-called systems approach they emphasize the input side, and the inputs are mostly the demands by groups placed upon government institutions.[3]

This bias is reflected in comparative government textbooks which give little if any systematic and theoretical treatment to the policy process concept. A typical book may include chapters on such diverse subjects as approaches to the discipline, political culture, voting, ideologies, interest groups, and parties, as well as the executive, legislature, and judiciary. But such a book reduces the policy process thread, which might tie so many of these parts together, mainly to a discussion of individual, group, and party pressures placed upon government institutions.[4]

Undoubtedly our understanding of other nations is enhanced by looking at the various pressures brought to bear on government institutions. But if one conceptualizes the comparative policy process as a byproduct of the demands made upon government and its decision makers—if one subordinates it to group activity—one focuses upon discrete phenomena which are obviously included in any elaboration of the policy process, but are not central to it. In other words, the policy process should not be conceptualized to encompass only demands upon government but should more broadly include within its orbit different sorts of conflicts, political actors, and government institutions. Without thinking in more macro-oriented terms about policy, it is difficult to grasp the process as a whole and achieve much from the standpoint of comparative theory.

## THE IMPORTANCE OF TYPOLOGIES

For a thorough understanding of the comparative policy process, policy should be viewed as an independent variable which affects individuals, groups, and institutional behavior; which encourages the three components of individual, group, and institution to cluster in certain rather predictable ways; and which therefore gives a special character to the process itself. In approaching the policy process from this perspective, we developed a typology of the comparative policy process which will hopefully lead to the growth of testable theoretical statements sufficiently general to cut across various political systems and consequently explain the policy process in diverse political orders.

Our typology is based upon the belief that the comparative policy process may best be understood according to the scope and intensity of conflict aroused over issues. We constructed four types of policies with a view that certain kinds of conflict affect the process by which issues are initiated and resolved. We explored in detail twelve case studies drawn from a total of sixty-four studies of cases which took place in various Western democracies (see Appendix) and organized the cases according to the four-fold typology of distribution, sectoral fragmentation, emotive symbolization, and redistribution. Briefly, we found that distributive issues display little conflict and are settled in legislative or executive committees; sectorally fragmented policies display moderate conflict among interests representing sectors and are settled on the legislative floor; emotive symbolic issues are deeply divisive ones, cutting across many social groupings, in which leaders tend to avoid staking out positions, party discipline is inoperative, and each legislator tends to go his own way; redistributive issues, finally, are highly conflictual class struggles and are settled by the topmost institutional leadership of the political, labor, and business worlds.

Therefore, we perceive certain patterns even in so diffuse and variable a concept as the policy process. That is, certain kinds of conflict, participants, and institutions cluster in fairly predictable ways, and their coming together offers some insight into the way policy is made. Keeping this point in mind, our most general proposition in this study is: issues involving different scopes and intensities of conflict activate special kinds of political actors and/or groups and are in turn settled by particular political institutions.

It is important to understand, however, that while typologies may suggest theoretical propositions, they cannot test them. Rather, their function is to "identify, simplify, and order the concrete data so that they may be described in terms that make them comparable."[5] For example, if someone were to judge our typology from the standpoint of the individual participants, he would probably argue that any given issue conflict may be perceived by some individuals as emotive symbolic, by others as redistributive, and by still others as sectorally fragmented. Empirically speaking, this observation about the opinions of discrete individuals may be valid, but it does not serve our intent. We sought to construct a typology which would express the policy process considered as a whole, not as a sum of the individual participants. It is the observer, not the participant, who must grasp the more salient aspects of the process.

Types present a methodological problem because it is exceedingly diffi-cult to make them isomorphic with (similar to) the phenomena they are intended to explain: a type is unlikely to provide a perfect fit to any set of data. Because we necessarily select out certain characteristics of the phenomena for emphasis in constructing types, individual types are rarely completely isomorphic with the data. Max Weber, with whom this type construction is most closely associated, concluded that "ideal types" are conscious deviations from concrete experience, so he sought to accentuate certain attributes useful for his own purposes. Because in this book we have hoped to approach empirical reality more closely than Weber's defi-nition implies, we share Professor John C. McKinney's less extreme view of "constructed types" as "a purposive, planned selection, abstraction, combination, and (sometimes) accentuation of a set of criteria with empiri-cal referents that serves as a basis for the comparison of empirical cases."[6] Typologies—as opposed to *single* types—may come much closer to achiev-ing a high correspondence between the individual type (as part of a typology) and the phenomena it studies.[7]

## THE PROBLEM OF CONFLICT

Although this study has stressed the role of issue conflicts in influencing the policy process the impact of different levels of conflict ("conflict social-ization") is most difficult to measure. In our discussion of the policy pro-cess typology, we easily comprehended the special kinds of participants (individuals, groups, associations) and the places where the issues were resolved (at least, in the short run), but relating participants and institu-tions to the precise level of conflict remains a difficult task. Are there rather specific, verifiable levels of discord which can be delineated in terms of low, medium, and high to express the attributes of policy types? Similarly, are there certain indicators of conflict socialization which can be linked with certain attributes of the typology? To put the matter in a slightly different way, is there a point in the growth of conflict which creates a different policy process in terms of participants and political institutions? As we move from the privatization of conflict through an ever-expanding scale of discord in Schattschneider's sense, are there cut-off points linking a particular issue conflict more precisely and systematically with other elements in the policy process pattern? Despite many social scientists' interest in Schattschneider's work, efforts to apply his major theoretical propositions are so far virtually nonexistent.[8]

Perhaps the case studies included in the previous chapters offer some clues for operationalizing Schattschneider's idea of the socialization of conflict. It will be recalled that the conflictual attributes of the policy types differ in essential ways. The class-oriented conflicts, as illustrated by the Matignon and Grenelle agreements, were characterized by riots and other illegal acts (lock-ins and sit-ins) as well as by more orthodox and legal behavior (strikes and peaceful demonstrations). While illegal activities were held to a minimum in the West German codetermination dispute, the struggle also led to widescale demonstrations and strikes. Contrasted with other types of policies, redistributive issues are more likely to generate broadly based overt acts of participation by ordinary, non-office-holding citizens.

With the exception of the American civil rights controversy—which had more than its share of riots and illegal demonstrations—the various emotive symbolic issues considered in this book reveal a dimension of large-scale conflicts rather different from the redistributive pattern. The bargaining process in redistributive cases takes place behind closed doors at the executive levels. While the legislature remains relatively passive in resolving such disputes, more vocal and intense activities occur within the larger society. Emotive symbolic disputes, however, are easily identified by the strong opposition and agitation they provoke among politicians in the legislative and executive branches of government. Thus, the broad scope and intensity of conflict produced by emotive symbolic disputes is more accurately gauged from a study of activities within executives and legislatures than from a consideration of larger social forces of workers, bourgeoisie, students, etc., outside the boundaries of the political system. This fact does not mean that the populace as a whole is unconcerned in cases of emotive symbolization: although opinion remains somewhat inactivated, surveys would probably show strong public awareness and concern. In fact, it is partly the fear of popular disapproval and potential retaliation at the polls which produces an impact upon political elites, drawing them so closely to mass opinion.

This point regarding the different elements of conflict must not be misunderstood, for after attributing a wide scope and intensity of conflict to both redistributive and emotive symbolic policy types throughout this book, we are not reversing ourselves and concluding that only redistributive type cases should be designated as widely conflictual. Rather, we are saying that one kind of policy especially activates the political class (e.g., legislators), whereas the other type leads to more agitation among the nonelected populace (e.g., workers, intellectuals, and students).

Similar difficulties also arise in distinguishing the moderately conflictual sectorally fragmented type from the largely nonconflictual distributive type. They are differentiated most clearly by conflict levels since sectoral fragmentation generates relatively greater legislative floor activity through the amending process.[9] But what if in a given issue committees are not controlling and resolving the issue (i.e., through a nondistributive policy process), and yet legislators are making little effort to amend the legislation on the floor? A daily reading of various newspapers, parliamentary journals, and other accounts may reaffirm that the process follows the sectorally fragmented pattern. Thus, if the amending process alone dominates the calculations, it is possible to lose a clear understanding of the issue's essence. An indicator of conflict, a technique, determines the policy type. Again, if issues of sectoral fragmentation are contrasted with those of emotive symbolization, one normally expects more amendments to be offered in emotive symbolization cases. Our own case studies, though, suggest that this is not always true. Finally, because explosive redistributive issues, which are not even acted out in the legislature, cannot be linked to the amending process at all, a single overriding indicator of conflict socialization is indeed difficult to establish. Thus, to give a greater quantitative precision to conflict socialization is fraught with complexity.

## ISSUE DEFINITION AND REDEFINITION

Another of E. E. Schattschneider's significant contributions is his discussion of the definition and redefinition of issues. He believed that the individual or group defining an issue to his or its own requirements is already far along in determining the ultimate outcome of the battle. To define an issue in American politics as socialistic, for example, is likely to assure victory to the antisocialists. Similarly, if the American government decides to nationalize the railways, it is unlikely to employ terminology such as "nationalization" or "socialization"; rather it will emphasize that its decision is a practical one which is applicable only to a specific industry with its own special needs. That way the decision will be perceived by the public in an essentially nonideological way.

Indeed, as the case studies of the previous chapters have shown, the way people define issues is highly significant in determining the scope and intensity of issue conflicts. For instance, to employ a terminology which encourages greater participation by large numbers of citizens will affect the outcome of a struggle in a rather different manner than if the acceptable definition of the issue calls for the solution by private groups and individuals.

Moreover, issues can be redefined and therefore changed from one kind of policy process into another kind—that is, changed from one cluster of conflict, participants, and institutions (or arena of conflict) into another cluster. For example, the dynamics of the May revolution of 1968 were altered once the workers and students linked hands at the Renault factory on the outskirts of Paris or at least when the proletariat began its own sit-ins and lock-ins. Until then the government had been criticized in the National Assembly by both the left and right benches, for the issue had been one of university reform, and public opinion had tolerated the student revolutionists. But once the revolt took this new turn, the government ranks were quickly reinforced by their previously critical backbenchers and their Independent Republican coalition partners.

Cases of issue redefinition are quite common, and Samuel Beer's discussion of the activities of the National Union of Teachers (NUT) in Great Britain[10] provides another illustration. The NUT, primarily a representative of elementary teachers, had interacted until 1954 with the Ministry of Education in distributive situations through a committee structure within the bureaucracy. At that time, however, the ministry decided to raise the teachers' superannuation fund while simultaneously agreeing to an increase in salaries.

The NUT was quite opposed to the proposal, and the government found it difficult to continue its usual game of distributive politics. The teachers readily gained support in Parliament from the opposition Labour party, which took a stand against the proposed bill. The Conservatives were also not immune to the teacher onslaught. Cabinet meetings dealt with the problem, but they produced no agreement. Finally, pressures became so intense that the resignation of the minister of education was announced. His replacement then quickly called for a withdrawal of the bill. Since a bargaining breakdown in committee meant that Parliament was now forced to resolve a dispute normally handled quietly behind the scenes, it could be said that the NUT successfully redefined the issue in terms of sectoral fragmentation.

Nevertheless, the redefinition process certainly does not always proceed from narrowly limited conflicts to progressively more expansive ones. Indeed, the redefinition of an issue may result in a desocialization of conflict. An example is the attempt in 1959 of French Premier Michel Debré to deal with that recurrent nemesis of the Fourth Republic—the argument over whether to subsidize church schools by public funds and to bring them under state supervision. At times in the past, the issue was framed in emotive symbolic terms; Debré, however, sought to redefine it in distributive terms.[11] He even had a word to convey the meaning of a shift from a largely conflicting to a nonconflicting arena: *"dépolitisation."* He hoped to take this particular problem out of politics by offering state aid to private schools in return for their acceptance of certain government-imposed restrictions. Private schools which opposed any controls were free to go their respective ways without financial help. Significantly, Debré's proposed alternatives were posed in such a way as to encourage individual schools to negotiate directly with the individual ministries. Whether intended or not, the Debré Law ultimately had the effect of shifting debate to distributive questions, enabling bureaucrats and school representatives to bargain quietly behind the scenes. Moreover, in this period there was little need to worry about Parliament, since the right was in control and supported the prime minister. Moderates, Gaullists, and Catholic Popular Republicans were sure to resist attempts to cripple the private schools in the name of anticlericalism.[12]

Successful issue redefinition is also likely to be highly dependent upon the nature of the participants and institutions involved. The British NUT could redefine an issue successfully by having another institution, the House of Commons, resolve its disagreements with the government. Unhappily, such flexibility is not possible for many interests. The support they count upon is relatively inelastic. For instance, French big business, with its rather compromised reputation after World War II, was restricted mostly to distributive politics. It was forced to work in the background, out of the public eye. Raising the level of conflict would have spelled disaster. Small business, on the other hand, probably had enough leeway and public empathy to move smoothly from one level of conflict to another.

It ought to be pointed out, finally, that the approach presented here neither postulates nor denies the existence of a so-called power elite. It is conceivable, for example, that such an elite operates with relative freedom either in the distributive or redistributive areas where institutionalization of conflict is advanced. Particularly in distributive decision making, major interests—which have greater access, money, knowledge, and time—may benefit from the secrecy which characterizes so much of committee work, while in cases of redistribution they dominate or actually occupy some of the most strategic command posts. However, in the latter the glare of publicity and the high level of activity may also serve to weaken them. In emotive symbolic and sectorally fragmented instances elite dominance may be much more limited due to the rapidly shifting alliances fostered by such issues. These issues lack that elemental secrecy necessary to gain victories which, if widely understood, would run the risk of creating much public resentment. As such, an elite might easily lose its ability to manage such conflicts.

Ultimately, the power of an elite depends upon its ability to utilize different conflict areas.[13] Thus, one may hypothesize that the greater the number of alternatives available, the greater the amount of power the given group possesses. From this point of view the fortunate interest which can redefine an issue one or more times not only limits its opponent's options but also expands its own possibilities for action.

If the relative degree of conflict is a major determinant in the way individuals, groups, and institutions cluster, it is therefore important to gain a more thorough understanding of the nature and role of issue conflicts. The manner in which issues are defined goes far in determining the scope of conflict, yet issue definition in itself gives a dynamic quality to the policy process which may all too easily elude one. Because the definition may change in relatively short periods of time, the same issue in the course of its historical development may ultimately reflect various types of policy. Thus, one kind of policy process may be at work as a bill winds its way through the legislature (e.g., sectoral fragmentation or emotive symbolization), but a quite different one may exist once the act is written into law (e.g., distribution). In each case a different constellation of political forces is activated. For instance, when a bill becomes law, its administration is taken over by the bureaucracy. The consequence is to reduce both the numbers of people involved and the salience of the issue by encouraging what Murray Edelman has called "political quiescence." As he suggests, "The fervent display of public wrath, or enthusiasm, in the course of the initial legislative attack on forces seen as threatening the 'little man' is a common American spectacle. It is about as predictable as the subsequent lapse of the same fervor."[14] Or, to put it another way, the issue becomes one of distribution.

# NOTES

1. For instance, see the recently founded quarterly, *Policy Studies Journal,* published by the Policy Studies Organization.

2. The group approach was debunked by leading comparativists at a time when it was quite popular among students of American government. See, for example, Joseph LaPalombara, "Utility and Limitations of Interest Group Theory in Non-American Field Situations," *Journal of Politics,* February 1960, pp. 29–49; and Roy C. Macridis, "Interest Groups in Comparative Analysis," *Journal of Politics,* February 1961, pp. 29–45.

3. This is the distinct impression one receives from reading the work of Gabriel Almond, which has had so much influence on students of comparative government. See his "Comparative Political Systems," *Journal of Politics,* August 1956, pp. 391–409; and his introductory essay in Gabriel A. Almond and James S. Coleman, eds., *The Politics of the Developing Areas* (Princeton: Princeton University Press, 1960), pp. 3–64.

4. One could take any number of examples but a study by Jorgen Rasmussen, *The Process of Politics* (New York: An Atherton Book, 1969) will suffice to make the point that inputs and group demands are basic to the study of policy among comparative politics scholars. Rasmussen, taking an avowedly structural-functional approach, deftly synthesizes much of the work in our field. But in two chapters entitled "Expressing and Focusing Demands for Authoritative Decisions" and "Policy-Making and Implementing Structures," he presents little if any knowledge about the *way* policy is made, despite what the chapter headings suggest. Rather, the author proceeds to analyze in a linear manner the behavioral characteristics of the citizenry to the topmost national institutions. Among other things, he discusses the individuals and groups that participate in politics and voting; the socioeconomic basis and types of party systems; and the disadvantages in altering constitutional forms. In short, he tells us about the surrounding environment within which policy is made, about those individuals and institutions which in some manner may affect policy, but he informs us little about the process itself.

5. John C. McKinney, *Constructive Typology and Social Theory* (New York: Appleton-Century-Crofts, 1966), p. 216.

6. Ibid., pp. 22–23, 25, 202.

7. For an interesting discussion of this point, see David Willer, *Scientific Sociology: Theory and Methods* (Englewood Cliffs, N.J.: Prentice-Hall, Inc., 1967), pp. 43–46.

8. Note, for example, David Adamany, "The Political Science of E. E. Schattschneider: A Review Essay," *American Political Science Review,* December 1972, pp. 1321–35.

9. One might do well to consult the previously cited work of Theodore J. Lowi, especially his "Decision Making vs. Policy Making: Toward an Antidote for Technocracy," *Public Administration Review,* May/June 1970, pp. 314–25.

10. Samuel Beer, "Pressure Groups and Parties in Britain," *American Political Science Review,* March 1956, pp. 6–9.

11. Certainly that is the impression received from a reading of Bernard E. Brown, "The Decision to Subsidize Private Schools," in James B. Christoph and Bernard E. Brown, eds., *Cases in Comparative Politics,* 2nd ed. (Boston: Little, Brown and Co., 1969), pp. 113–47.

12. A study of the French right in this period may be found in T. Alexander Smith, "Algeria and the French *Modérés:* The Politics of Immoderation?" *Western Political Quarterly,* March 1965, pp. 116–34.

13. Note the difference of this perspective from that of Gabriel A. Almond and G. Bingham Powell, Jr., *Comparative Politics: A Developmental Approach* (Boston: Little, Brown and Co., 1966), pp. 88–90.

14. Murray Edelman, *The Symbolic Uses of Politics* (Urbana, Ill.: The University of Illinois Press, 1967), p. 25.

# APPENDIX

*The following is a list of case studies*
*utilized in preparing this book*

| ISSUE | NATION | POLICY PROCESS |
|---|---|---|
| 1. Agriculture Act (1955) (Landwirtschaftsgesetz) | West Germany | Distributive |
| 2. Common Market Adjustment Act (1965) (EWG-Anpassungsgesetz) | West Germany | Distributive |
| 3. Fair Labor Standards Amendment (1961) | U.S.A. | Distributive |
| 4. Family Law Reform Bill (1969) | Great Britain | Distributive |
| 5. Federal Reserve Board Bill (1970) | U.S.A. | Distributive |
| 6. Freedom of Publications Bill (1969) | Great Britain | Distributive |
| 7. Interior Appropriations Bill (1965) | U.S.A. | Distributive |
| 8. Juvenile Delinquency Bill (1968) | U.S.A. | Distributive |
| 9. Kenya Independence Bill (1963) | Great Britain | Distributive |
| 10. Military Construction Authorization Bill (1966) | U.S.A. | Distributive |
| 11. Pensions Bill (1962) | Great Britain | Distributive |
| 12. Post Office Savings Bank Bill (1966) | Great Britain | Distributive |
| 13. Regional Development Bill (1963) | Great Britain | Distributive |
| 14. Sea Fishing and Industry Bill (1962) | Great Britain | Distributive |
| 15. Smoot-Hawley Tariff Act (1930) | U.S.A. | Distributive |
| 16. Southern Rhodesia Bill (1961) | Great Britain | Distributive |
| 17. Teacher Training Colleges Bill (1962) | Great Britain | Distributive |

| ISSUE | NATION | POLICY PROCESS |
|---|---|---|
| 18. Trades Union (Amalgamation) Bill (1964) | Great Britain | Distributive |
| 19. War Damages Bill (1965) | Great Britain | Distributive |
| 20. Anti-Ballistic Missile Bill (1970) | U.S.A. | Sectoral Fragmentation |
| 21. Broadcasting Bill (1964) | France | Sectoral Fragmentation |
| 22. The Budgetary Debate (1972) | Canada | Sectoral Fragmentation |
| 23. Cartel Act (1957) (Kartellgesetz) | West Germany | Sectoral Fragmentation |
| 24. Central Arizona Project Bill (1967) | U.S.A. | Sectoral Fragmentation |
| 25. Cigarette Labeling and Advertising Bill (1965) | U.S.A. | Sectoral Fragmentation |
| 26. Civil Rights Act (1961) | U.S.A. | Sectoral Fragmentation |
| 27. Commercial Television Debate (1954) | Great Britain | Sectoral Fragmentation |
| 28. Crime Control Bill (1968) | U.S.A. | Sectoral Fragmentation |
| 29. Debré Law (1959) | France | Sectoral Fragmentation |
| 30. Divorce Reform Bill (1969) | Great Britain | Sectoral Fragmentation |
| 31. Draft Lottery Bill (1968) | U.S.A. | Sectoral Fragmentation |
| 32. "Emergency Powers" Bill (1966) | Great Britain | Sectoral Fragmentation |
| 33. Gun Control Bill (1968) | U.S.A. | Sectoral Fragmentation |
| 34. Kennedy Trade Bill (1962) | U.S.A. | Sectoral Fragmentation |
| 35. London Government Bill (1967) | Great Britain | Sectoral Fragmentation |
| 36. Market Structure Act (1969) (Marktstrukturgesetz) | West Germany | Sectoral Fragmentation |
| 37. Medicare Bill (1965) | U.S.A. | Sectoral Fragmentation |
| 38. Personnel Representation Act (1956) (Personalvertretungsgesetz) | West Germany | Sectoral Fragmentation |
| 39. Race Relations Bill (1965) | Great Britain | Sectoral Fragmentation |
| 40. Ratification of Nonproliferation Treaty (1969) | U.S.A. | Sectoral Fragmentation |
| 41. Resale Price Maintenance (1964) | Great Britain | Sectoral Fragmentation |
| 42. South Africa Bill (1962) | Great Britain | Sectoral Fragmentation |
| 43. Strike Bill (1963) | France | Sectoral Fragmentation |
| 44. Succession Bill (1964) | Great Britain | Sectoral Fragmentation |

| ISSUE | NATION | POLICY PROCESS |
|---|---|---|
| 45. Superannuation Fund Debate (1954) | Great Britain | Sectoral Fragmentation |
| 46. Surtax Extension (1969) | U.S.A. | Sectoral Fragmentation |
| 47. Taft-Hartley Bill (1947) | U.S.A. | Sectoral Fragmentation |
| 48. Tax Reform Bill (1969) | U.S.A. | Sectoral Fragmentation |
| 49. Transportation Finance Act (1955) (Verkehrsfinanzgesetz) | West Germany | Sectoral Fragmentation |
| 50. Value-Added Tax Bill (1965) | France | Sectoral Fragmentation |
| 51. Capital Punishment Bill (1948) | Great Britain | Emotive Symbolization |
| 52. Capital Punishment Bill (1956) | Great Britain | Emotive Symbolization |
| 53. Civil Rights Bill (1964) | U.S.A. | Emotive Symbolization |
| 54. Eastern Treaties Bill (1972) (Ostverträge) | West Germany | Emotive Symbolization |
| 55. Emergency Powers Act (1968) (Notstandsgesetz) | West Germany | Emotive Symbolization |
| 56. European Defense Bill (1954) | France | Emotive Symbolization |
| 57. Great Flag Debate (1964) | Canada | Emotive Symbolization |
| 58. Murder Bill (1964) | Great Britain | Emotive Symbolization |
| 59. School Prayer Amendment (1961) | U.S.A. | Emotive Symbolization |
| 60. Sexual Offenses Bill (1966) | Great Britain | Emotive Symbolization |
| 61. Grenelle Agreement (1968) | France | Redistributive |
| 62. Matignon Agreement (1936) | France | Redistributive |
| 63. Special Codetermination Act (1951) (Montanmitbestimmungsgesetz) | West Germany | Redistributive |
| 64. Works Constitution Act (1952) (Betriebsverfassungsgesetz) | West Germany | Redistributive |

# Index

# INDEX